Y0-EDO-283

INTERESTING
AND
AUTHENTIC NARRATIVES
OF THE MOST
REMARKABLE SHIPWRECKS,

The Life Boat rescuing the Passengers from the wreck of the Isabella.

INTERESTING
AND
AUTHENTIC NARRATIVES
OF THE MOST
REMARKABLE SHIPWRECKS,

FIRES, FAMINES, CALAMITIES, PROVIDENTIAL DELIVERANCES, AND LAMENTABLE DISASTERS ON THE SEAS,

IN MOST PARTS OF

THE WORLD.

By R. THOMAS, A. M.

Embellished with numerous plates from original designs

BOOKS FOR LIBRARIES PRESS
FREEPORT, NEW YORK

First Published 1835
Reprinted 1970

STANDARD BOOK NUMBER:
8369-5178-6

LIBRARY OF CONGRESS CATALOG CARD NUMBER:
70-106022

PRINTED IN THE UNITED STATES OF AMERICA

THE

REMARKABLE SHIPWRECKS.

LOSS OF THE GROSVENOR INDIAMAN.

On the Coast of Caffraria, August 4, 1782.

In the melancholy catalogue of human woes, few things appear more eminently disastrous than the general fate of the Grosvenor's crew. Shipwreck is always, even in its mildest form, a calamity which fills the mind with horror; but, what is instant death, compared to the situation of those who had hunger, thirst, and nakedness to contend with; who only escaped the fury of the waves to enter into conflicts with the savages of the forest, or the greater savages of the human race; who were cut off from all civiiized society, and felt the prolongation of life to be only the lengthened pains of death?

The Grosvenor sailed from Trinicomale, June 13th, 1782, on her homeward bound voyage, and met with no memorable occurrence till the 4th of August, the fatal day on which she went on shore.

During the two preceding days it had blown very hard, the sky was overcast, so that they were unable to take an observation; and it is likewise probable, that from their vicinity to the shore, they had been carried out of their course by currents. The combination of these circumstances may account for the error in their reckoning, which occasioned the loss of the ship. It appears that captain Coxson had declared, a few hours before the disaster took place, that he computed the ship to be at least one hundred leagues from the nearest land, and this opinion lulled them into a false security.

John Hynes, one of the survivors, being aloft with some others, in the night-watch, saw breakers ahead, and asked his companions if they did not think land was near. In this opinion they all coincided, and hastened to inform the third mate, who was the officer of the watch. The infatuated young man only laughed at their apprehensions; upon which one of them ran to the cabin to acquaint the captain, who instantly ordered to wear ship. But before this could be accomplished, her keel struck with great force; in an instant every person on board hastened on the deck, and apprehension and horror were impressed on every countenance.

The captain endeavored to dispel the fears of the passengers, and begged them to be composed. The pumps were sounded, but no water found in the hold, as the ship's stern lay high on the rocks. In a few minutes the wind blew off the shore, which filled them with apprehensions lest they should be driven out to sea, and thus lose the only chance they had of escaping. The powder room was by this time full of water, the masts were cut away, without any effect, and the ship being driven within a cable's length of the shore, all hopes of saving her vanished.

This dismal prospect produced distraction and despair, and it is impossible to describe the scene that ensued. Those who were most composed set about forming a raft, hoping by means of it to convey the women, the children, and the sick to land. Meanwhile three men attempted to swim to the shore with the deep-sea line; one perished in the attempt, but the other two succeeded. By these a hawser was, at length, carried to the shore and fastened round the rocks, in which operation they were assisted by great numbers of the natives, who had come down to the water's edge to witness the uncommon sight.

The raft being by this time completed, was launched overboard, and four men got upon it to assist the ladies; but they had scarcely taken their station before the hawser, which was fastened around it, snapped in two, by

Wreck of the Grosvenor. *Page* 6.

which accident it was upset, and three of the men drowned. In this dilemma, every one began to think of the best means of saving himself. The yawl and jolly boat had already been dashed to pieces by the violence of the surf; so that the only means of preservation now left was by the hawser made fast to the rocks, hand over hand. Several got safe on shore in this manner, while others, to the number of fifteen, perished in the difficult attempt.

The ship soon separated just before the main-mast. The wind, at the same time, providentially shifted to the old quarter, and blew directly to the land; a circumstance which contributed greatly to the preservation of those on board, who all got on the poop, as being nearest to the shore. The wind and surges now impelling them, that part of the wreck on which the people were rent asunder fore and aft, the deck splitting in two. In this distress they crowded upon the starboard quarter, which soon floated into shoal water, the other parts of the wreck breaking off those heavy seas which would otherwise have ingulphed or dashed them to pieces. Through this fortunate incident, all on board, even the ladies and children, got safe on shore, except the cook's mate, a black, who, being drunk, could not be prevailed upon to leave the wreck.

Before this arduous business was well effected night came on, and the natives having retired, several fires were lighted with fuel from the wreck, and the whole company supped on such provisions as they picked up on the shore. Two tents were formed of sails that had drifted to the shore, and in these the ladies were left to repose, while the men wandered about in search of such articles as might be of service.

On the morning of the 5th, the natives returned, and, without ceremony, carried off whatever suited their fancy. This conduct excited a thousand apprehensions, particularly in the minds of the females, for their personal safety; but observing that the savages contented themselves with plunder, their fears were somewhat allayed.

The next day was employed in collecting together all

the articles that might be useful in their journey to the Cape, to which they imprudently resolved to direct their course; a resolution which involved them in complicated misery, and which can be justified by no wise principle From the wreck they might easily have built a vessel capable of containing them all, and by coasting along, they might have reached the nearest of the Dutch settlements with half the danger or risk to which they were then exposing themselves. Distress, however, sometimes deprives men of all presence of mind; so the crew of the Grosvenor, having just escaped the dangers of the sea, appear to have considered land as the most desirable alternative, without reflecting on the almost insuperable obstacles that lay in their way.

On examining their stores, they found themselves in possession of two casks of flour and a tub of pork, that had been washed on the beach, and some arrack, which the captain prudently ordered to be staved, lest the natives should get at it, and by intoxication increase their natural ferocity.

Captain Coxson now called together the survivors, and having divided the provisions among them, asked if they consented to his continuing in the command, to which they unanimously agreed. He then informed them, that from the best calculation he could make, he was in hopes of being able to reach some of the Dutch settlements in fifteen or sixteen days. In this calculation the captain was probably not much mistaken. Subsequent observations prove that the Grosvenor must have been wrecked between the twenty-seventh and twenty-eighth degrees of south latitude; and as the Dutch colonies extend beyond the thirty-first degree, they might have accomplished the journey within the time specified, had not rivers intervened and retarded their progress.

Every thing being arranged, they set out on their journey on the seventh, leaving behind only an old East-India soldier, who, being lame, preferred trusting himself to the natives till some more favorable opportunity of getting away should present itself; adding, that he might as well die with them as end his life on the way with pain and hunger.

As they moved forward they were followed by some of the natives, while others remained at the wreck. Those who accompanied them plundered them, from time to time, of whatever they liked, and sometimes threw stones at them. After proceeding a few miles they were met by a party of about thirty of the natives, whose hair was fastened up in a comical form, and their faces painted red. Among these was a man who spoke Dutch, who, it afterwards appeared, was a runaway slave from the Cape, on account of some crimes, and was named Trout. When this man came up to the English he inquired who they were, and whither they were going. Finding by their answers that they had been cast away, he informed them, that their intended journey to the Cape would be attended with unspeakable difficulties from the natives, the wild beasts, and the nature of the country through which they would have to pass.

Though this did not contribute to raise their spirits they tried to engage him as a guide, but no arguments could prevail upon him to comply with their wishes. Finding all their solicitations fruitless, they pursued their journey for four or five days, during which they were constantly surrounded by the natives, who took from them whatever they pleased, but invariably retired on the approach of night.

As they proceeded they saw many villages, which they carefully avoided, that they might be less exposed to the insults of the natives. At length they came to a deep gully, where they were met by three Caffres, armed with lances, which they held several times to the captain's throat. Irritated beyond all patience by their conduct, he wrenched one of the lances from their hands and broke it. Of this the natives seemed to take no notice, and went away; but the next day, on coming to a large village, they there found the three men, with three or four hundred of their countrymen, all armed with lances and targets. As the English advanced they were stopped by these people, who began to pilfer and insult them, and at last fell upon and beat them.

Conceiving that it was the intention of the natives to

kill them, they formed a resolution to defend themselves to the last extremity. Accordingly, placing the women, the children, and the sick at some distance, the remainder, to the number of eighty or ninety, engaged their opponents in a kind of running fight for upwards of two hours, when our countrymen, gaining an eminence, where they could not be surrounded, a kind of parley took place. In this unfortunate encounter many were wounded on both sides, but none killed. After a pacification had taken place, the English cut the buttons from their coats, and presented them to the natives, upon which they went away and returned no more.

The following night they were terrified with the noise of wild beasts, so that the men were obliged to keep watch to prevent their too near approach. What a dreadful situation, especially for females of delicate habits, and so lately possessing all the luxuries that eastern refinement could afford!

When morning arrived they were again joined by Trout, who had been on board the wreck, and had loaded himself with various articles of iron and copper, which he was carrying to his habitation. He cautioned them against making any resistance in future, for as they were not furnished with any weapons of defence, opposition would only tend to irritate the natives and increase obstructions. With this advice he left them.

Having made some progress during the day, they agreed to pass the night near a deep gully, but were so disturbed by the howlings of wild beasts that they could get but little sleep. Though a large fire was kept up to intimidate these unwelcome visiters, they came so near as to occasion a general alarm.

The next day, as they were advancing, a party of natives came down upon them, and plundered them, among other things, of their tinder-box, flint, and steel, which proved an irreparable loss. They were now obliged to carry with them a firebrand by turns, the natives following them until it was almost dark. At length they came to a small river, where they determined to stop during the night. Before the natives retired they became more insolent than ever, robbing the gentlemen of their watches, and the ladies of the diamonds which they had secreted in their hair. Opposition was in vain; the attempt to resist these outrages being productive of fresh insults, and even blows.

The following day they crossed the river. Here their provisions being nearly expended, and the delay and fatigue occasioned by travelling with the women and children being very great, the sailors began to murmur, and each seemed resolved to shift for himself. Accordingly the captain, with Mr. Logie, the first mate, and his wife, the third mate, colonel James and lady, Mr. and Mrs. Hosea, Mr. Newman, a passenger, the purser, the surgeon, and five of the children, agreed to keep together, and travel as before; many of the sailors were also prevailed upon to attend them, by the liberal promises of the passengers.

On the other hand, Mr. Shaw, the second mate, Mr. Trotter, the fourth, Mr. Harris, the fifth, captain Talbot, Messrs. Williams and Taylor, M. D'Espinette, several other gentlemen, and their servants, together with a number of the seamen, in all forty-three persons, among whom was Hynes, from whom much information was afterwards obtained, resolved to hasten forward. A young gentleman of the name of Law, seven or eight years of age, crying after one of the passengers, they agreed to take him with them, and to carry him by turns when tired.

This separation was equally fatal, cruel, and impolitic; however, the second mate's party having been stopped by a river, they once more joined with great satisfaction, and travelled in company the whole of that day and part of the next.

They now arrived at a large village, where they found Trout, who introduced his wife and child to them, and begged a piece of pork. He informed them that this was his residence, and repeated his former declaration, that the natives would not suffer him to depart, even if he were inclined to return to his own country. He, however, communicated various articles of information relative to their journey, for which they made due acknowledgments; but it is to be lamented that he could not be induced to extend his services, or rather that his crimes and character rendered him dangerous to be trusted, and fearful of trusting himself among Christians.

During their conversation with Trout, the natives surrounded them in numbers, and continued to follow them till dusk. The two companies passed the night together, but that distress, which ought to have been the bond of unity, was unfortunately perverted into an occasion for disaffection and complaint.

Their provisions running very short, a party went down to the sea-side to seek for shell-fish on the rocks, and found a considerable quantity of oysters, muscles, and limpets. These were divided among the women, the children, and the sick; for the tide happening to come in before they had collected a sufficient stock, some of the wretched troop were obliged to put up with a very scanty allowance. After a repast which rather excited than gratified their appetites, they continued their march, and about noon reached a small village, where an old man approached them, armed with a lance, which he levelled, making at the same time a noise somewhat resembling the report of a musket. From this circumstance, it is probable, he was acquainted with the use of fire-arms, and apprehended they would kill his cattle, for he immediately drove his herd into the kraall; an inclosure, where they are always secured upon the appearance of danger, and during the night. The old man took no farther notice of the English, but they were followed by some of the other inhabitants of the village, who behaved extremely ill.

The final separation now took place; they parted to meet no more. In adopting this resolution they appear to have been influenced by motives which had, at least, the specious appearance of reason. They conceived, that by pursuing different routes, and travelling in small parties, they should be less the object of jealousy to the natives, and could the more easily procure subsistence.

To counterbalance these advantages, however, they lost that unity of action, that systematic direction, which a prudent superior can communicate to those under his care; and by rejecting established authority, they soon split into parties, guided only by caprice, and swayed by temporary views. After all, they did not part without evincing those emotions so honorable to human nature: their misfortunes had, in some measure, levelled distinctions, and the services of the lowest were regarded as tokens of friendship, not expressions of duty.

From this period the fate of the captain, and his associates, is almost wholly unknown. But imagination cannot form a scene of deeper distress than what the delicate and tender sex, and the innocent children, must have experienced. From the accounts of some of the party who survived their distresses, and subsequent inquiries, it is probable, that the hand of death soon released them from their accumulated ills; though the public mind was long harassed with the belief that a few had been doomed to worse than death among the natives.

The separation being decided upon, the party which had attached itself to the second mate travelled till it was quite dark, when, arriving at a convenient spot, they kindled a fire and reposed for the night.

Next day they proceeded, as they conjectured, thirty miles; and though they saw great numbers of the natives they received from them not the least molestation. Towards the close of the day they reached an extensive wood, and being fearful of entering it, lest they might lose their way, they spent a restless night on its verge, being terribly alarmed by the howlings of wild beasts.

They continued their route the following day till noon, without any other food than wild sorrel and such berries as they observed the birds to peck at. None of the natives made their appearance. The wanderers, having reached a point of the rocks, found some shell-fish, and after refreshing themselves they advanced till they came to the banks of a large river, where they reposed.

Next morning, finding the river very broad and deep,

and several of the company being unable to swim, they resolved to follow its windings, and seek some place where it was fordable. In their way they passed many villages, the inhabitants of which were too much alarmed to yield them any assistance. Pursuing the course of the river a considerable way, and not finding it become narrower, they determined to construct catamarans, a kind of raft, in order to cross it. This being effected, with such materials as they found on the banks, those who could not swim were placed upon the float, which being impelled by the others, they all crossed it in safety, though the river was computed to be not less than two miles over.

It was now three days since they had left the sea, and during that period they had scarcely taken any nourishment but water and a little wild sorrel. They therefore again directed their course to the shore, where they were fortunate enough to find abundance of shell-fish, which afforded them a very seasonable refreshment.

After following the trendings of the coast for three or four days, during which the natives suffered them to pass without molestation, penetrating a pathless wood, where, perhaps, no human being ever trod, uncertain which way to proceed, incommoded by the heat, and exhausted by the fatigues of their march, they were almost ready to sink, when they reached the summit of a hill. Here they rested, and had the satisfaction to see a spacious plain before them, through which a fine stream meandered. As the wild beasts, however, were accustomed, in their nocturnal prowlings, to resort to this place for water, the situation of the travellers was perilous, and subject to continual alarms.

In the morning one of the party ascended a lofty tree to observe the trendings of the coast, after which they resumed their course, and entered another wood just as the night set in. Having passed it by paths which the wild beasts alone had made, they again reached the sea-coast. Here they made fires, which, after the fatigues they had undergone, was a toilsome business, and threw into them the oysters they had collected, to make them open, as they had not a single knife remaining among them. On this spot they reposed, but found no water.

Next day, the wanderers, in the course of their journey, had the good fortune to discover a dead whale, which sight in their present situation afforded them no little satisfaction. The want of a knife to cut it up prevented them from taking full advantage of this accidental supply; some of them, though in the extremity of hunger, nauseated this food: while others, making a fire on the carcass, dug out the part thus roasted, with oyster-shells, and made a hearty meal.

A fine, level country now presented itself, the sight of which caused them to believe that their fatigues were near a termination, and that they had reached the northernmost part of the Dutch colonies. Here new dissensions arose, some advising that they should penetrate inland, while others persevered in the original plan of keeping in the vicinity of the sea-coast.

After many disputes another division of the party took place. Mr. Shaw, the fourth mate, Mr. Harris, the fifth, Messrs. Williams and Taylor, captain Talbot, and seamen, to the number of twenty-two persons, among whom was Hynes, the reporter, resolved to proceed inland. The carpenter, the ship's steward, M. D'Espinette, M. Olivier, with about twenty-four seamen, continued to follow the shore.

The party which took the interior proceeded for three days through a very pleasant country, where they saw a great number of deserted kraals. During this time they had nothing to subsist on but a few oysters, which they carried with them, and some berries and wild sorrel gathered on the way. The effects of hunger soon compelled them to return to the coast, where, as usual, they found a supply of shell-fish. As they were proceeding up a steep hill, soon after their separation, captain Talbot complained of great lassitude, and repeatedly sat down to rest himself. The company several times indulged him by doing the same; but perceiving that he was quite exhausted, they went on, leaving him and his faithful servant, Blair, sitting beside each other, and neither of them was heard of any more.

Having reposed near the shore, the next day, about noon, they arrived at a small river, where they found two of the carpenter's party, who, being unable to swim, had been left behind. The joy of these poor creatures, at the sight of their comrades, was excessive. They were preserved since they had been in this place almost by a miracle, for while they were gathering shell-fish on the beach their fire went out, so that it was wonderful how they escaped being devoured by the wild beasts.

They were with difficulty got over the river, and travelling on for four days more the party came to another river, of such breadth that none of them would attempt to pass it. Having no alternative, they marched along its banks in hopes of finding a practicable passage, and arrived at a village, where the natives showed them the inside of a watch, which some of the carpenter's party had given for a little milk. Mr. Shaw conceiving that such a traffic would not be unacceptable, offered them the inside of his watch for a calf. To these terms they assented, but no sooner had they obtained possession of the price than they withheld the calf, which was immediately driven out of the village.

They continued their march along the river for several days, and passed through several villages without molestation from the inhabitants, till they came to a part where they conceived they should be able to cross. Having constructed a catamaran, as before, they all passed the river in safety, excepting the two who had been left behind by the carpenter's party, and who were afraid to venture. These unfortunate men were never seen afterwards.

Having gained the opposite bank, the company now proceeded, in an oblique direction, towards the shore, which they reached about noon on the third day. The next morning, at the ebbing of the tide, they procured some shell-fish, and having refreshed themselves, they pursued their journey.

In the course of that day's march they fell in with a party of the natives, belonging, as they imagined, to a new nation, by whom they were beaten, and extremely ill treated. To avoid their persecutions they concealed themselves in the woods till the savages had retired when they assembled again and resumed their march They had not proceeded far before they perceived th prints of human feet in the sand, from which they concluded that their late companions were before them. In the hope of rejoining them they traced their supposed footsteps for a while, but soon lost them among the rocks and grass.

After some time they came to another river, not very broad, but of considerable depth, which they passed in safety on a catamaran, as before. Nothing remarkable occurred during the three following days; but at the expiration of that period they overtook the carpenter's party, whose sufferings they found had been even more severe than their own. The carpenter himself had been poisoned by eating some kind of fruit, with the nature of which he was unacquainted: M. D'Espinette and M. Olivier, worn out with famine and fatigue, had been left to their fate. The unfortunate little traveller, Law, was still with them, and had hitherto supported every hardship in an astonishing manner.

Thus once more united they proceeded together til they came to a sandy beach, where they found a couple of planks with a spike nail in each. This convinced them that some European ships had been nea the coast, or that they were in the vicinity of some settlement. The nails were prizes of the first consequence; these, being flattened between two stones, were shaped into something like knives, and, to men in their situation, were considered a most valuable acquisition.

In a short time they came to another river, on whose banks they accidentally found fresh water, which induced them to rest there for the night. In the morning they crossed the river, and on examining the sea-shore they found another dead whale, which diffused a general joy, till a large party of natives, armed with lances, came down upon them. These people, however, perceiving the deplorable condition of the travellers, conducted themselves in such a pacific manner as to dispel their apprehensions. One of them even lent those who were employed upon the whale his lance, by means of which, and their two knives, they cut it into junks, and carried off a considerable quantity, till they could find wood and water to dress it.

On coming to a river the following day, another of the party drooped, and they were under the cruel necessity of leaving him behind. Having plenty of provisions, they now proceeded four days without intermission, and procuring a stick, they set about making a kind of calendar, by cutting a notch for every day; but, in crossing a river, this register of time was lost, and the care they had taken to compute their melancholy days was of no avail.

They soon reached a new river, where they halted for the night. The frequent impediments of rivers much retarded their progress. Few of these, however, are of very great magnitude at any distance from the sea; but as the travellers derived all their subsistence from the watery element, they were obliged to submit to the inconvenience of passing them in general where the tide flowed. This will account for difficulties, from which, had it been practicable, a more inland course would have exempted them.

As the weather was very unfavorable next morning, some of the company were afraid to cross the river, upon which Hynes, and about ten more, being impatient to proceed, swam across, leaving the rest, among whom was master Law, behind them. Having gained the opposite shore, they proceeded till they came to a place where they met with shell-fish, wood, and water. Here they halted two days, in expectation of the arrival of the others; but as it still blew fresh, they concluded that their more timorous companions had not ventured to cross the river; therefore thinking it in vain to wait any longer, they went forward.

They had not travelled many hours before they had the good fortune to discover a dead seal on the beach. One of the knives being in possession of this party, they cut up their prey, dressed part of the flesh on the spot, and carried the rest with them.

The next morning the party left behind overtook them. It was now conducted by the ship's steward, and in the interval from the recent separation it appeared that they had suffered extremely from the natives, from hunger, and fatigue, and that five of them were no more. Thus these unfortunate men were rapidly losing some of their body; yet the reflection of their forlorn condition did not rouse them to the good effects of unanimity, which alone, had it been either a permanent principle, or enforced by an authority to which they ought to have submitted, might have saved them many distresses, and would have tended to the preservation of numbers. Concord is always strength; the contrary, even in the happiest circumstances, is weakness and ruin.

Having shared the remainder of the seal among them, and taken some repose, they again proceeded in one body, and after some time came to a lofty mountain, which it was necessary to cross, or go round the bluff point of a rock on which the surf beat with great violence. The latter appearing to be much the shortest passage, they chose it, but had reason to repent their determination, as they had a miraculous escape with their lives. Some of them not only lost their provisions, but their firebrands, which they had hitherto carefully carried with them, were extinguished by the waves.

Dispirited by this essential loss, which was their chief protection from the wild beasts, they felt the misery of their situation with aggravated force, and an additional gloom clouded their future prospects. Marching along in this disconsolate mood, they fell in with some female natives, who immediately fled. When the travellers came up to the spot where these women had been first descried, they had the satisfaction to find that the fire on which they had been dressing muscles was not extinguished. With joy they lighted their brands, and after a few hours' repose pursued their course.

Next day they arrived at a village, where the natives offered to barter a young bullock with them. The inside of a watch, some buttons, and other trifles, were offered and readily accepted in exchange; the beast being delivered up, was despatched by the lance of one of the natives. The Caffres were pleased to receive back the entrails, and the carcass being divided in the most impartial manner, our people took up their abode for that night near the village, and the next morning passed another river on a catamarah.

The bullock was the only sustenance they had hitherto received from the natives, by barter or favor, excepting that the women sometimes gave the poor child who accompanied them some milk. Among the most barbarous nations, the females, to the honor of their sex, are always found to be comparatively humane, and never was there a more just object of commiseration than master Law. Hitherto he had got on tolerably well, through the benevolent attention of his companions. He walked when able, and when tired they carried him in turn without a murmur. None ever obtained any food without allowing him a share. When the rest were collecting shell-fish he was left to watch the fire, and on their return he participated in the spoils.

They now entered a sandy desert, which they were ten days in passing. In this desolate tract they had many rivers to pass; and had it not been for the supply of food they carried with them, they must all have perished. However, they had wood in abundance, seldom failed to find water by digging in the sand, and being safe from the apprehensions of the natives, this appears to have been the most pleasant part of their journey.

Having crossed the desert, they entered the territories of a new nation, by whom they were sometimes maltreated, and at others were suffered to pass without molestation. Being now on the borders of the ocean, they fell in with a party of the natives, who, by signs, advised them to go inland: and complying with their directions, they soon arrived at a village, where they found only women and children. The women brought out a little milk, which they gave to master Law. It was contained in a small basket. curiously formed of rushes, and so compact as to hold any kind of liquid. Here they had an opportunity of examining several huts, and observed the mode in which the natives churn their butter. The milk is put into a leather bag, which is suspended in the middle of the tent, and pushed backward and forward by two persons, till the butter arrives at a proper consistence. When thus prepared, they mix it with soot, and anoint themselves with the composition, which proves a defence against the intense heat of the climate, and renders their limbs uncommonly pliant and active.

While the travellers were resting themselves, the men belonging to the village returned from hunting, each bearing upon the point of his spear a piece of deer's flesh. They formed a ring round the strangers, and seemed to gaze on them with admiration. After having satisfied their curiosity, they produced two bowls of milk, which they appeared willing to barter; but as our wretched countrymen had nothing to give in exchange, they drank it up themselves.

Scarcely had they finished their meal, when they all rose up, and in an instant went off into the woods, leaving the English under some apprehensions as to the cause of this sudden motion. In a short time, however, they returned with a deer, and though our people earnestly entreated to be permitted to partake of the spoil, the natives not only disregarded their solicitations, but likewise insisted on their quitting the kraal. This they were obliged to comply with, and after walking a few miles they lay down to rest.

For several days they pursued their journey without any remarkable occurrence. They frequently fell in with the natives, who had great numbers of oxen, but they would part with nothing without a return, which was not in the power of the travellers to make. They had, however, the negative satisfaction of not being annoyed in their progress. They now came to another river, where they saw three or four huts, containing only women and children. The flesh of sea-cows and sea-lions was hanging up to dry, of which the women gave the travellers a part. They slept that night at a small distance from these huts.

Next morning, Hynes and nine others swam across the river, but the rest were too timorous to make the attempt. Those who had crossed the river soon afterwards had the good fortune to observe a seal asleep, just at high-water mark, and having cut off his retreat, they found means to kill him. Having divided the flesh, they travelled four or five days, occasionally falling in with the natives, who, upon the whole, behaved with tolerable forbearance.

They now arrived at another river, which they were obliged to cross, and proceeding on their route, the next day found a whale; and thus being well supplied with provisions they resolved to halt for their companions; but after waiting in vain two days they proceeded without them. They afterwards found that their companions had taken a more inland route, and had got before them. Having, therefore, cut up as much of the whale as they could carry, and being much refreshed, they proceeded with alacrity, having now no necessity to loiter in quest of food.

Thus they travelled for more than a week, and in their way discovered some pieces of rags, which satisfied them that their late associates had got the start of them. They now entered an extensive sandy desert, and finding, towards the close of the first day, but little prospect of obtaining either wood or water, they were much disheartened. To their joy, however, at the entrance of a deep gully they saw the following words traced on the sand: *Turn in here and you will find plenty of wood and water.* This cheered them like a revelation from heaven, and on entering the gully they found the notification verified, and the remains of several fires, which assured them that their late companions had reposed in the same place.

They proceeded several days, proportionably exhausted with fatigue as they advanced, but without any memorable occurrence. They now came to a bluff point of a rock, which projected so far into the sea as to obstruct their progress, so that they were obliged to direct their course more inland. To add to their distress, their provisions were again exhausted, when, arriving at a large pond, they luckily found a number of land-crabs, snails, and some sorrel in the vicinity, and on these they made a satisfactory meal.

As soon as it dawned they resumed their journey, and entering a wood, they observed many of the trees torn up by the roots. While they were lost in amazement at this phenomenon, to their terror and astonishment thirty or forty large elephants started up out of the long grass, with which the ground was covered. The travellers stood some moments in suspense, whether they would retreat or advance; but, by taking a circuitous course, they passed these enormous creatures without any injury. The grass in which they lay was not less than eight or nine feet high. This may appear strange to those who are not acquainted with the luxuriant vegetation of tropical climates, but other travellers, of unquestionable veracity, have made the same remarks on Africa.

Having reached the sea-shore that night, our travellers were miserably disappointed by the state of the tide, which deprived them of their usual supplies of shell-fish. To such extremities were they, in consequence, reduced, that some of them, who had made shoes of the hide of the bullock obtained in barter from the natives, singed off the hair, broiled and eat them. This unsavory dish they rendered as palatable as possible by means of some wild celery they found on the spot, and the whole party partook of it.

At low water they went as usual to the rocks to procure shell-fish; and as they proceeded they often perceived evident traces of that division of their party which had got the start of them. In two days' time they fell in with a hunting party of the natives, who offered no molestation to our people as they passed, and for several days they everywhere behaved with the same forbearance.

After passing two rivers, and finding no fresh water near them, they entered a sterile country, where the natives appeared to have nothing to subsist on but what they derived from hunting and fishing. What then must have been the situation of our travellers! They had not a drop of water for several days; and a few berries which they occasionally picked up were the only alleviation of their burning thirst. However, they soon reached Caffraria, properly so called, which they found to be a fine and populous country.

During their march through this territory our travellers were absolutely starving in the midst of plenty. They saw abundance of cattle, but so tenacious were the natives of their property, that they would not part with any thing gratuitously, and our people had nothing to give in barter. So apprehensive were the Caffres, lest these poor vagrants might commit depredations, that they constantly secured their cattle as they approached, and even used violence to keep them at a distance. So true it is that in all countries poverty is considered rather as a crime than a misfortune, and that he who has nothing to bestow is immediately suspected of an intention to take away.

But the Caffres have been characterized as a humane and inoffensive people. How are we then to reconcile this description with the conduct they displayed to our countrymen? May not the idea, that they were Dutchmen, solve the difficulty? Between the Caffres and the Dutch colonists an inveterate enmity subsisted at that period. The Caffres had been treated with unparalleled cruelty and oppression by the white people, with whom they were conversant; all white people were, therefore, probably regarded as enemies. Among uncivilized nations, wherever any intercourse has been established with Europeans, the characters of the latter, in general, have been determined from the conduct of a worthless few. Thus, as on other important occasions, many suffer for the vices of individuals.

Our travellers, everywhere repelled, or regarded with apprehension, at length came to a river, and having crossed it, were met by a party of the natives, one of whom had adorned his hair with a piece of a silver buckle, which was known to have belonged to the ship's cook. It seems the cook, who set a particular value upon his buckles, had covered them with bits of cloth, to conceal them from the natives; but at length hunger had compelled him to break them up, in order to barter them for food: but no sooner was the price deposited than the natives broke their engagement, as had been their general practice, except in one solitary instance, and drove the claimants away.

Hynes and his party were roughly handled by the natives they had fallen in with. To avoid their persecution, they travelled till late at night, and after reposing for a few hours, they recommenced their journey before it was light, that they might escape a repetition of their ill treatment.

Next day, about noon, they reached a spot where there was good water, and a probability of finding an abundance of shell-fish; here, being much fatigued, they determined to spend the night. While in this situation they were overtaken by a tremendous storm of thunder and lightning, and the rain poured down in such torrents that they were obliged to hold up their canvass frocks over the fire to save it from being extinguished. Next day, at low water, they found shell-fish, as usual, staid some time to dry their clothes, and then resumed their journey. Coming to a large village the inhabitants fell upon them with such fury, that several of them were wounded, in consequence of which, one man died soon afterwards. Hynes received a wound in his leg from a lance, and being knocked down, was left senseless on the spot by his companions, who supposed him to be dead. However, in a few hours, to their great joy, he rejoined his countrymen, who had despaired of ever seeing him again.

From this time they lost sight of the habitations of the natives, and entered a sandy desert, where it was with the utmost difficulty they could procure any sustenance. At intervals, indeed, they experienced the usual bounty of the sea, and having collected as many shell-fish as possible, they opened them in the fire, and taking out the animal, left the shells, which greatly diminished the labor of carriage.

Having passed the desert, they arrived at a large river, which, as they afterwards learned from the Dutch, is called Bosjesman's river. Here they found Thomas Lewis, one of the party which had gone before them, who, having been taken ill, was abandoned to his fate. He informed them that he had travelled inland and seen many huts, at one of which he obtained a little milk, and at another was beaten away. He added, that having reached the place where he now was, he found himself too weak to cross the river, and was, therefore, determined to return to the nearest kraal, indifferent as to his reception or his life. In vain his companions strove to overcome this determination. They flattered him with the hope of yet being able to reach the Cape, but their encouragement was ineffectual. Both his body and mind were broken down; he had drained the cup of affliction to the dregs; despair had laid her iron hand upon him, and sealed him for her own. In spite of all their entreaties he went back to the natives, and once more had the good fortune to receive assistance, when he could least of all expect it, and in such a shape as proved effectual to his preservation. But we are anticipating events.

On exploring the sea-coast, our people, to their great joy, discovered another whale, and having cut the flesh into junks, took with them as much of it as they were able to carry. Again losing sight of the natives and their huts, they were kept in perpetual alarm by the wild beasts, which were here more numerous than in any part of the country through which they had hitherto passed.

On the fourth day, after passing the river, they overtook the ship's steward and master Law, who still survived inexpressible hardships. From them they learned that the cooper had been buried the preceding evening in the sand; but when Hynes and the steward went to take a farewell view of the spot, they found, to their surprise and horror, that the body had been carried off by some carnivorous animal, which had evidently dragged it to a considerable distance.

Hynes' party presented the steward and child with some of the flesh of the whale, by which they were much refreshed; and for eight or ten days more they all proceeded in company. At length they came to a point of rocks, and as the whale was by this time wholly consumed, they went round the edge in search of such sustenance as the sea might afford. This took up so much time that they were obliged to sleep on the rock, where they could procure no water but what was very brackish. In the morning the steward and child were both taken ill, and being unable to proceed, the party agreed to halt till the next day. The extreme coldness of the rock on which they had slept produced a sensible effect on them all: the steward and child still continued very ill. Their companions, therefore, agreed to wait another day, when, if no favorable turn took place, they would be under the painful necessity of abandoning them to their fate. But their humanity was not put to this severe test, for in the course of the following night this poor child resigned his breath, and ceased any longer to share their fatigues and sorrows. They had left him, as they supposed, asleep, near the fire round which they had all rested during the night; but when they had made their arrangements for breakfast, and wished to call him to participate, they found that his soul had taken its flight to another world.

Forgetting their own misery they sensibly felt for the loss of this tender youth, and the affliction of the steward in particular was inexpressible. This child had been the object of his fondest care, during a long and perilous journey, and it was with the utmost difficulty that his companions could tear him from the spot.

They had not proceeded far before one of the party asked for a shell of water, which being given him, he solicited a second, and as soon as he had drunk it, lay down and instantly expired. So much were they habituated to scenes of distress, that, by this time, death had ceased to be regarded as shocking; it was even considered by them as a consummation rather to be wished for than dreaded. They left the poor man where he dropped, and had not advanced far, when another complained of extreme weakness, and sat down upon the sand by the sea-side. Him too they left, compelled by severe necessity, in order to seek for wood and water, promising, if they were successful, to return to assist him.

Having sought in vain for a comfortable resting-place for the night, they were all obliged to repose on the sands. Recollecting the situation of their comrade, one of the party went back to the spot where he had been left, but the unhappy man was not to be found; and as he had nothing to shelter or protect him, it is more than probable that he was carried off by wild beasts.

With the first approach of day they resumed their journey, but their situation was now more deplorable than ever. Having had no water since the middle of the preceding day, they suffered exceedingly from thirst, the glands of their throats and their mouths were much swollen; and in the extremity of thirst they were induced to swallow their own urine.

This was the crisis of calamity. The misery they now underwent was too shocking to relate. Having existed for two days without food or water, they were reduced to such an extremity that when any of them could not furnish himself with a draught of urine, he would borrow a shell full of his more fortunate companion till he was able to repay it. The steward, whose benevolence ought to immortalize his memory, now followed his little favorite to another world. In short, to such a state of wretchedness were they now reduced, that death was stripped of all its terrors.

Next morning two more of the party were reduced to a very languid state; one of them, unable to proceed a step farther, lay down, and his companions, incapable of affording him any assistance, took an affectionate farewell, and left him to expire.

Towards evening they reached a deep gully, which they entered, in the hope of meeting with fresh water. Here they found another of the Grosvenor's crew lying dead, with his right hand cut off at the wrist. A circumstance so singular could not fail to attract the notice of his companions, especially as they recollected that it had been the common asseveration of the deceased,—*May the devil cut my right arm off if it be not true!* It had a sensible effect upon his comrades for a time, as they superstitiously imagined that Providence had interfered, by a miracle, to show its indignation against his profaneness. One of the company, who had lost his own clothes in crossing a river, took the opportunity of supplying himself by stripping the dead man, and then they proceeded till night, without any other sustenance than what their own water afforded them.

Next day brought no alleviation of their miseries. Necessity impelled them to proceed, though hope scarcely darted a ray through the gloom of their prospects. The whole party was, at last, reduced to three persons, Hynes, Evans, and Wormington, and these could hope to survive their companions only a very few days. Their faculties rapidly declined, they could scarcely hear or see, and a vertical sun darted its beams so intensely upon them, that it was with the utmost difficulty they could proceed.

Their misery, from thirst, now became so intolerable, that Wormington earnestly importuned his companions to determine by lot which of them should die, in order that the others might be preserved by drinking his blood. Hynes, though almost childish, was shocked at the proposal; his tears flowed abundantly, and he declared, that as long as he was able to walk he could not think of casting lots; but that, if he should be obliged to drop, they might then use him as they pleased. Upon this, Wormington, shaking hands with Hynes and Evans, suffered them to proceed without him.

Every hour now seemed to throw a deeper gloom over their fate; nature could support no more. Hynes and Evans, however, made another effort to advance, without even indulging a hope of the possibility of relief. They this day saw something before them which had the appearance of large birds, but their surprise may be conceived, when upon a nearer approach they discovered them to be men. Nearly blind and idiots, they did not at first recollect their newly found companions, but after some time they recognised in them four of the steward's party from which they had been separated. One of them, a boy, named Price, advanced to meet them, and gave them the pleasing information, that his associates had fresh water in their possession. This inspired them with new life, and reciprocal inquiries were made relative to the fate of their lost companions. The three men whom Hynes and his companion had overtaken were named Berney, Leary, and De Lasso, who hearing that Wormington was left behind, the two latter went in search of him, charging those who remained not to suffer Hynes and Evans to drink too freely of the water, as several had expired from the eagerness with which they swallowed that fluid after long abstinence.

Wormington was recovered by the humanity of those who went in search of him, and a painful detail of sufferings succeeded. It appeared that the captain's steward had been buried in the sand of the last desert over which they passed, and that the survivors were reduced to such extremity, that after his interment two of the party were sent back to cut off his flesh for their immediate support; but while proceeding upon this horrid errand, they had the good fortune to discover a young seal, newly driven on shore, and fresh bleeding, which proved a most seasonable relief. They farther stated, that they had obtained shell-fish in the sand, when none were to be seen upon it, by observing the manner in which the birds scratched for them. Without this discovery they must inevitably have perished.

Hynes and Evans, recounting their adventures to the party they had joined, among other circumstances mentioned that the ship's steward, whom they had left to expire on the road, had on very decent clothes. This tempted one of them to propose to Evans, who was by this time pretty well recovered, to go back to the spot and strip the body, but the steward could not be found, and they concluded that the wild beasts had anticipated their design. In the evening Evans returned, but without his companion, who had been so indolent and advanced with such a slow pace, that the former was obliged to leave him behind. As he was never seen afterwards, no doubt can be entertained but that he likewise fell a victim to the ravenous beasts. These were so numerous as to be seen in troops of twenty or more; and it was the common and effectual practice of the travellers to shout as loud as possible to drive away those formidable animals.

Having now arrived at a favorable spot for water and shell-fish, they employed two days in collecting provisions for their future march, and in refreshing themselves. Rest and food had an astonishing effect in restoring not only the powers of the body, but of the mind; and in a short time they thought themselves qualified to encounter new fatigues.

With extreme difficulty and danger they passed a large river, supposed to be the Sontag, on a catamaran, and having reached the opposite shore, they looked back with terror and amazement on their fortunate escape from being driven out to sea by the rapidity of the stream. Here they likewise found a kind of shell-fish which buries itself in the sand, and which increased their supplies.

The united party, consisting of six persons, pursued their route over a desert country, where neither hut nor native was to be seen, and in six days reached the Schwartz river, as they afterwards learned, on the banks of which they took up their abode for the night.

The country, at length, began to assume a fertile and cultivated appearance, and some huts appeared at a distance from the shore. While contemplating with pleasure this change of prospect, the grass near them took fire, and spread with great rapidity. They all used every effort to extinguish it, lest this involuntary mischief should provoke the resentment of the natives, or the blaze call them to the spot.

Next morning they swam over the river in safety, and soon discovered another dead whale lying on the seashore. Thus supplied with food they purposed resting here a few days, if they could have found fresh water, but that necessary article being wanting, they cut up as much of the whale as they could carry, and proceeded on their route. In two hours they came to a thicket, where they met with water, and halted to rest.

Next morning four of the party went back to the whale for a larger supply, De Lasso and Price being left in charge of the fire. As Price was collecting fuel he perceived at a little distance two men with guns, and being intimidated at the sight, he returned hastily to the fire, whither the welcome intruders pursued him. These men belonged to a Dutch settlement in the neighborhood, and were in search of some strayed cattle. One of them, named John Battores, supposed to be a Portuguese, was able to converse with De Lasso, the Italian, so as to be understood; a circumstance as fortunate as it was little to be expected. Battores having learned the outline of their melancholy story, accompanied them to the whale, where their companions were employed in cutting away the flesh. Affected at the sight of these miserable objects, he desired them to throw away what they had been collecting, promising them better fare when they reached the habitation to which he belonged.

In vain shall we attempt to describe the sensations of the shipwrecked wanderers on receiving this intelligence, and that they were within four hundred miles of the Cape. The joy that instantly filled every bosom produced effects as various as extraordinary: one man laughed, another wept, and the third danced with transport.

On reaching the house of Mynheer Christopher Rcostooff, to whom Battores was bailiff, they were treated with the kindest attention. The master, on being acquainted with their distress, immediately ordered bread and milk to be set before them; but acting rather on principles of humanity than prudence, he furnished them such a quantity that their weak stomachs were overloaded. After their meal, sacks were spread upon the ground for them to repose on.

It had been so long since they had known any thing

of the calculation of time, that they were unacquainted even with the name of the month; and they were given to understand, that the day of their deliverance was the twenty-ninth of November; so that one hundred and seventeen days had revolved their melancholy hours since they were shipwrecked; a period of suffering almost unparalleled, and during which they had often been miraculously preserved.

Next morning Mynheer Roostooff killed a sheep for the entertainment of his guests, and another Dutchman, of the name of Quin, came with a cart and six horses to convey them towards the Cape. The boy, Price, being lame, from the hardships he had undergone, was detained at Roostooff's house, who kindly undertook his cure, and promised to send him after the others when he had recovered. The rest of the party proceeded to Quin's house, where they were hospitably entertained four days.

From that time they were forwarded in carts, from one settlement to another, till they arrived at Swellendam, about one hundred miles from the Cape. Wherever they passed they experienced the humanity of the farmers, and their wants were relieved with a liberal hand.

At Swellendam they were detained till orders should be received from the governor at the Cape, in regard to their future destiny, Holland and Great Britain being at that time at war. At length two of the party were ordered to be forwarded to the Cape, in order to be examined, while the rest were to remain at Swellendam. Accordingly Wormington, and Leary proceeded to the Cape, where, after being strictly interrogated, they were sent on board a Dutch man-of-war lying in the bay, with orders that they should be set to work. While in this situation, Wormington having discovered that the boatswain was engaged in some fraudulent practices, imprudently threatened to give information, on which the boatswain, desiring him and his companion to step into a boat, conveyed them on board a Danish East Indiaman, just getting under way, and by this fortunate incident they first reached their native land.

But to return to the fate of the rest. Though the flames of war were raging between the two nations, the Dutch government, at the Cape, being informed of the particulars of the loss of the Grosvenor, with a humanity which does them infinite honor, despatched a large party in quest of the unhappy wanderers. This detachment consisted of one hundred Europeans, and three hundred Hottentots, attended by a great number of wagons, each drawn by eight bullocks. The command was given to captain Muller, with orders to proceed, if possible, to the wreck, and load with such articles as might be saved, and to endeavor to discover such of the sufferers as were still wandering about the country, or in the hands of the natives.

De Lasso and Evans accompanied this expedition as guides; but Hynes, being still very weak, was left at Swellendam. The party was well provided with such articles as were most likely to insure them a favorable reception from the natives, and procure the liberty of the unfortunate persons they might find in their way. They proceeded with spirit and alacrity, till the Caffres, in consequence of their antipathy to the colonists, interrupted the expedition. In their progress they found Thomas Lewis, who had been abandoned by his companions, as before mentioned, and William Hatterly, who was servant to the second mate, and had continued with that party till he alone survived. Thus the fate of one division was ascertained.

At other places on the road they met with seven lascars, and two black women, one of whom was servant to Mrs. Logie, and the other to Mrs. Hosea. From these women they learned, that soon after Hynes' party had left the captain and the ladies, they also took separate routes; the latter intending to join the lascars, but what became of them after this separation was unknown. They, indeed, saw the captain's coat on one of the natives, but whether he died or was killed could never be discovered.

After the enmity of the natives prevented the progress of the wagons, some of the party travelled forward fifteen days on horseback, in the prosecution of their plan, but the Caffres still continuing to harass them, they were obliged to return, after an absence of about three months.

Captain Muller returned to Swellendam, with the three Englishmen, the seven lascars, and two black women, the boy, Price, and the two guides, De Lasso and Evans. The people of color were detained at Swellendam; but the English were forwarded to the Cape, where, after being examined by the governor, they were permitted to take their passage to Europe in a Danish ship, the captain of which promised to land them in England: but, excepting Price, who was set on shore at Weymouth, they were all carried to Copenhagen, from whence they at last found their way to England.

Such was the termination of the adventures of these unfortunate people; but the inquiry concerning the fate of the captain and his party was not dropped. Though it is probable that before the first Dutch expedition could have reached them they had all paid the debt of nature; rumors had been spread that several of the English were still in captivity among the natives, and these obtained such general belief, that M. Vailant, whose philanthropy equalled his genius and resolution, made another attempt to discover the reputed captives; but he could learn nothing decisive as to their situation or final fate.

The public mind, however, continued still to be agitated, and the interest which all nations took in the fate of the unhappy persons, particularly the women, some of whom it was reported had been seen, induced a second party of Dutch colonists, with the sanction of government, to make another effort to explore the country and to reach the wreck.

These men, amply provided, set out on the twenty-fourth of August, 1793, from Kaffer Keyl's river, towards cape Natal, on the coast of which the Grosvenor was supposed to have been wrecked. Of this expedition we have a journal kept by Van Reenen, one of the party, and published by captain Riou. It would not be generally interesting to the reader to give the meagre details of distance travelled, and elephants killed; of danger encountered, and rivers crossed; we shall therefore confine ourselves to such incidents as appear to deserve notice, or are connected with the melancholy subject of our narrative.

After proceeding an immense way, on the third of November they arrived among the Hambonaas, a nation quite different from the Caffres. They have a yellow complexion, and their long, coarse hair is frizzled up in the form of a turban. Some of these people informed our adventurers, that, subject to them, there was a village of bastard Christians, descended from people shipwrecked on the coast, of whom three old women were still alive and married to a Hambonaa chief. This intelligence roused their curiosity, and they were fortunate enough to obtain an interview with the old women in question, who said they were sisters, but having been shipwrecked when children, they could not say to what nation they originally belonged. The Dutch adventurers offered to take them and their children back on their return, at which they seemed much pleased. It appears probable, that the reports which had been spread, in regard to some European women being among the natives, originated from this circumstance, and as the existence of any other white people in this quarter was neither known nor suspected, it was naturally concluded that they must have belonged to the Grosvenor.

The Dutch afterwards fell in with Trout, whose name has been mentioned in the preceding narrative. He at first engaged to conduct them to the spot where the Grosvenor was wrecked, and informed them that nothing was then to be seen, excepting some cannon, iron, ballast, and lead: adding, that all the unfortunate crew of that ship had perished, some by the hands of the natives and the rest of hunger.

Trout, who, it is to be feared, was guilty of much duplicity from the first, pretended that he was a freeman, and had sailed in an English ship from Malacca; but finding himself likely to be detected, and probably apprehensive of being carried back to the Cape, he cautiously avoided the Dutch in the sequel, and left them to find their way to the wreck in the best manner they were able.

As they were proceeding to the spot, one of the party, named Houltshausen, unfortunately fell into a pit of burnt stakes, by which he was terribly wounded in the palm of one of his hands, which eventually produced a locked jaw, and terminated in his death. These pits are dug by the natives, and being covered over with branches of trees and grass, serve as snares for the elephants, which frequently fall into them, and are thus taken.

Several of the party, however, proceeded on horseback to the wreck, and found nothing more than what Trout had described remaining. It was plainly perceived that fires had been made in the vicinity, and on a rising ground, between two woods, was a pit, where things had been buried and dug out again. This likewise tallied with the information of Trout, who told them that all the articles collected from the wreck had been dispersed over the country, and that most of them had been carried to Rio de la Goa, to be sold. That place was represented to be about four days' journey from the scene of the catastrophe.

The natives in the neighborhood expressed great astonishment that the Dutch had been at such infinite pains to come in search of the unfortunate crew, and they all promised, that in case of any similar disaster they would protect such people as might be thrown upon the coast, if they could be assured of obtaining beads, copper, and iron, for their trouble, which was liberally promised by the Dutch.

These intrepid adventurers, who were now four hundred and thirty-seven leagues distant from the Cape, and two hundred twenty-six beyond any Christian habitation, finding that nothing farther was to be discovered relative to the wreck, or the fate of the persons who had reached the shore, determined to return, particularly as Houltshausen's illness increased.

On their way back they called at the bastard Christian village, and would have taken under their protection the three old women, who seemed desirous of living

4

among Christians, but they wished first to gather in their crops; adding, when that business was accomplished, their whole race, to the number of four hundred, would be happy to depart from their present settlement. Every indulgence was promised them in case they should be disposed to emigrate to the Cape. On seeing people of the same complexion as themselves they appeared to be exceedingly agitated.

On their homeward journey the Dutch shot many elephants and sea-cows; but on the first of December they met with a terrible accident, while employed in cutting up the sea-cows killed the preceding day. "As we were thus engaged, (says the journalist,) a large elephant made up to the wagons; we instantly pursued and attacked him, when, having received several shot, by which he twice fell, he crept into a very thick underwood. Thinking we had killed him, Tjaart Vander Valdt, Lodewyk Prins, and Ignatus Mulder, advanced to the spot, when he rushed out furiously from the thicket, and catching hold of Prins with his trunk, trod him to death, driving one of his tusks through the body, and throwing it up into the air to the height of thirty feet.

"The others, perceiving that there was no possibility of escaping on horseback, dismounted, and crept into the thicket to hide themselves. The elephant seeing nothing in view but one of the horses, followed him for some time, and then turning about came back to the spot where the dead man was left. At this instant our whole party renewed the attack, and after he had received several more wounds, again escaped into the thickest part of the wood.

"We now supposed ourselves safe, but while we were digging a grave for our unfortunate companion, the elephant rushed out again, and drove us all from the place. Tjaart Vander Valdt got another shot at him; a joint attack being commenced, he began to stagger, and falling, the Hottentots despatched him as he lay on the ground."

The rest of their journey afforded little worth notice. In January, 1791, they reached their respective homes, after surmounting incredible difficulties, in an expedition to which they were prompted solely by a principle of humanity, and the desire of relieving, if any remained alive, such of our countrymen as might be among the natives. No intelligence of this kind could, however, after the most diligent inquiries, be obtained. They were, indeed, informed that the ship's cook had been alive about two years before the period of their journey, but that he then caught the small-pox and died.

We cannot conclude this mournful narrative better than with the sensible reflections of captain Riou.

"Had the party (says he) that set out in search of these shipwrecked people, in 1783, prosecuted their journey with the same degree of zeal and resolution that Van Reenen's party manifested, it is possible they might have discovered and relieved some who have since perished. Yet, as they could not have arrived at the place of the wreck in less than six months after the disaster happened, there is no great probability for supposing, that after such a length of time had elapsed, any great number of the unfortunate sufferers could be remaining alive.

"But what we have most to regret is, that, perhaps, the failure of the endeavors of the unfortunate crew to save their lives was owing to their own misconduct. It is too often the case, that disorder and confusion are the consequences of extreme distress, and that despair, seizing on the unprincipled mind, hurries it on to a subversion of all good order and discipline: so that at the moment when the joint efforts of the whole are most necessary for the general good, each desponding, thoughtless member acts from the impulse of the moment, in whatever manner his tumultuous feelings may direct; and from an erroneous idea of self-interest, or, wonderful as it may appear, from a desire of gratifying a rebellious and turbulent spirit, at a time when it can be done with impunity, is always ready to overturn every plan that may be proposed by his superiors, and the considerate few that happen to be of the party.

"Such must have been, and such we are indeed told

was, the situation of the crew of the Grosvenor subsequent to their shipwreck.

"Though it may be said to be very easy to see errors when their consequences are apparent, it will not surely be too much to assert, that when this ship's crew was once safely on shore, with the advantage of such articles as they could procure from the wreck, their situation, however deplorable, could not be considered as hopeless. For had a chosen body of ten or twenty men marched a few days to the northward, they must have fallen in with Rio de la Goa, where it seldom happens that there is not a French or Portuguese slave ship. But allowing captain Coxson was much out of his reckoning, and that he supposed himself much nearer to the Cape than he really was, they might then have existed on the sea-coast, in that climate, sheltered by huts, till ready to set out, and by preserving order and discipline, and conducting themselves properly in regard to the natives, they might gradually have proceeded in safety to the territories of the Dutch.

"Had the crew continued under the orders of their officers, either of those objects might have been accomplished, by men whose minds were not wholly resigned to despair; or they might have subsisted on what provision they could pick up from the wreck, together with what they could purchase from the natives, till a boat could have been constructed and sent to solicit assistance from the Cape.

"These reflections have been extended by considering the circumstances in which the shipwrecked people were placed; from all which it may fairly be concluded, that the greater part might have effected a return to their native land, had they been guided by any idea of the advantages of discipline and subordination.

"It is to be hoped, then, that the fatal consequences attending disorderly conduct on these calamitous occasions, will impress on the minds of seamen this incontrovertible truth, that their only hope of safety must depend upon obedience."

LOSS OF THE EAST-INDIAMAN, THE FATTYSALEM,

On the Coast of Coromandel, August 28th, 1761.

THE following narrative of the loss of the Fattysalem is given in a letter from M. de Kearney, a captain in Lally's regiment, who was taken prisoner by the English, to the count D'Estaing, lieutenant-general, commanding the French troops in the East Indies, during the war of 1756.

Some time after your departure from India, (says M. de Kearney,) I was taken prisoner by the English, at the battle of Vandevachy, a small fort between Madras and Pondicherry. My conquerors treated me with the greatest generosity, and even did all in their power to save my effects. But I lost every thing I had taken with me for the campaign; the sepoys plundered me without mercy. You are acquainted with that undisciplined militia: they do not comprehend that it is possible to treat as friends; that is, to spare as much as possible those who have been, and may again be, their enemies.

I slept one night in the English camp, and colonel Calliot paid me the greatest attention. The next day I obtained permission to go on my parole to Pondicherry, where I remained several months, and made every possible exertion to procure my exchange. When the place was invested by the English, I was summoned, together with the other prisoners of war, to repair to Madras. I accordingly went to that place, where I found almost two thirds of the officers of the king's army, taken on different occasions. I was, therefore, at Madras when the English, having made themselves masters of Pondicherry, resolved to send all the French officers to England. I was, in consequence, directed to hold myself in readiness for embarking; lord Pigott, the governor of Madras, kindly permitted me to choose the way by which I wished to be conveyed to England. I chose that of Bengal, on account of the good accommodations which lord Pigott had provided me on board the Hawk, and I shall never forget the favors and civilities he conferred upon me. By this arrangement I hoped to alleviate the hardships and fatigues of my passage to Europe. The apprehensions arising from the prospect of such a long voyage, with upwards of fifty prisoners of war, of all descriptions, confined within a narrow compass, and suffering many inconveniences; but, above all, the necessity to which, as I was informed, we should be reduced, of living seven or eight months on salt provisions, though the company had given orders to the contrary, induced me to take this step, as the safest under such circumstances. It was, however, the cause of all my subsequent misfortunes.

The Hawk, in which I was to be conveyed to Europe, proceeded without me from Madras to Bengal, because I had not yet settled all my affairs. I was, therefore, ordered to prepare to join her by the first opportunity that should offer, and which could not be far distant in a season when vessels were sailing every week for the gulf.

The first ship that happened to depart was the Fattysalem, which had been built at Bombay, and had never been employed but in the India seas. She was intended to carry great part of the stores taken by the English, and near five hundred troops, which had been thought fit to send to Bengal, because, after the reduction of Pondicherry, they were not wanted on that coast.

In this unfortunate vessel I embarked on the 26th of August, 1761, and the same day set sail. On the 28th, between ten and eleven in the morning, the captain of the ship, in confidence, told major Gordon, the principal officer of the troops, that there were seven feet water in the hold, that, notwithstanding the exertions of the men, the water continued to gain upon them, and that the ship could not live above two hours longer.

When the people had been nearly two hours employed

lightening the vessel, by throwing every thing overboard, I kept a watchful eye upon the captain. I saw him speaking to the major, with an air of consternation, denoting the greatest misfortune. I advanced towards them and asked in a whisper, in English, what was the matter. Major Gordon with a tremulous voice repeated what he had just heard of the captain. Struck with the dreadful intelligence, but not deprived of the power of acting, I instantly formed my resolution. Cutting short all useless words, I only asked the captain if we might not save ourselves by taking possession of the boat which was laden with pigs, and in tow astern of the vessel. He replied, with the most dejected and discouraging look, that this expedient would only cause us to survive a few hours those we should leave on board; and he did not think this measure practicable among so many soldiers and sailors. This answer convinced me that the pusillanimous captain had no resource. I told him we would undertake the execution of the design, and that for his part he had only to observe two points, not to mention it to others, and to follow when he should see us in the fatal boat. He immediately left us. The major and I being left together, concerted our escape from the vessel, which we executed in less than two minutes. He descended from the deck by a private ladder into the great cabin, to inform the officers of his regiment, who might chance to be there, of our design, for the moments were too precious to go elsewhere to seek them. For my part, I called my servant, a trusty fellow, on whom I could depend. He had been a soldier in my company, and had likewise been taken prisoner; but I had obtained his liberty of lord Pigott. I told him in few words our intention. I immediately shut the door, that the people might not see us from the forecastle. As the ship, though very large, had no gallery, I directed my servant to go out at one of the windows of the cabin, and by means of a rope he let himself down into the boat. I had previously furnished him with my sword and a hatchet, ordering him to despatch without mercy all that attempted to get into the boat, excepting they came from the spot where I was stationed to conduct our descent. Every thing was executed in the best manner; this intelligent servant kept the boat for us till all those whom it was intended to receive had descended, and our little embarkation was effected with such success and expedition that he was not under the necessity of making use of his weapons. As soon as the captain, who through his irresolution had nearly lost the boat, had entered with the rest, the first thing we did was to cut the rope by which she was fastened to the vessel, and to push off, so that in a short time we had got a considerable distance.

We were now in an open boat, abandoned to the impulse of the wind and waves, to the number of twenty-five persons, among whom were two young ladies, the wives of English officers, in Coote's regiment, all badly accommodated, ill-clothed, and mixed promiscuously with the hogs. Our first purpose was to make room, for which purpose we began to throw the pigs overboard; but a lucky reflection of one of the company caused us to keep seven, in order that, at all events, we might not be reduced to the horrible necessity of devouring each other, which must have been the case without this wretched resource. Having thus cleared the boat a little, we were obliged to attend to another point equally pressing. Each of us took off his coat or waistcoat, to make a sail to our bark, and even the ladies were each obliged to give one of the petticoats they had on, which were only of muslin. All these things, being joined and tied together, with our handkerchiefs torn into slips, formed a kind of sail, equally weak and awkward.

While we were thus employed, the unfortunate crew kept making signals that every thing was repaired, with a view to induce us to return. This artifice was employed by our wretched companions, in the hope of saving themselves in our boat. If we had been so weak as to listen to our captain, who fell into such an evident snare, we should have gone back, and all have perished together. We, however, took care not to go near them, and it was fortunate for us that we did; for a few minutes afterwards the ship presented the most distressing spectacle. She was no longer under government; sometimes she drifted away, and at others she turned round like a whirlwind. Soon afterwards one of the masts went by the board; another followed, and the third went next. The ship was now a sheer-hulk, still floating at the will of the waves; but which appeared to be kept afloat only by the incessant exertions of the poor wretches, whose piercing cries filled us with horror. A fog came on; we could no longer distinguish the vessel, and she must in a short time have gone to the bottom.

It is always by comparison that we are fortunate or miserable. What great reason had we to thank Heaven for having preserved us from the fate to which between five and six hundred persons left on board were doomed. But what was the price of our escape? For what miseries reserved? And, how melancholy our situation! In the open sea, in a crazy boat, which a single wave would have sent to the bottom, in the hand of Providence, without compass, or any other rigging than our little sail, which required all our attention.

We had not a drop of water, nor provisions of any kind. Constantly wet with the waves which entered our boat, and continually employed in baling the water, with which we were incessantly inundated; and, notwithstanding this fatiguing labor, were shivering with cold, because we had very few clothes to cover ourselves, and those few were thoroughly soaked. In this state we floated at the mercy of the waves seven days and seven nights.

Our only nourishment was a spoonful and a half of pig's blood, distributed to each every twenty-four hours; for, in order to allow two spoonfuls, it was necessary to mix with it a little salt water; and never was any thing more exactly measured than this scanty pittance. Many of us, whose appetites and stomachs were equally good, eat the flesh of the pigs quite raw, and we killed one each day, so that on the seventh we had nothing left. My principal regale was the liver, or coagulated blood, which I only sucked, and then spit it out. My servant, our butcher, always reserved that part for me.

Soon after twelve o'clock of the seventh night, we thought we heard a noise, that at first appeared very strange, but which we afterwards judged to proceed from the dashing of breakers against the rocks, or against some shore. We floated between fear and joy, and impatiently waited for daylight. That light, so slow in its approach, at length arrived, and every thing disappeared. Judge of the revolution produced in our minds and bodies by this vain hope destroyed, as soon as conceived. It plunged us into such profound consternation, that we should not have been able to bear up against it, had not the hand of the Almighty speedily afforded relief.

About seven the same morning, one of the company cried out, "Land, or something like it." We now distinguished in the horizon a speck which our ardent desire to meet with land actually caused us to take for such. Nature was once more animated by a ray of hope. We directed our course towards the point which appeared in the horizon, and at nine began to distinguish hills, but saw no land till we were on the beach, because the shore is so extremely low. It is impossible to describe the effect this cheering sight produced upon us. I will, however, endeavor to give you some idea of it. We all immediately experienced a certain impression of joy, vigor of life, with which our souls were penetrated, as a person is penetrated by the heat, when, after enduring excessive cold, he comes to a good fire, whose genial influence reanimates his benumbed powers. We felt a delicious sensation of our feeble existence, and this sensation, diffused through all our faculties, seemed to restore us to new life. It is only those who have been in the same situation that can know the inexpressible enjoyment of a moment of which assuredly no other situation in life can afford an idea.

The question now was how to disembark. Here we were under some embarrassment; for the surf was very strong, and the desert appearance of the coast, on which we discovered neither house, nor inhabitants, nor *chelinguis*, (small boats which are used in the East Indies for embarking and going on shore,) was a more convincing proof than the assertion of the pusillanimous captain, that no European boat had ever landed there. A consultation was held, in which it was resolved to make the attempt to let those save themselves who could. This opinion, supported by those who could swim, and particularly by the captain, who even declared that he was sure of getting on shore safe, was too contrary to humanity to be adopted by good sense. It was the same as condemning those who unfortunately were not familiar with the water, and in particular the two females and myself, who knew no more how to swim than they, to almost inevitable death, at least, excepting the Almighty should work a new miracle in our behalf. I reprobated the measure, and told the captain in a firm tone that it should not be executed as long as I had breath; that since part of the company were in the same predicament with myself, and my servant, whose life was as dear to me as my own, it was their duty to steer the boat in such a manner, that we might all get to land in safety. I added, holding my sword drawn before him, that he should answer with his life for that of every individual.

At these words an English officer, of the name of Scott, a hotheaded man, and almost inclined to the most violent measures, exclaimed, "What! does a single Frenchman, and prisoner of war, here pretend to give law to us, and dare to call us barbarians?" "Sir," said I, calmly, "our common misfortune renders us all equal; I am free here as well as you, and repeat it at the risk of all the satisfaction that may be demanded of me when on shore, the captain shall answer with his life for the lives of all our companions."

The captain being intimidated, ordered two lascars, good swimmers, that had escaped with us, to place themselves beside me, and not to quit me till I was on shore. He then went to the helm, and managed so skilfully, or rather with such good fortune, that we ran aground without any accident. In consequence, however, of a very natural impatience, twelve of our companions, the moment the boat struck, leaped into the water, and even some of those who could swim nearly perished. They were besides separated from us, the boat being thrown by two waves into a river, which we did not perceive till we had entered it. This river was so rapid that our boat was soon driven aground, and we thus had an opportunity of getting on shore.

I wish I could describe this moment; but how shall I trace it, with all its circumstances, with the simplicity, the energy, the truth of nature? We scarcely felt the ground, when each, occupied only with himself and the single sentiment of his own preservation, no longer thought of his companions. Our eyes sought only fresh water, and something to prolong our existence. We perceived a small lake, and we instantly ran to its banks, plunging overhead in the water like ducks, to allay a dreadful thirst, a thirst of seven whole days, to which the heat of a burning fever bears no comparison. It would be necessary to have endured, for the same length of time, the devouring fire of thirst, of all human wants the most insupportable, and the most pressing, to form any conception of ours, and our eagerness to appease it. In such a situation, the sufferer would give for a glass of water all the gold and all the diamonds of India; he would give the world. From this you may judge of our protracted sufferings, our transports on the banks of the lake, and the delight we experienced. Having drank our fill, we began some to eat the grass, and others the shell-fish, which fortunately happened to be on the spot where we landed, and during forty-eight hours we had no other nourishment.

We now began to be distressed at our separation into two parties. We endeavored to join each other again, but being prevented by the depth of the torrent that separated us, each company began to march towards the interior of the country, in quest of some habitation. The country belonged to the dominions of the Rajah of Arsapour, situated near the mouth of the Ganges. We had not advanced far, when a snare was laid for us by the natives, that they might the more easily get us into their power. Two fishermen, by whom we had been discovered, were directed to tell us to remain where we were. They assured us that the sovereign of the place was informed of our arrival in his dominions, that he was acquainted with our disaster, and our unfortunate situation, and that, being a prince of a benevolent disposition, he would very soon send us relief of every kind. A few hours afterwards a quantity of rice and hog's lard was actually brought us, with the Rajah's compliments, and a promise that the following day we should be sheltered from the inclemency of the air, and particularly the night dews, which was very dangerous in that climate. This promise they punctually performed, for the next day people came to fetch us, but it was for the purpose of conducting us to a small island, to be kept as prisoners. Each of the two divisions was conducted by a different route, and we knew not what had become of the other. There we remained seven weeks, having no other nourishment than black rice, on paying for it, and twice a week detestable salt fish; and to procure even this we were obliged to sell every thing we had about us. We, however, found means to tame two blacks, to whose care we were consigned, and to procure of them some indulgences. One of our ladies, Mrs. Tait, a native of Ireland, who had a good voice, sung them some English songs, to which they listened with great pleasure, though they understood not a word of them. This complaisance obtained us from time to time some fruits and other refreshments. The water we had to drink was so unwholesome, that out of the two companies thirteen died, and the twelve survivors were all attacked with fevers or dropsies, and were either livid or yellow, and so disfigured, that no one would have taken us for Europeans.

But as no distress is so great as to deprive men of all hope or the power of relieving themselves from it, so our attention was incessantly directed towards the means of escaping from our island. The two lascars who were in our company appeared likely to aid us in the design. With a pencil, which one of the ladies chanced to have

5

preserved, we wrote a note to Barasole, where the English have a small factory. This we prevailed upon the lascars to take, promising them a considerable sum of money, if we should be released from captivity, and on our arrival at the first European settlement. The lascars complied with our desire, and notwithstanding the difficulties of the journey, they set off. They were obliged to swim across three or four very large rivers, and always to travel in the night, to prevent being discovered by the natives. Having escaped many dangers by their dexterity, or surmounted them by their boldness and perseverance, they at length arrived at Cattack, the residence of a Rajah, or chief of the Mahrattas. On their arrival at that place they were carried before the Rajah, and being interrogated respecting their business there, they gave an account of our shipwreck, the manner in which we had escaped, the distresses we had since experienced, and our confinement by the Rajah of Arsapour. They did not forget to add that we had with us two young white women, and that the men were people of consequence. The Mahratta chief then inquired if the men were proper for soldiers; likewise asked whether the women were very fair, and handsome enough for his seraglio. The lascars having satisfied him relative to these particulars, the Rajah immediately sent for the son of the Rajah of Arsapour, who was then his hostage, and ordered him to write to his father, to send off to Cattack, immediately on the receipt of his letter, the Europeans, both men and women, whom he had, for two months, kept prisoners in an island. Conformably to the policy of all the petty sovereigns of India, he likewise took care to order that we might be sent by the worst and least frequented roads, to conceal us as much as possible from the sight of the natives. The order for departure having been given separately to the two parties, we set off with our guides, and had proceeded some hours when we met. We had been parted two months, and during this interval had received no tidings of each other; you may therefore conceive how great was our joy on seeing one another again. We mutually learned the death of those of our companions which each party had lost; and skeletons, walking spectres, that could scarcely walk, congratulated each other on being still alive.

The distance to Cattack was fourteen days' journey; this we travelled on foot, and almost without shoes. Our journeys were very short, because we were all ill, and exhausted with fatigue; besides, our way led almost continually through marshes, up to our waists in mud. We had several large rivers to cross, in the passage of which those who could swim assisted the others. The two young English women, who certainly were not formed for such hardships, were in a most deplorable condition, and the sufferings of these poor creatures seemed to aggravate our own distresses. One of them, Mrs. Nelson, died four days before we reached Cattack, but the other, though three months advanced in her pregnancy, was so fortunate as to arrive at that place in safety.

Although exhausted with fatigue at the end of each day's journey, we were obliged to pass the night under trees, because the people of the country would not permit us to set foot in their houses, the exercise of hospitality towards Europeans being prohibited by their religion. We, at length, arrived at Cattack, but some several days before the others. There we learned that the English had a factory in the place, and repaired thither immediately; but we found only some sepoys in the Company's pay, and not a single European. The sepoys received us with great kindness, and, moved by our situation, they first went to the bazar, or market, to procure us some bread. This we greedily devoured, drinking water, which they gave us, and thus made a delicious repast. We congratulated one another on finding ourselves under a roof, and sheltered from the inclemency of the air; we then lay down and slept. We expected the next day that the Mahratta chief would send some orders relative to us, but he was then on a tour in the country. His minister took no notice of us, and allowed us nothing to subsist upon. The sepoys, therefore, continued to maintain us in the best manner they were able.

During our journey from the island in which we had been confined to Cattack, the two lascars who had effected our release, and had concealed from the Mahratta chief the commission with which they were intrusted by us, proceeded on their route, and arrived at Barrasole, where they acquainted the English with our situation. They then went to Calcutta, and called upon Mr. Van Sittart, the English governor of Bengal. The governor lost no time in sending us relief; but, on account of the distance, we did not receive it till twenty or twenty-five days after our arrival at Cattack. He used all his influence with the Mahrattas to obtain our liberty, but as they were not, at that time, on very good terms with the Company, they refused to grant this favor to merchants. It was, therefore, necessary that colonel Coote, the conqueror of India, should demand our release, which he obtained without difficulty.

Our company was soon anxious to repair to Barrasole, at the distance of six days' journey. As for me and my faithful servant we did not wait for the general order to depart, but set off before the rest. I had found at Cattack an European, a native of Russia, who had been a gunner in M. De Bussy's army, and was now an artillery officer in the service of the Mahrattas. As he understood and could speak the French language, I endeavored, without informing him who I was, to learn his sentiments relative to M. De Bussy. He assured me that it was he who had given the Asiatics the highest idea of the Europeans, that he should regret him all his life, and should never cease to adore him; these were his expressions. On this I told him I was a Frenchman, and prisoner of war to the English; that I had with me a servant, to whom I was strongly attached, and that I was desirous of leaving Cattack as speedily as possible. He replied that he would procure me permission to leave the place, provided the others should know nothing of the matter till the moment of our departure. I kept the secret, and he actually obtained a kind of permission for me and my servant. I immediately hired two dooleys, a kind of handbarrow carried by men. To pay for these and to support us on our journey, I sold my stock buckle and sleeve buttons, the only things I had left. I then took leave of my companions, frankly informing them how and by what means I had obtained permission to depart, that they might employ the same method.

Our journey to Barrasole had nearly proved fatal to us; being twice attacked by tigers, and had the pain to see a Moor, that had been very serviceable to us several times in our distress, carried off, at the distance of a few paces from us, by one of these cruel animals. The same tiger, after despatching the unfortunate man, came again out of the wood, and gazed on us with a most terrible look, but keeping close together, our firmness, and the noise we made, obliged him to retire.

On my arrival at Barrasole, I met with some Englishmen going to embark for Bengal. They proposed to me to accompany them. I had scarcely time to drink a glass, and went on board.

We were six or seven days in reaching Calcutta, it being so very difficult to ascend the Ganges, and were again near perishing in this short passage, where you meet with rocks upon rocks, and dangers upon dangers. When we had arrived at Goupil, I saw several of the East India Company's ships, and begged the English to let me go on board one of them. They perceived that both myself and my servant were sick, exhausted, and in want of every thing; therefore, at the expense of two rupees, all the money I had left, I procured a boat to carry me on board the Plassy, commanded by captain Ward. When I had got on board this ship, I imagined my hardships at an end, and every thing was almost forgotten. The first person I spoke to was Mr. White, a captain of the Company's troops. He took my servant and me for two soldiers who had been robbed; our figure and dress, equally worthy of pity, announced the most miserable condition. This generous Englishman, addressing himself to me, said, in his own language,—"Poor soldier! you are badly equipped. Who are you, and whence do you come?" I replied in English, "You are right, I am a soldier, and my servant there is one likewise; we think ourselves very fortunate in being still in existence." I added, that I was one out of twelve who had escaped from the ship Fattysalem, which had been lost, together with the crew, on the coast of Coromandel; that I was indebted for my life, in the first place, to my soldier's courage, and in the next to the exertions of my servant, whom he saw overwhelmed with disease, and unable to stand; and concluded with telling him my name and rank. Mr. White immediately went to his cabin, and brought me a change of clothes from head to foot, of which I certainly stood in great need, for I had for ten weeks worn the same shirt, all in tatters; my servant only dipped it from time to time in water, to ease me a little. The poor fellow, who was quite naked, was likewise supplied with clothes. Mr. White then presented me with some chocolate and something to eat; but I was so weak that the smell only of the chocolate had nearly made me faint, and I could not eat any thing. I drank some tea, and that was all I could get down. I received a thousand other civilities from this worthy man, and the captain showed me equal kindness. When I had changed my things and taken my tea, those gentlemen proposed to me to go up the Ganges to Calcutta with them, in a vessel that was just going to set off. I consented, but not without great regret, at being obliged to leave behind me in the vessel my faithful companion, who was attacked with a violent fever. However, as there was no other alternative, and as the kindness of those gentlemen, both to him and to me, rendered me easy with regard to his fate, I left him, but not without great reluctance. He died soon afterwards in the English hospital at Calcutta.

We arrived at that place the next day. I went to the governor, Mr. Van Sittart, who received me with great humanity, and assigned me, as a prisoner of war, one hundred and twenty rupees per month for my subsistence. I was in great want, and he did not make me any advance. I had recourse to my benefactor, Mr. White, who lent me three hundred rupees, which I expended in the purchase of linen and clothes. I was two months without drawing the allowance assigned me by the governor. I was about to receive it, when I suddenly received an order to embark in the Hawk, which was still on the coast. I was sick, and had no linen made up, nor any thing necessary to set out on so long a voyage. I was, however, pressed to set off. Colonel Coote had the kindness to defer my departure, and the Hawk sailed without me. I therefore had time to equip myself. I flattered myself that Mr. Van Sittart, to whom, in the quality of an officer of the king's etat-major and captain of his forces, I offered the necessary securities, or bills of exchange on the French East India Company, would advance me a sum to pay the debts which my situation had obliged me to contract: but in this hope I found myself mistaken. I mentioned this subject shortly before my departure to colonel Coote, who sent me three hundred rupees. The governor hearing of it, likewise transmitted me four hundred. This was all I received from him, and I could not help receiving this scanty relief, that I might leave no debts behind me.

On the 2d of February, I left Calcutta and returned to Goupil, on the Ganges, where I embarked in the Holdernesse, commanded by captain Brooke. I was received with great kindness by the captain, who had on board thirteen or fourteen other French officers, prisoners like myself. The ship arrived without accident, and after a month's residence at London I was permitted to return to France.

LOSS OF THE AMERICAN SHIP HERCULES,

On the Coast of Caffraria, the 16th of June, 1796.

THE account of the fate of the American ship Hercules, (and of the adventures and sufferings of her crew,) which set out on her voyage from Bengal in the month of December, 1795, involves so much interest, as cannot fail to prove extremely entertaining; nor can it be better detailed than from the account given by the commander, captain Benjamin Stout; whose intention it was, to take in a private freight for Hamburgh, but not finding one that would answer his expectations, he chartered his ship to the British East India Company, who were at that time busily employed in shipping rice for England. Intelligence having reached the settlements in India that a failure of corn throughout the whole of Great Britain was likely to produce a famine, the most active and laudable exertions were made in India to supply the markets at home with rice; and he received on board unwards of nine thousand bags, with directions to proceed to London with every possible despatch. The crew, most of which having been engaged in India, consisted Americans, Danes, Swedes, Dutch, Portuguese, but chiefly lascars, amounting in the whole, men and boys, to about sixty-four. The necessary arrangements for the voyage being completed, they sailed from Sugar-Roads on the 17th of March, 1796.

Nothing material occurred during the voyage until the 1st of June following, at which time they reached the latitude of about 35° south, and 28°, 40′, east longitude. It then began to blow a gale from the westward, which obliged them to lay to under their mizzen stay-sail for six days. During this time the gale continued to blow from the west, but increased progressively until the 7th, when the contentions of the sea and winds presented a scene of horror, of which, perhaps, the annals of marine history give us no example. "Although bred to the sea (says captain Stout) from my earliest life, yet all I had ever seen before, all I had ever heard of or read, gave me no adequate idea of those sublime effects which the violence and raging of the elements produce, and which, at this tremendous hour, seemed to threaten nature itself with dissolution." The ship, raised on mountains of water, was in a moment precipitated into an abyss, where she appeared to wait until the coming sea raised her again into the clouds. The perpetual roaring of the elements echoing through the void, produced such an awful sensation in the minds of the most experienced of the seamen, that several of them appeared for some time in a state of stupefaction; and those less accustomed to the dangers of the sea added to this scene of misery by their shriekings and exclamations.

The terrors of the day could only be surpassed by those of the night. When the darkness came on, it is impossible for man to describe, or human imagination to conceive, a scene of more transcendent and complicated horror. To fill up the measure of their calamities, about the hour of midnight a sudden shift of wind threw the ship into the trough of the sea, which struck her aft, tore away the rudder, started the stern post from the hauden ends, and shattered the whole of her stern frame. The pumps were immediately sounded, and in the course of a few minutes the water had increased to four feet. A gang was immediately ordered to the pumps, and the remainder were employed in getting up rice out of the run of the ship, and heaving it overboard, in order, if possible, to get at the leak. After three or four hundred bags were thrown into the sea, the principal leak was discovered, and the water poured in with astonishing rapidity. In order, therefore, to decrease as much as possible the influx of water, sheets, shirts, jackets, bales of muslin, and every thing of the like description were thrust into the aperture. Had not these exertions been attended with some success, the ship must certainly have gone down, although the pumps delivered fifty tons of water an hour.

As the next day advanced, the weather began to moderate. The men worked incessantly at the pumps, and every exertion was made to keep the ship afloat. They were at this time about two hundred miles from the eastern coast of Africa.

On the 9th, although the violence of the tempest had in a great measure subsided, yet the swell of the sea was tremendous. The longboat was ordered out; but the captain having reason to suspect that some of the crew would endeavor to make off with her, he directed the second mate and three seamen to take possession of her; at the same time giving them arms and express orders to shoot the first man who attempted to board her without his permission. They were also instructed to keep astern, but to stick by the ship until they came to an anchor.

The men having taken their station in the boat, a raft was ordered to be made of all the large spars, which was accordingly done. The whole when lashed together measured about thirty-five feet in length, and fifteen in breadth. At this time the captain apprehended the ship could not make the land, and being convinced, in case of her going down, that all the people could not be received into the longboat, determined not to neglect any measure that presented even a chance of saving the whole.

When the second mate was preparing to obey the orders he had received, and take command of the longboat, the carpenter addressed the captain in a respectful manner, and earnestly entreated him to leave the ship. On being reprimanded for not attending to the pumps, the man burst into tears, and declared, that the whole of the stern frame was shook and loosened in such a manner, that he expected every minute she would go down. The miserable appearance of this man, and the affecting tone of voice in which he delivered his apprehensions, considerably increased the terrors of the crew;

whereupon the captain thought it necessary to declare that he would perform his duty and stick to the ship until he was convinced from his own observation that all hope of saving her was at an end. The carpenter repeated his solicitations, when he was ordered to his post, and assured, at the same time, that unless he made every exertion to encourage the people in their duty at the pumps, he should be immediately thrown into the sea. He retired, and exerted himself afterwards with a manly perseverance.

The captain was immediately addressed on the departure of the carpenter by many of the sailors, and on the same subject. They were so clamorous, and diffused so much in their opinions, that he was nearly going to extremes with some of them.

These circumstances are mentioned as a caution to future navigators, who are intrusted with a command. They too frequently listen to the opinion of their people in time of danger, who are generally for quitting the ship, and taking to boats, masts, yards and spars formed into rafts, or whatever timbers they can lash together; indeed, as the prejudices and sentiments of the common sailors on these occasions are so various, it is not to be supposed that any thing can arise from such a mistaken conduct but confusion and misfortune.

A crew, such as composed that of the Hercules, which consisted of people of various nations, require indeed from their commander a peculiar attention. It may happen, that by humoring their religious prejudices at a particular moment, an essential service may be obtained; and the following remarkable anecdote will tend to elucidate this opinion.

At a period when the tempest raged with the utmost violence, the captain directed most of the crew below, particularly the lascars, to work the pumps. One of them, however, was perceived coming up the gangway, with a handkerchief in his hand; and on being questioned what he was about, he answered in a tone of voice that discovered a perfect confidence in the measure he proposed, that he was going to make an offering to his god. "This handkerchief," said he, "contains a certain quantity of rice, and all the rupees I am worth; suffer me to lash it to the mizzen-top, and rely upon it, sir, we shall all be saved." The captain was going to order him back to the pumps, but recollecting that in so doing he might throw both him and his countrymen into a state of despondency, and thereby lose the benefits of their exertions, he acquiesced. The lascar thanked him, and he soon beheld the child of prejudice mount the tottering ladder without discovering a single apprehension. He lashed the handkerchief to the mizzen top-mast head, fearless of all danger, and arrived in safety on the deck. Confident now that his god was the captain's friend, he went below to inform his brethren that he had done his duty; all the lascars seemed transported with joy, embraced their virtuous companion, and then labored at the pumps with as much alacrity and perseverance as if they had encountered, before, neither apprehension nor fatigue. To their unceasing labors was owing, in a great measure, the preservation of his people.

The shift of wind which threw the ship into the trough of the sea and tore away the rudder, was fortunately a squall of but short duration, not continuing above a quarter of an hour. Had it lasted but a little longer, the ship must have been torn to pieces. The wind came round to its former quarter, and moderated gradually.

After the longboat had been delivered to the care of the second mate, and the raft completed, the captain held a consultation with the officers, and they were all decidedly of opinion that it was impossible to save the ship, and that they had no other chance to preserve their lives than to make the land and run her on shore.

The people, when informed of the issue of this consultation, appeared to work with renovated spirits. This disposition was kept up by being assured they would soon be within sight of land, and that by constantly working at the pumps, the ship would be kept afloat until they reached the shore.

She remained for some time unmanageable, frequently

standing with her head from the land, which all their efforts could not prevent. The captain got a rudder made out of the top-mast, and fixed in the place of the one they had lost; but it was found of little use without the help of the longboat, which he ordered therefore to be hauled athwart her stern, and this served, although with the greatest difficulty, to get her head towards the shore, the wind being variable from the eastward. A cable could have been got out, that might have answered tolerably well to steer the ship; but the people could not be spared from the pumps to attend roussing in on the tackles, or guise, as occasion might require.

On the evening, however, of the 15th, they discovered land at about six leagues' distance. All on board at this moment expressed their joy in shouts and acclamations. The ship still kept nearing the shore, with five feet water in her hold.

On the 16th, in the morning, being then about two miles from the land, and the wind from the westward, the captain ordered the anchor to be let go, that a last effort might be made to stop the leaks, and, if possible, save the ship. But her stern was shattered in such a manner, that after holding another consultation with his officers, it was finally resolved to run the ship on the coast then opposite to them. Another gale threatened them, and no time was to be lost.

The captain immediately ordered his second mate, who was in the boat, to come on board, and he then delivered into his custody the ship's register, and all the papers of consequence he had. After providing him and his three men with water and provisions, he ordered him into the boat again, with directions to keep in the offing; and that after they had run the ship on shore, provided they got safe to land, he would search for some inlet into which he might run with safety. They desired him also to look out for signals which would be occasionally thrown out from the shore to direct his course. The mate faithfully promised to obey his instructions, and then returned to his boat.

They were now on the coast of Caffraria, within a

few leagues where the Infanta river empties itself into the sea. A dreadful crisis approached, and they agreed to meet it with becoming fortitude. The captain therefore gave directions to set the head sail, to heave the spring well taught, in order to get her head towards the shore, and then to cut the cable and the spring. His orders were obeyed with the greatest promptitude.

After running until within something less than half a mile of the shore, she struck on a cluster of rocks. The swell at this moment was tremendous; and from the ship's thumping so violently, it was scarcely possible for the men to hold on. In this situation she remained for about three or four minutes, when a sea took her over the rocks, and carried her about a cable's length nearer the shore, where she again struck, and kept heaving in with a dreadful surf, which every moment made a breach over her.

The lashings that held the raft having given way, and the spars carried to a considerable distance from the ship, they lost all hope from that quarter. At length one of the crew, who was a black, plunged into the waves, and by exertions which seemed more than human, gained and seated himself on the raft. He scarcely remained in that situation for ten minutes, when the whole was turned over and the man completely enveloped in the sea. In a few moments, however, they perceived him in his former seat. Again he endured a similar misfortune; and a third succeeded. Still he buffeted the waves, and gained the raft, until at length, after suffering two hours of fatigue, which, until then, the captain could not possibly imagine human nature could survive, he drifted on land.

The natives, who had kindled several fires, appeared in great numbers on the shore. They were mostly clothed in skins, armed with spears, and accompanied by a vast number of dogs. A party of them seized the man who had landed, and conducted him behind the sand-hills that line the coast, and which hid him entirely from their view.

Twelve of the crew now launched themselves on different spars, and whatever pieces of timber they could find. They braved all difficulties and at last gained the land. No sooner had they reached the beach than the natives came down, seized and conducted them also behind the sand-hills. As it was impossible for those who remained on board to discover what they were about, and observing several parties of the natives appear at different times on the shore, but not accompanied by any of the people, they conceived all those who had landed were massacred, and that a similar fate awaited the whole of them. They who had remained on board the ship were obliged to shelter themselves in the forecastle, as the wreck becoming a fixed object, the sea made over her, and there was no other part where they could remain, even for a moment, in a state of security.

Suspense and apprehension reigned during the whole of the night. Some were of opinion, that to avoid being tortured by the savages, and perhaps thrown into the fires they had perceived on shore, it would be more advisable to resign themselves to a watery element, as in that situation they should only endure a few struggles, and then life would be no more. Others entertained different sentiments, and were for making the shore in as compact a body as possible. "We shall then," said they, "attack the savages with stones, or whatever we can find." This was overruled as a measure impracticable; there was no possibility of six men keeping together; but if such a number could, by a miracle, get on shore without being divided, the natives could destroy them in a moment with their spears. The whole of this miserable night was spent in such consultations; and as the next sun was to light them to their fate, they trembled at its approaching the horizon.

As soon as morning appeared, they looked towards the shore; but not an individual was to be seen. Distraction was now visible in every countenance, and what death to choose the principal consideration. At length, about the hour of nine, the scene changed in a moment. A delirium of ecstasy succeeded, which no pencil can portray, no being can conceive, but those who beheld it.

All the people who had landed the day before were observed making towards the shore; and they soon perceived them beckoning and inviting them to land. In a few minutes, every spar, grating, and piece of timber that could be procured, were afloat, and completely occupied; some with two people, others with more, according to the size. "I immediately (says the captain) stripped off my shirt, put on a short jacket, wrapped a shawl round my waist, in the corner of which I put a gold watch, and keeping my breeches on, seized a spar and launched into the sea. For nearly three quarters of an hour I preserved my hold, and drifted towards the shore. Sometimes I was cast so near as to touch the rocks with my feet, then hurried away to a considerable distance; again I was precipitated forward, and in a moment afterwards carried off by the returning sea. At length a sudden jerk, occasioned by the swell, strained both my arms, and I was compelled to quit the spar. At this instant, although a considerable distance from the beach, a wave that was proceeding rapidly towards the shore bore me along, and in a few moments cast me senseless on the sand. My people who were on shore observed my situation; they ran down, and snatching me from the danger of the coming waves, bore me to a place of security. I was insensible at this time, but soon revived, as they placed me near a fire, and used every means in their power for my recovery. The first subject of inquiry, when my faculties returned, was, of course, the fate of my unfortunate crew; and I enjoyed the heart-felt pleasure of beholding them all around me, except them in the longboat, and one man, who perished near the shore. I then addressed myself to the natives; but on this occasion I labored under the difficulty of not being understood. I knew nothing of their language, and for some time I endeavored to explain myself by signs. Fortunately there was a Hottentot present, who had lived with the Dutch farmers, and could speak their language. My third mate was a Dutchman, and these served as interpreters.

"This difficulty being happily removed, I endeavored

Loss of the Hercules. *Page* 64.

by every means in my power to secure the friendship of the natives. I thanked them in the name of my whole crew, and on the part of my nation, for the liberal and humane assistance they had afforded us in the hour of our misfortune, and solicited their future kindness and support.

"This being, as I conceived, at no great distance from the spot where the Grosvenor was lost in 1782, I inquired of the natives whether any of them remembered such a catastrophe. Most of them answered in the affirmative, and, ascending one of the sand-hills, pointed to the place where the Grosvenor suffered.

"I then desired to know of them whether they had received any certain accounts respecting the fate of captain Coxson, who commanded the Grosvenor, and who was proceeding on his way to the Cape, with several men and women passengers, who were saved from the wreck. They answered, that captain Coxson and his men were slain. One of the chiefs having insisted on taking two of the white ladies to his kraal, the captain and people resisted, and not being armed, were immediately destroyed. The natives, at the same time, gave me to understand, that at the period when the Grosvenor was wrecked, their nation was at war with the colonists; and as the captain and his crew were whites, they could not tell, provided they had reached the Christian farms, but they would assist the colonies in the war. This affected my situation so directly, that I desired to know on what terms the Caffres and the colonists then stood. 'We are friends,' said they, 'and it will be their fault if we are not always so.'

"This answer relieved me from a very serious embarrassment; but the fate of the two unfortunate ladies gave me so much uneasiness, that I most earnestly requested of them to tell me all they knew of their situation; whether they were alive or dead; and if living, in what part of the country they were situated. They replied, and with apparent concern, that one of the ladies had died a short time after her arrival at the kraal; but they understood the other was living, and had several children by the chief. 'Where she now is,' said they, 'we know not.'

"After I had received every possible information on this melancholy subject, we employed ourselves principally during the remainder of the day in assisting the natives to save whatever came on shore from the wreck. When they got a piece of timber, they placed it immediately on the fire, as the readiest method of procuring the iron, which they sought after with the most persevering diligence."

When night came on, the natives retired, and they left us to sleep under the sand-hills, without covering, and without food. The weather was boisterous, and a strong wind from the westward, and the cold severe: a consultation was held in what manner they should dispose of themselves until morning, and they at length resolved that some of them should keep watch during the night, and the rest place themselves near the fire, and, if possible, obtain a little rest.

The night passed without any of the unfortunate sufferers enjoying a moment of repose. Their bodies on one side were heated by the fire, but the cold chilled the other in such a manner as to render the pain hardly supportable. The sand, driven by the winds in prodigious quantities, filled their eyes, ears, and mouths, as they lay under the banks, and kept them in perpetual motion. They likewise entertained apprehensions respecting the natives.

At length day appeared, and the Caffres returned in great numbers. The chief, knowing they were in want of food, brought a bullock, which they immediately slaughtered by knocking the animal on the head with clubs, and penetrating its sides with their spears. It was skinned almost in a moment, and they cut it up in lumps, which they placed on the fire to singe, rather than to roast, and then devoured their respective shares with the highest satisfaction. The beast, as it was given to the famished crew, it might be supposed would be left for their own disposal; but the Caffres were hungry, and they knew nothing of European etiquette. It is true they presented the bullock to them as a donation; but they saw no reason why they should not dispose of the greater part of it.

On cutting up the animal, it was observed they paid more than ordinary attention to the paunch. Several of the Caffres laid violent hands on it; and after giving it a shake for the purpose of emptying the contents, they tore the greater part in slits with their teeth, and swallowed the whole as it came warm from the beast.

Their meal, such as it was, being finished, part of the crew proceeded to the shore, and the longboat was observed at a considerable distance. The ship was dividing very fast, and the gale increasing; many things were therefore cast on shore, which the Caffres were indefatigable in procuring. A cask, however, was thrown on the beach, which considerably excited the captain's anxiety: it contained sixty gallons of rum, a quantity sufficient to have intoxicated the whole of the natives, although they amounted to at least three hundred. The predilection for such liquor is well known, and the consequences of their intoxication were particularly dreaded by the captain. The only way left was to steal to the spot where the cask lay, and stave in the head without being perceived by them. This was happily accomplished, and they afterwards stripped the vessel of the iron hoops, without discovering what had been done, or what it formerly contained.

In the general search on the shore, one of the Caffres had picked up the ship's compass. Not knowing what it was, yet pleased with its formation, he delivered it to the chief, who immediately took it to pieces; and after contemplating the various parts, took the copper ring in which it hung, and suspended it from his neck. He appeared highly pleased with the ornament; and this circumstance induced the captain to present him with one still more glittering, and of course, in his estimation, more valuable: recollecting that he had in his possession a pair of paste knee-buckles, he presented them to the chief, and hung one upon each of his ears.

The moment this was done, the chief stalked about

with an air of uncommon dignity. His people seemed to pay him greater reverence than before, and they were employed for some time in gazing at the brilliancy of the ornaments, and contemplating the august deportment of their chief magistrate.

Towards evening the captain again addressed the chief on the subject of their departure. He requested he would send a guide with them through the deserts to the first Christian settlement, and that nothing should be wanting on his part to recompense his kindness. The Caffre paused for a moment, and then very coolly replied, that he would gratify the captain's wishes; and being desired to name the time when he would suffer them to depart, he gravely answered, "When I consider that matter you shall be made acquainted with my determination." This answer alarmed the unfortunate sufferers. The countenance of the savage appeared to discover some hostile measure that was lurking in his mind; and yet his former conduct was so liberal and humane, that they had no just ground for suspecting his integrity. The natives, however, were perceived consulting together in parties, and from their gestures nothing favorable could be perceived. When the day was drawing to a close, the crew was left to rest under the sand-hills, as on the former night.

The fire was recruited with some timber from the wreck, and sentinels placed as before. The wind blowing hard from the same quarter, they were again tormented with clouds of sand, and a chilling atmosphere. June being one of the winter months, they had to encounter the severities of the season. It was impossible to shift their quarters, as they could not procure timber to light new fires, and the Caffres might be displeased at their not remaining in their former situation. The night passed in consultations and gloomy predictions. The captain told his people not to do any thing that might have the least tendency to displease the natives; to give them every thing they asked for, as the inhabitants of these deserts were only to be dreaded when provoked; but at the same time, if, contrary to their expectation, they made an attack, or endeavored to detain them after a certain time, then he hoped they would firmly unite, and either force their way or perish in the conflict.

When the sun made its appearance, they mounted the most elevated of the sand-hills to look out for the long-boat; but she was not to be discovered in any direction. In a short time they perceived the Caffres advancing. Most of them had assagays in their hands; others were furnished with clubs; some were decorated with ostrich feathers, and their chief wore a leopard-skin, with the captain's knee-buckles suspended as before. They saluted the crew in a very friendly manner, and were accompanied by them to the beach. The wind had increased during the night, and several parts of the ship came on shore. One of the people had picked up a handsaw, and as he perceived the Caffres were indefatigable in procuring iron, he hid it in the sands. This was a valuable acquisition, and became of infinite service to them in the course of their proceedings.

Having secured all they could obtain from the wreck, the captain requested the chief to order some of his people to display their skill in the use of the assagays. This is a spear of about four feet six inches in length, made of an elastic wood, and pointed with iron, which the natives contrive to poison so effectually, that if it wounds either man or beast, death is the inevitable consequence.

The captain's wishes were immediately gratified. The Caffres first placed a block of wood on the ground, and then retired about seventy yards from the spot where it lay. The chief then said they would now behold their manner of fighting when engaged in battle. These compliances, as they seemed to remove former suspicions, gave great satisfaction to the sufferers. A party of about thirty began their manœuvring. They first ran to a considerable distance; then fell, as if motionless, on the ground; in a moment they started up, divided, joined again, and ran in a compact body to the spot from whence they originally set out. After halting for about a minute, they let fly a shower of assagays at the mark, and with a precision that was truly astonishing.

Not a word more passed this day about the departure of the crew. The natives retired as usual on the approach of night. All were employed to gather wood; and after procuring a sufficient quantity, they stretched themselves on the ground, and in spite of wind, sand, and cold, slept until morning.

When day appeared, all were again employed in looking out for the longboat; but she was not to be seen, nor did they ever hear of her again.

The Caffres did not make their appearance this day until the sun had proceeded two hours in its course. As little now was to be procured from the wreck, captain Stout begged the chief to appoint a guide for himself and crew, as he proposed taking his departure on the next day. "I shall furnish you with two," said the chief. These joyful tidings were delivered with so much frankness, that the captain was relieved at once from all apprehension and suspicion.

Desirous of having the Hottentot who served as an interpreter to accompany them through the desert, the chief was given to understand how much the services of this man would not only contribute to their pleasure, but also to their safety. The honest savage, however, had anticipated their wishes; he had previously mentioned it to the Hottentot, who had consented to proceed to the first Christian farm. Another of the tribe, who was better acquainted with the country, had likewise agreed to be of the party; and this information, which was communicated to the crew, diffused a general joy and satisfaction.

After assuring the chief and the Caffres in general of our unalterable friendship, and that the guides should be rewarded to the extent of their wishes, "I told him, (says the captain,) we had endured great distress for want of water, and begged to know where we could procure some. 'I will conduct you,' said he, 'to a spring of excellent water; it is not far from this place; and, if you think proper, we will proceed directly to the spot.' No sooner was the proposal made than we set out; the Caffres singing and dancing as they proceeded, and my people, although not without suspicion, in tolerable spirits."

After travelling westward about four miles through a delightful country, they came at last to a wood, in the bosom of which was discovered a hollow. The Caffres descended first, and when they all arrived at the bottom, the chief pointed to the brook. They drank of the water and found it delicious. After allaying their thirst, they looked about, and from the dismal appearance of the place, were again in a state of apprehension; being mostly of opinion, that nothing less was intended by the Caffres than to massacre the whole party in this sequestered place; that they were decoyed here for the purpose; and that every man should prepare to defend his life. The captain, however, endeavored to quiet their apprehensions, and at last succeeded.

The Caffres having invited the party to remain on this spot during the night, they began to prepare wood for the fires. All hands went to work, and by the assistance of a *handsaw*, they procured some dry trees and underwood, that afforded a very comfortable fire. One of the Hottentots, who was so rich as to possess a tinder-box, struck a light; and this accommodation being not only highly useful, but unexpected, gave new spirits to the whole party.

The natives, as the night came on, did not retire as usual to their kraal. This gave a fresh alarm, which did not appear to be without some cause; situated as the party then were, they were obliged to abide the event, and therefore prepared for the worst that could happen. The watch was set as formerly; but the Caffres, huddling together, were soon lost in sleep. This place, however dismal in its appearance, afforded a tolerable shelter for the night; clouds of sand were no longer troublesome, and the severities of the wind and cold were mitigated by the friendly shade afforded by the trees.

"We were roused," says the captain, "by the savages, as the sun appeared, and we departed from this supposed Golgotha in tolerable spirits. We had, however, consumed the last pound of our bullock, before we left the sand-hills, and our party began to dread an approaching famine. I mentioned the distress of my people to the chief, and he promised to relieve us. We had journeyed but a few miles, when the Caffres told us we must remain where we were that night. We accordingly set to work to procure firewood, and had scarcely completed this necessary business, when the chief presented us with another bullock. It was soon despatched, skinned, cut into pieces of about four pounds each, and we then proceeded to dress them as provision for our journey. This was a business of so much importance, that most of the day was spent in accomplishing it.

"The night passed with less apprehension than before, and when the morning came, we prepared for our departure.

"The moment now arrived when the real intentions of the Caffres were to be developed. The natives came about us, and assisted in dividing the provisions. Each man was to carry his own stock, which amounted to about three or four pounds of beef; this, with some biscuits, which a few of my people had contrived to preserve from the wreck, was to serve us until we reached a Christian settlement. So far from any appearance of hostility, the natives seemed to view our departure with regret. I took the chief by the hand, and thanked him for his great and friendly attentions to me and my unfortunate crew; assuring him at the same time, that if I survived the journey, it would ever be my first consideration to render him and his people some essential service. He thanked me, and then requested I would tell the colonists our ship was lost at sea, and so distant from the land that no part of her could possibly reach the shore. He also desired me to place the utmost confidence in my guides, as they would certainly direct me for the best. After my people and the natives had exchanged some mutual civilities, we parted, and gave one another a last and affectionate adieu."

They did not take their departure on the morning of the 23d until the sun was well up. The guides were intelligent, and gave them to understand that they must on no account travel early, as the wild beasts constantly rose with the sun, and then ranged the deserts in quest of their prey. As they were all unarmed, a single lion, leopard, or panther could have destroyed most of them. It became, therefore, highly necessary they should not stir until these animals had satisfied their hunger, and were retired for the day.

Notwithstanding this cautious and necessary advice, and which was given with a laudable earnestness for their preservation, still the people were so desirous of getting on, that they grew uneasy; but the guides could not be induced to quit the fires until about nine o'clock, at which time they all proceeded, and in good spirits.

Not more than three or four of the party were at this moment in possession of shoes. They had many hundred miles to travel through unknown countries, to ascend mountains of stupendous elevation, penetrate woods, traverse deserts, and ford rivers; and yet they were to combat all these difficulties barefooted, not having saved above four pair of shoes, and even these but in a sad condition.

"As my feet were naked," says the captain, "like most of my people, one of them offered me an old pair of boots which he then wore; but I refused them. My habiliments were a short jacket, a tablecloth, which I found on the shore, wrapt round my loins; a shawl over it; four shirts, which I wore at the same time; a pair of trousers, and a hat. We bore to the westward on our setting out, for the purpose of obtaining fresh water in the course of our journey. Our guides observed, that near the coast the water was generally brackish; we therefore struck into the interior, and were not entirely disappointed in our expectations."

They now travelled through a country beautifully variegated with hills, dales, extensive plains finely watered, but less wooded than the former. The grass appeared of an extraordinary height; but in the course they pursued, not a human footstep could be traced; no cattle, nor sign of cultivation, could be observed. They were not interrupted by any beast of prey, although they constantly perceived their dung. At length, after travelling about thirty-five miles, they began to feel the want of water.

Having searched for this indispensable aliment, with the utmost anxiety and attention, they were so fortunate as to discover, before sunset, a brook that ran near the corner of a wood; and here they determined to rest for the night. They began, therefore, to prepare a sufficient quantity of fuel. The wood was chiefly composed of trees that partook in some degree of the nature of thorn: they cut several, and arranged their fires. One of the Caffres struck a light, and the whole, in a few minutes, was in a blaze. The tinder which he provided was of a particular description; it consisted of a pitchy substance, extracted from a reed, and so tenacious of fire, that a single spark from the steel caught it in a moment. The weather being cold, they resolved to sleep close to one another; but the guides told them the place they had fixed upon to rest during the night was known to be infested with leopards, and that, if they scented the party, nothing could prevent them from destroying some of them. This intelligence induced them to enlarge their fires, and they began to consult upon other measures that were likely to contribute also to their preservation. But such is the powerful influence of Morpheus over the harassed soul, that their conversation had scarcely commenced on this important subject, when they were all relieved from any sense of danger, by gently falling into a sound sleep, in which they remained in perfect security until morning.

No sooner had the sun peeped above the horizon, than they were all roused by the tremendous roaring of lions. Never were men in a situation more truly alarming. Had they discovered them during the night, they must have been torn to pieces when sleeping, as not an individual could attend the watch, or keep awake even for an hour. They therefore congratulated one another on finding they had all escaped, and set out about seven in the morning in company with their guides. They soon arrived at the bank of a small river, which, being perfectly dry, they crossed without difficulty. Shortly after they came to another, which they likewise passed in a few minutes. They reached at length some islands, from the tops of which they discovered several beautiful vales, clothed with long dry grass, and clusters of trees; in other places, forests of considerable extent, and skirting mountains of different elevations. In the course of the day they were in great distress for want of water, and lost much time in the pursuit of it. Indeed they almost despaired of finding any, as the earth appeared so dry as to exhaust all the brooks they had visited. Luckily, however, about sunset, they discovered a small rivulet that ran near the skirt of a forest; and, although the water was not good, yet it still relieved them from a dreadful situation.

Having travelled this day about thirty miles, they determined to remain where they were during the night. All hands, therefore, went immediately to work, for the purpose of getting fuel. They had seen no wild animals in the course of the day, but frequently observed the dung of the elephant and the rhinoceros.

As their situation for this night was as dangerous and deplorable as on the preceding one, they determined to enlarge their fires, as the only means of safety they had left. This was accordingly done, and they had the pleasure to find, when the day appeared, that not an individual was missing of the whole party.

They proceeded on their journey shortly after sunrise; and, as they were to travel through a wood of considerable extent, the guides told them to be upon their guard, as they would certainly be interrupted by wild animals, which resorted to that place in prodigious numbers. They determined, notwithstanding, to brave all dangers, and accordingly proceeded. They indeed escaped the lions, the panthers, the rhinoceros, the elephant, &c. but, unfortunately, about noon, came up with a horde of Caffres, that were distinguished by their own countrymen as a bad tribe. They spoke at first to some Caffre women, who behaved kindly, and gave them one or two baskets of milk. These baskets are made of twigs, wove so closely together as to hold water.

Having proceeded but a short way, after receiving this instance of female liberality, they were stopped by twelve Caffre men, armed with spears, and clothed in leopard-skins. Their guides, alarmed at the appearance of these savages, flew to the banks of the great Fish river, which at that time was not more than two hundred yards from the place where they stood. They repeatedly called on them to return, but in vain; they immediately crossed the bed of the river, which was dry, and having reached the opposite shore, ascended an adjoining mountain with the utmost precipitation. The savages brandished their spears, and appeared by their gestures to menace the destruction of the people. They could not understand them, but supposed they demanded from them whatever articles they possessed; and as these principally consisted of the little stock of provisions they had left, and their clothes, they determined not to part with either.

One of the captain's people had a knife, which was slung over his shoulder. A Caffre perceiving it, made a snatch at the handle; but the owner resisting it, he lost his hold. This so enraged the savage, that he lifted up his assagay with an apparent intention of despatching the object of his resentment. At the moment he stood in this attitude, a more finished picture of horror, or what may be conceived of the infernals, was perhaps never seen before. The savage wore a leopard's skin; his black countenance bedaubed with red ochre; his eyes, inflamed with rage, appeared as if starting from their sockets; his mouth expanded, and his teeth gnashing and grinning with all the fury of an exasperated demon. He was, however, diverted from his purpose, and dropped the assagay.

The crew instantly proceeded to the river, and crossed it in pursuit of their guides, who were standing on the summit of the mountain; when they came up, the guides expressed the utmost satisfaction at their escape. They gave them a terrible description of the people they had just left, and assured them, if the remainder of their horde had not been hunting at the time they got to the Fish river, not a man of them would have survived.

They also declared, that they were the most abominable horde throughout the whole of Caffraria.

Their conversation lasted but a few minutes, when they resolved to descend the mountain, and pursue their journey. Scarcely had they put themselves in motion, when a scene of the most extensive and luxuriant beauties burst in a moment on their view. The danger they had just escaped engaged their attention so entirely, when they gained the summit, that they did not immediately perceive the world of beauties that now lay spread before them. All stood for some time in a state of rapture and amazement. The country was mostly a level, yet pleasingly diversified with gentle elevations, on the tops of which they could perceive clumps of the mimosa tree, and the sides clothed with shrubs of various denominations. A thousand rivulets seemed to meander through this second Eden; frequently skirting or appearing to encircle a plantation of wood; then suddenly taking a different direction, glided through a plain of considerable extent, until it came to a gentle declivity; here it formed a natural cascade, and then, following its course, proceeded in an endless variety throughout the whole of the country.

As they stood gazing on this sylvan scene, they perceived innumerable herds of animals, particularly of the species of the gazelle, scouring over the plains; some darting through the woods, others feeding, or drinking at the rivulets. As far as the eye travelled in pursuit of new beauties, it was most amply gratified, until at length the whole gradually faded on the view, and became lost on the horizon. They were so wrapt in ecstasy in contemplating this landscape, that they forgot their danger, and remained too long upon the mountain. They at length descended and proceeded on their journey.

Before the day closed they fixed on a place where they were to remain until the morning. It was near a wood, mostly composed of that kind of thorn already mentioned. Several of these they immediately cut, not only for the purpose of fuel, but to form a barricade or defence against the wild animals during the night.

After completing their fortification, lighting the fires, and supping in the best manner possible, they lay down to rest; but their sleep was constantly disturbed during the night by a herd of elephants brushing through the wood, passing and returning almost every moment. Had not the fence been erected the preceding evening, they would in all probability have been trampled to death by these monstrous animals. They had the good fortune however to escape; and, about seven the next morning, proceeded on their journey, in company with the guides.

They travelled this day through a delightful country. The land, in some places, seemed to be composed of a red and yellow clay, and the valleys appeared covered with a very thick and long grass, but not a sign of agriculture was to be observed. In the course of the day they perceived a few deserted huts, one of which they entered, but paid severely for their curiosity, as those who ventured in were in a moment entirely covered with fleas.

Water was found sometimes, but it was brackish, although they were at least fifty miles from the sea. They kept at this distance during most of the journey.

They brought up for the night, after travelling about thirty-five miles, at the skirt of a small forest, and provided fuel, with a temporary defence, as before. The provisions being nearly exhausted, they were obliged to eat sparingly, although most of them were ravenously hungry.

About seven in the morning they again set out; but many of the people dropped astern in the course of the day, being almost worn out with fatigue. In this situation it was thought advisable for such of the party as could travel to get forward, and provide a place where wood and water could be had. The captain was of this company; and, that all those who remained behind might find their way, he ordered the Caffre guides to set fire to the long grass, which served during the night as a point of direction. He was likewise in expectation of their coming up before morning, but was sadly disappointed. They remained stationary until the sun appeared, and then went on.

Not one of the people left behind appeared this morning; but the guides were of opinion they would reach a Christian settlement in the course of the day, where assistance would certainly be had. This intelligence gave them new spirits; and they travelled with unusual alertness until they came to a farm-house. Here relief was expected, but none was to be found: the whole place had been deserted for some time; they were obliged, therefore, to sleep again in the air, and leave their absent and miserable companions to all the horrors of the desert.

This was not a night of sleep, but lamentation. They sat round the fire, and spoke of nothing but their absent messmates, and their unfortunate situation. They were left defenceless, without food, hardly able to stand erect, and in a country where the ferocious animals were most numerous. They were likewise every hour in danger of an attack from the Boshis-men, who swarm in these parts, and destroy the unhappy objects of their vengeance with arrows that are poisoned. The sensibility of the people on this melancholy occasion displayed the genuine character of a sailor. Men who could brave all the dangers of the tempest, and face death without a trembling nerve, even in the cannon's mouth, could not, however, speak of their distressed and absent brethren without a tear. Their own misfortunes were forgotten, and their only consideration, during the night, was their unhappy messmates, whom they never expected to behold again.

They remained here for more than an hour after the rising of the sun. Out of sixty, that composed the party when they departed from the beach, thirty-six were so maimed and worn down by fatigue as to be unable to travel: these remained in the desert, if not already destroyed, and had no hope of preservation but by the exertions of the party who were able to proceed. The guides were now certain that a Christian habitation was at hand. The last they saw had been destroyed by the Caffres in the war with the colonists: it was therefore determined to proceed to a place where relief could be obtained, with every possible despatch. The people proceeded with redoubled energy; the salvation of their companions was the incentive, and that consideration banished every idea of danger or fatigue.

They travelled without a single halt for about three hours, when one of the guides, who was advanced, roared out, in a transport of joy, "I see a Hottentot, attending a flock of sheep." It was the voice of a seraph proceeding from a Caffre. They all ran to the place where he stood, and, at a considerable distance, observed a man attending a flock of at least four thousand. They moved in a body towards the shepherd, who seemed at first to be alarmed; but perceiving that they were mostly whites, and unarmed, he stopped until they came up. The captain requested of him to direct them the nearest way to the first settlement, which he did, and at the same time informed us the proprietor was a good man; the distance, he said, was about three miles. The pleasure diffused through the party, on receiving this information, it is impossible to describe. The captain embraced this opportunity, and went on; a general joy succeeded, and who should be foremost was the principal consideration.

At length—ecstatic reflection!—they came within sight of a Christian farm. "Come on, my lads," said the captain, "we are safely moored at last; and our people in the deserts will be soon relieved." Some tottered as they stood, overcome with joy, and could not move; others appeared as in a trance, until at length about ten followed him, and they entered the house of Jan du Pliesies.

Fortunately, this was a settler of the best order, about sixty years old, born in Holland, but who had resided in Africa for many years; humane, generous, and possessing a heart that appeared to be the constant mansion of a virtuous sympathy. His cottage was formed of clay, thatched with a kind of reed, and furnished with a few stools, a table, and some kitchen utensils. His family consisted of five or six sons, their wives and children, together with a daughter, making together about twenty people. His stock, however, was considerable, not less than twelve thousand sheep, and one thousand oxen.

After the alarm which their first appearance occasioned had subsided, the captain told the story of their melancholy disaster, and implored his assistance for the relief of the unhappy people who were left behind. This good man could not listen to the relation without discovering by his countenance the tenderness of his nature. His face, which was naturally pallid, became at certain intervals of a crimson hue: these emotions appeared as the effervescence of sensibility, and to exhibit, in glowing colors, the complexion of virtue.

As no time, he said, should be lost in preparing for the relief of the unfortunate people, he immediately directed two of his sons to harness eight oxen to a wagon. His orders were obeyed with a cheerfulness that evinced an hereditary goodness, and that it had descended, unimpaired, from the sire to his children. They were directed to travel all night; and the guides described the spot so minutely as to avoid all possibility of a mistake. The wagon was soon out of sight, and they all sat down to partake of a sheep, which our liberal host had ordered to be killed for their entertainment.

When the meal was over, the worthy colonist began to interrogate them respecting their journey through Crffraria. He could not possibly conceive, he said, how the Tambochis could be induced to suffer their departure. They were such a horrid race, that nothing was so gratifying to their nature as the shedding of human blood. The Boshis-men, he also observed, were so numerous, and so perpetually on the look-out, that he was amazed at their travelling with any degree of security; but when he considered that they came through a part of Caffraria so infested with carnivorous animals that people could never travel safely but in parties, and well armed, he declared their being then in his house appeared to him a kind of miracle.

The captain took this opportunity of giving our worthy host a proper idea of the Tambochis. His mind had been poisoned by some of his depredating neighbors, and never going on such parties himself, he had entertained these prejudices without having an opportunity of knowing the contrary. He appeared much pleased at the conduct of the Tambochis during our abode in their country, and declared this circumstance alone would relieve him from many hours of uneasiness.

His sequestered mansion was nearly surrounded by trees, on which were hung to dry the skins of lions, tigers, panthers, and other destructive animals killed in the vicinity of his own habitation. The carcasses of two enormous creatures were observed lying near the door, which had the appearance of being recently destroyed. They were two rhinoceroses that the farmer's sons had killed, but the day before, on their own land. This gave rise to a narrative respecting these animals, which the good man related with great circumspection, and which appeared very extraordinary.

"These creatures," said the farmer, "are more savage, and infinitely more to be dreaded, than any other animal of the deserts. Even the lion, when he perceives a rhinoceros, will fly from him in an instant. I had a proof of this," said he, "about two years ago. As I was traversing my lands in the morning, I perceived a lion entering a thicket, about the distance of half a mile from the place where I stood. In a few minutes after I observed a second, then a third, and a fourth came; they seemed to follow one another at their leisure, and, in less than an hour, I counted nine that entered the same wood. Never having seen so many of the same species together, I was desirous to know the event of their meeting, and I concealed myself for the purpose. After waiting for rather more than an hour in my lurking place, without either seeing any of them or hearing any noise from the quarter where they lay, I began to despair of having my curiosity in the least gratified. At length I perceived a rhinoceros of uncommon magnitude approach the wood. He stood motionless for about five minutes when he arrived at a small distance from the thicket, then tossed up his nose, and at last scented the animals that lay concealed. In an instant I saw him dart into the wood, and in the space of about five minutes afterwards I observed all the lions scamper away in different directions, and apparently in the greatest consternation. The rhinoceros beat about the wood in pursuit of his enemies for a considerable time; but not finding any, he broke covert at last and appeared on the plain. He then looked around him, enraged at his disappointment, began tearing up the earth, and discovered every sign of madness and desperation. I remained quietly in my retreat until the animal disappeared, and then returned to my house."

The travellers slept this night on sacks, which their host had arranged for their accommodation. At breakfast on the succeeding morning, their benefactor entertained them with some very interesting observations respecting the country where he resided. He particularly stated the hardships which the colonists endured from the restrictive orders and persecuting conduct of the government at the Cape. "I have lead ore," said he, "on my own farm, so near the surface that we can scrape it up with our hands, and yet we dare not touch it. If we were known to melt and use a single pound of it, we should all be transported, for life, to Batavia."

Before they had finished their meal, their benefactor despatched messengers to his neighboring friends, desiring their assistance to get the crew to the Cape. Several of them came and behaved with the greatest tenderness and liberality. They went so far as to say, that such as were desirous of remaining in the country till they were perfectly recovered, should be accommodated at their houses; and as they travelled once in every year to the Cape, they would take the first opportunity of conveying them thither. The captain thanked them for their kindness, but declined accepting their proposal, as his intention was to make the Cape with every possible expedition.

This conversation was interrupted by a Hottentot servant who ran into the house and declared the "wagon was in sight." All flew to meet it, and the captain had the heart-felt consolation of perceiving twenty-three of his unfortunate people, chiefly lascars, lying down in the machine. On their arrival, the two sons of Pliesies said they found them near a wood, perfectly resigned to their fate, having given up all hopes of relief. The preceding thirteen of their companions had separated from them; but where they had strayed to not one of them could even guess at. These poor fellows, after enduring for a long time the most unexampled miseries, all arrived in safety at the Cape.

They were now forty-seven in number, and as they were to proceed in wagons, such as were afflicted with sore feet, or weak, through hunger and fatigue, would not again be separated from their companions.

Their benevolent host now provided them with a wagon and two sets of oxen, each set containing eight. They were occasionally to relieve each other on the way, and two or three Hottentot servants were appointed as drivers, and to take charge of the relaying cattle. One of the farmer's sons, completely armed, was likewise directed to attend them, and the wagon was stored with provisions and water sufficient for them until they should arrive at the next settlement.

They took their departure from the hospitable mansion of the benevolent Du Pliesies on the morning of the 2d of July. The guard was perpetually on the watch, lest the Boshis-men or the wild animals might dart upon them unperceived. About eight o'clock in the evening, however, they reached the second farm in perfect security. The distance travelled was about thirty-five miles this day, and all the people in good spirits.

The owner, whose name was Cornelius Englebrock, they found also a benevolent character. His cottage was poor indeed, but all that he could afford he gave with cheerfulness. His neighbor's letter was produced, which he read with great attention, and then said, "My friend is a good man, and I always valued him; but you wanted no other recommendation to my poor services than your misfortunes."

They remained here during the night, after partaking of a frugal repast which their host had provided, and which was given with many innocent apologies for its scantiness.

Before their departure on the ensuing morning, the farmer generously presented them with nine sheep. The poor man lamented that he could not let them have a morsel of bread. "We live, (said he,) the year round chiefly on mutton and game, but seldom enjoy the luxury of a loaf." He insisted, however, on the captain's taking the sheep, which he accepted with many thanks, and they then departed on their journey.

During the four or five succeeding days, they travelled on from house to house, generally at fifteen or sixteen miles' distance from each other, and were received at all of them with a disinterested hospitality. These occurrences are related with a scrupulous attention to fidelity, because the colonists, without distinction, have been frequently represented as a ferocious banditti, scarcely to be kept within the pale of authority.

During several days' travelling they could get but little bread, and not much water. The countries were alternately hill and dale, and often afforded the most romantic prospects. They frequently perceived vast quantities of wolves, and such droves of that species of deer which the farmers call spring-buck, that one flock alone could not contain less than from twelve to fourteen thousand. Indeed many of the settlers said they had seen double that number at one time, and frequently killed three at a single shot. . Our travellers likewise saw vast quantities of guinea-fowl, which after a shower of rain are easily caught by the farmers' dogs.

The zebra, or wild ass, is common in these advanced colonies, and many of them were seen. Ostriches were likewise very numerous. They had such plenty of venison at the houses where they stopped, that their stock of nine sheep, furnished by honest Englebrock, was diminished but three in the course of six days.

From the 8th to the 14th of July, their journey was not interrupted by any disagreeable occurrence. The countries through which they passed displayed at every mile a new change of beauties. The mountains were in many places of stupendous height, and the valleys, decorated with wood, were astonishingly fertile in vegetable productions. One of the most extensive of these valleys took them no less than three days and a half in passing. It is called by the settlers Long Cluff, and affords, perhaps, as many romantic scenes as can be found in any spot of the same extent on the face of the earth.

The hills, for seventy or eighty miles, run parallel to each other. The lands between are wonderfully rich, and produce vast quantities of a plant similar in its taste and smell to our thyme. On this fragrant herb are fed immense quantities of sheep and cattle; they devour it with great eagerness, and it gives the mutton a flavor so like our venison, that an epicure might be deceived in the taste. The valleys are generally level, from four to eight miles in breadth, and in several places intersected with rivulets, on the borders of which are frequently perceived whole groves of the aloe-tree.

On or about the 14th, they reached the settlement of an old and blind man. He had a large family, and appeared to possess a comfortable independence. When he heard the story of the travellers, the good farmer burst into tears, and ordered a glass of brandy to be given to each of the crew. After this unusual and cheering repast, he directed some mutton to be delivered to the people, and gave them a pot to dress it in. He then requested the captain to mess with the family, which was complied with, and when supper was ended, this worthy creature said he was so pleased with their escaping the dangers of the seas, and the Caffres, that he would celebrate the meeting with a song. He immediately began and sung with the voice of a Stentor. A general plaudit succeeded; and then the honest benefactor said, "Now, captain, I have a favor to ask of you. Pray, desire all your people to sing." It was impossible to help laughing at this whimsical request; but it was thought good-humor, at such a moment, should not be interrupted; therefore an American sailor was desired to sing one of his best songs. He no sooner began than all the lascars tuned their pipes; this set agoing the Swedes, Portuguese, and Dutchmen, and all the crew; each party sung in their different languages, and at the same time. Such a concert was never heard before; the liberal and merry old colonist was so entertained with their music, that he had nearly dropped from his chair in a fit of laughter.

The captain was provided this night with a sheepskin, on which he rested under the roof of the farmer's cottage; but there was not room for all, and therefore most of the poor fellows were obliged to sleep in the air. A similar inconvenience had happened so frequently since they reached the colonies, that they determined to separate.

On the morning of the 17th they separated, and the captain took with him his chief and third mate, together with one or two more, who were solicitous to accompany him. The country, as they advanced, increased in population; and the farm-houses were, in several places, not more than two miles' distance from each other. Many of them were beautifully situated, and the lands produced grain, oranges, figs, and lemons in abundance. Their grapes likewise appeared to flourish, and supplied them with wine and brandies, which they vended chiefly at the Cape. Vast herds of deer, and partridges out of all number, were seen, and immense tracts of land covered entirely with aloe-trees

From the 17th to the 21st, they travelled a mountainous country; but the valleys constantly presented farms and habitations where the industry of the husbandman was amply rewarded. The flocks of sheep were prodigious; but the cattle were not so numerous, nor in such good condition, as those seen in the more advanced colonies.

On the 22d they arrived at Zwellingdam, and proceeded to the landorse-house. The landorse is the chief man of the place, and his settlement consists of about sixteen or eighteen houses, surrounded by a delightful country, and producing grain, vegetables for culinary purposes, grapes, and fruits of almost every description.

This gentleman gave them a very hospitable reception, and the next morning furnished the captain with a horse and guide, to conduct him to his brother-in-law's. That nothing might be omitted on his part to secure a favorable reception at the Cape, the captain's worthy host gave them a very kind letter to his friend general Craig, commander in chief, acquainting him with the loss of the ship, and the miseries endured by the crew in their travels through the desert. He also requested the general would do them every kindness in his power, which he would acknowledge as an obligation conferred upon himself.

They arrived at the settlement of Johannes Brinch, at Stallen Bush, on the third or fourth day, after travelling a country highly cultivated, and producing immense forests of the aloe-tree. The farmers live here in affluence, and the crew continued to experience the most liberal and kind attention during the remainder of their journey.

On their arrival at Stallen Bush, the captain waited on Mr. Brinch, whose reception can never be mentioned but in terms of the most fervent gratitude and esteem. His residence is one of those delightful places which, from its natural situation and fertility, wraps the beholder, the moment he sees it, in a kind of ecstasy. The vines there are reared with great attention, and are highly productive. Grain, vegetation, and fruits, yield abundant crops; and camphor-trees of very large dimensions thrive also in the settlement. Indeed, the whole settlement seemed to be so precisely what it should be, that any alteration must be a deformity. The people here dress well, but nearer the English than the Dutch style. They have nothing of that sullen taciturnity belonging to the character of the Hollander, but are sprightly and good-humored.

"I remained two days (says the captain) under the roof of this liberal and benevolent gentleman. He pressed me to stay longer; but I was desirous of reaching the Cape, and therefore declined his hospitable invitation. In the morning, therefore, he provided me with a horse and guide, and I took my departure from Stallen Bush, on the 30th, in the morning. Our journey was but short, as we arrived the same evening at the Cape of Good Hope; and although emaciated in my frame yet in tolerable health."

LOSS OF HIS MAJESTY'S SHIP LITCHFIELD,

Of Fifty Guns, on the Coast of Barbary, Nov. 30, 1758.

THE Litchfield, captain Barton, left Ireland on the 11th of November, 1758, in company with several other men-of-war and transports, under the command of commodore Keppel, intended for the reduction of Goree. The voyage was prosperous till the 29th, when at eight in the evening I took charge of the watch, and the weather turned out very squally, with rain. At nine it was extremely dark, with much lightning, the wind varying from S. W. to W. N. W. At half past nine, had a very hard squall. Captain Barton came upon deck and staid till ten; and then left orders to keep sight of the commodore, and make what sail the weather would permit. At eleven saw the commodore bearing south, but the squalls coming on so heavy, we were obliged to hand the main top-sail, and at twelve o'clock were under our courses.

November 30th, at one in the morning, I left the deck in charge of the first lieutenant; the light, which we took to be the commodore's, right ahead, bearing S., wind W. S. W., blowing very hard. At six in the morning I was awaked by a great shock, and a confused noise of the men on deck. I ran up, thinking some ship had run foul of us, for by my own reckoning, and that of every other person in the ship, we were at least thirty-five leagues distant from land; but, before I could reach the quarter-deck, the ship gave a great stroke upon the ground, and the sea broke over her. Just after this I could perceive the land, rocky, rugged and uneven, about two cables' length from us. The ship lying with her broadside to windward. the masts soon went overboard.

carrying some men with them. It is impossible for any but a sufferer to feel our distress at this time; the masts, yards, and sails hanging alongside in a confused heap; the ship beating violently upon the rocks; the waves curling up to an incredible height, then dashing down with such force as if they would immediately have split the ship to pieces, which we, indeed, every moment expected. Having a little recovered from our confusion, we saw it necessary to get every thing we could over to the larboard side, to prevent the ship from heeling off, and exposing the deck to the sea. Some of the people were very earnest to get the boats out, contrary to advice; and, after much entreaty, notwithstanding a most terrible sea, one of the boats was launched, and eight of the best men jumped into her; but she had scarcely got to the ship's stern when she was hurled to the bottom, and every soul in her perished. The rest of the boats were soon washed to pieces on the deck. We then made a raft with the davit, capstan-bars, and some boards, and waited with resignation for Providence to assist us. The ship soon filled with water, so that we had no time to get any provisions up; the quarter-deck and poop were now the only places we could stand upon with security, the waves being mostly spent by the time they reached us, owing to their breaking over the fore part of the ship.

At four in the afternoon, perceiving the sea to be much abated, one of our people attempted to swim, and got safe on shore. There were numbers of Moors upon the rocks ready to take hold of any one, and beckoned much for us to come ashore, which, at first, we took for kindness; but they soon undeceived us, for they had not the humanity to assist any that was entirely naked, but would fly to those who had any thing about them, and strip them before they were quite out of the water, wrangling among themselves about the plunder. In the mean time the poor wretches were left to crawl up the rocks if they were able, if not, they perished unregarded. The second lieutenant and myself, with about sixty-five others, got ashore before dark, but were left exposed to the weather on the cold sand. To preserve ourselves from perishing of cold, we were obliged to go down to the shore, and to bring up pieces of the wreck to make a fire. While thus employed, if we happened to pick up a shirt or handkerchief, and did not give it to the Moors at the first demand, the next thing was a dagger presented to our breasts.

They allowed us a piece of an old sail, which they did not think worth carrying off: with this we made two tents, and crowded ourselves into them, sitting between one another's legs to preserve warmth, and make room. In this uneasy situation, continually bewailing our misery, and that of our poor shipmates on the wreck, we passed a most tedious night, without so much as a drop of water to refresh ourselves, excepting what we caught through our sail-cloth covering.

November 30th, at six in the morning, went down with a number of our men upon the rocks, to assist our shipmates in coming ashore, and found the ship had been greatly shattered in the night. It being now low water, many attempted to swim ashore; some arrived, but others perished. The people on board got the raft into the water, and about fifteen men placed themselves upon it. They had no sooner put off from the wreck than it overturned; most of them recovered again, but scarcely were they on, before it was a second time overturned. Only three or four got hold of it again, and all the rest perished. In the mean time, a good swimmer brought with much difficulty a rope, which I had the good fortune to catch hold of, just when he was quite spent, and had thoughts of quitting it. Some people coming to my assistance, we pulled a large rope ashore with that, and made it fast round a rock. We found this gave great spirits to the poor souls upon the wreck; for, it being hauled taught from the upper part of the stern, made an easy descent to any who had art enough to walk or slide upon a rope, with a smaller rope fixed above to hold by. This was the means of saving a number of lives, though many were washed off by the impetuous surf, and perished. The flood coming on, raised the surf, and prevented any more from coming at that time, so that the ropes could be of no further use. We then retired from the rocks; and hunger prevailing, we set about broiling some of the drowned turkeys, &c. which, with some flour mixed into a paste, and baked upon the coals, constituted our first meal upon this barbarous coast. We found a well of fresh water about half a mile off, which very much refreshed us. But we had scarcely finished this coarse repast, when the Moors, who were now grown numerous, drove us all down to the rocks to bring up empty iron-bound casks, pieces of the wreck which had the most iron about them, and other articles.

About three o'clock in the afternoon we made another meal on the drowned poultry, and finding that this was the best provision we were likely to have, some were ordered to save all they could find, others to raise a larger tent, and the rest sent down to the rocks to look for people coming ashore. The surf greatly increasing with the flood, and breaking upon the fore part of the ship, she was divided into three parts; the fore part turned keel up, the middle part soon dashed into a thousand pieces; the fore part of the poop likewise fell at this time, and about thirty men with it, eight of whom got ashore with our help, but so bruised that we despaired of their recovery. Nothing but the after part of the poop now remained above water, and a very small part of the other decks, on which our captain, and about one hundred and thirty more, remained, expecting every wave to be their last. Every shock threw some off; few or none of whom came on shore alive. During this distress, the Moors laughed uncommonly, and seemed much diverted when a wave, larger than usual, threatened the destruction of the poor wretches on the wreck. Between four and five o'clock the sea was much decreased with the ebb: the rope being still secure, the people began to venture upon it; some tumbled off and perished, but others reached the shore in safety.

About five, we beckoned as much as possible for the captain to come upon the rope, as this seemed to be as good an opportunity as any we had seen; and many arrived in safety with our assistance. Some told us that the captain was determined to stay till all the men had quitted the wreck; however, we still continued to beckon for him, and before it was dark saw him come upon the rope. He was closely followed by a good able seaman, who did all he could to keep up his spirits and assist him in warping. As he could not swim, and had been so many hours without refreshment, with the surf hurling him violently along, he was unable to resist the force of the waves, had lost his hold of the great rope, and must inevitably have perished, had not a wave thrown him within the reach of our ropes, which he had barely sufficient sense to catch hold of. We pulled him up, and after resting a short time on the rocks, he came to himself, and walked up to the tent, desiring us to continue to assist the rest of the people in coming on shore. The villains, the Moors, would have stripped him, though he had nothing on but a plain waistcoat and breeches, if we had not plucked up a little spirit and opposed them; upon which they thought proper to desist. The people continued to come ashore, though many perished in the attempt. The Moors, at length, growing tired with waiting for so little plunder, would not suffer us to remain on the rocks, but drove us all away. I then, with the captain's approbation, went, and by signs made humble supplication to the bashaw, who was in the tent dividing the valuable plunder. He understood us at last, and gave us permission to go down, at the same time sending some Moors with us. We carried firebrands down to let the poor souls on the wreck see that we were still there in readiness to assist them. About nine at night, finding that no more men would venture upon the rope, as the surf was again greatly increased, we retired to the tent, leaving, by the account of the last man that arrived, between thirty and forty souls upon the wreck. We now thought of stowing every body in the tent, and began by fixing the captain in the middle; then made every man lie down on his side, as we could not afford them each a breadth; but, after all, many took easier lodgings in empty casks.

The next morning the weather was moderate and fair. We found the wreck all in pieces on the rocks, and the shore covered with lumber. The people upon the wreck all perished about one in the morning. In the afternoon we called a muster, and found the number of the survivors to be two hundred and twenty; so that one hundred and thirty perished on this melancholy occasion.

On the 2d of December, the weather still continued moderate. We subsisted entirely on the drowned stock, and a little pork to relish it, and the flour made into cakes; all of which we issued regularly and sparingly, being ignorant whether the Moors would furnish us with any thing, they being still very troublesome, and even wanting to rob us of the canvass which covered our tent. At two in the afternoon a black servant arrived, sent by Mr. Butler, a Dane, factor to the American Company at Saffy, a town at the distance of about thirty miles, to inquire into our condition and to offer us assistance. The man having brought pens, ink and paper, the captain sent back a letter by him. Finding there was one who offered us help, it greatly refreshed our afflicted hearts.

In the afternoon of the following day we received a letter from Mr. Butler, with some bread, and a few other necessaries. On the 4th the people were employed in picking up pieces of sails, and whatever else the Moors would permit them. We divided the crew into messes, and served the necessaries we received the preceding day. They had bread, and the flesh of the drowned stock. In the afternoon we received another letter from Mr. Butler, and one at the same time from Mr. Andrews, an Irish gentleman, a merchant at Saffy. The Moors were not so troublesome now as before, most of them going off with what they had got.

On the 5th the drowned stock was entirely consumed, and at low water the people were employed in collecting muscles. At ten in the morning Mr. Andrews arrived, bringing a French surgeon with medicines and plasters, of which some of the men, who had been dreadfully bruised, stood in great need. The following day we served out one of the blankets of the country to every two men, and pampooses, a kind of slippers, to those who were in most want of them. These supplies were likewise brought us by Mr. Andrews. The people were now obliged to live upon muscles and bread, the Moors, who promised us a supply of cattle, having deceived us, and never returned.

The people on the 7th were still employed in collecting muscles and limpets. The Moors began to be a little civil to us, for fear the emperor should punish them for their cruel treatment to us. In the afternoon a messenger arrived from the emperor at Sallee, with general orders to the people to supply us with provisions. They accordingly brought us some lean bullocks and sheep, which Mr. Andrews purchased for us; but at this time we had no pots to make broth in, and the cattle were scarcely fit for any thing else.

In the morning of the 10th we made preparations for marching to Morocco, the emperor having sent orders for that purpose, and camels to carry the lame and the necessaries. At nine, set off with about thirty camels, having got all our liquor with us, divided into hogsheads, for the convenience of carriage on the camels. At noon, joined the crews of one of the transports, and a bomb-tender, that had been wrecked about three leagues to the northward of us. We were then all mounted upon camels, excepting the captain, who was furnished with a horse. We never stopped till seven in the evening, when they procured us two tents only, which would not contain one third of the men, so that most of them lay exposed to the dew, which was very heavy, and extremely cold. We found our whole number to be three hundred and thirty-eight, including officers, men, boys, and three women and a child, which one of the women brought ashore in her teeth.

On the 11th continued our journey, attended by a number of Moors on horseback. At six in the evening we came to our resting-place for that night, and were furnished with tents sufficient to cover all our men.

At five in the morning of the 12th, we set out as before, and, at two in the afternoon, saw the emperor's cavalcade at a distance. At three, a relation of the emperor's, named Muli Adrix, came to us, and told the captain it was the emperor's orders he should that instant write a letter to our governor at Gibraltar, to send to his Britannic majesty to inquire whether he would settle a peace with him or not. Captain Barton immediately sat down upon the grass and wrote a letter, which, being given to Muli Adrix, he went and joined the emperor again. At six in the evening came to our resting-place for the night, and were well furnished with tents, but very little provisions.

We were, the following day, desired to continue on the same spot, till the men were refreshed, and this repose they greatly needed, and we received a better supply of provisions. That morning lieutenant Harrison, commanding the soldiers belonging to lord Forbes' regiment, died suddenly in the tent. In the evening, while employed with his interment, the inhuman Moors disturbed us by throwing stones and mocking us. The next day we found that they had opened the grave and stripped the body.

On the 16th we continued our journey, came to our resting-place at four in the afternoon, pitched the tents, and served out the provisions. Here our people were ill-treated by some of the country Moors. As they were taking water from a brook, the Moors would always spit into the vessel before they would suffer them to take it away. Upon this some of us went down to inquire into the affair, but were immediately saluted with a shower of stones. We ran in upon them, beat some of them pretty soundly, put them to flight, and brought away one, who thought to defend himself with a long knife This fellow was severely punished by the officer who had the charge of conducting us.

The two succeeding days continued our journey, and, at three in the afternoon of the 18th, arrived at the city of Morocco, without having seen a single habitation during the whole journey. Here we were insulted by the rabble, and, at five, were carried before the emperor, surrounded by five or six hundred of his guards. He was on horseback before the gate of his palace, that being the place where he distributes justice to his people. He told captain Barton, by an interpreter, that he was neither at peace nor war with England, and he would detain us till an ambassador arrived from that country to conclude a permanent treaty. The captain then desired that we might not be treated as slaves. He answered hastily, that we should be taken care of. We were then immediately hurried out of his presence, conveyed to two old ruinous houses, shut up amidst dirt and innumerable vermin of every description. Mr. Butler being at Morocco on business, came and supplied us with victuals and drink, and procured liberty for the captain to go home with him to his lodgings. He likewise sent some blankets for the officers, and we made shift to pass the night with tolerable comfort, being very much fatigued.

At nine in the morning of the 21st, the emperor sent orders for the captain and every officer to appear before him. We immediately repaired to his palace; we remained waiting in an outer yard two hours; in the mean time he diverted himself with seeing a clumsy Dutch boat rowed about in a pond by four of our petty officers. About noon we were called before him, and placed in a line about thirty yards from him. He was sitting in a chair by the side of the pond, accompanied only by two of his chief alcaids. Having viewed us some time, he ordered the captain to come forward, and after asking him a good many questions concerning our navy, and destination of the squadron to which we had belonged, we were also called forward by two and three at a time as we stood according to our rank. He then asked most of us some very insignificant questions, and took some to be Portuguese because they had black hair, and others to be Swedes because their hair was light. He judged none of us to be English excepting the captain, the second lieutenant, the ensign of the soldiers, and myself. But assuring him we were all English, he cried *Bonno*, and gave a nod for our departure, to which we

9

returned a very low bow, and were glad to return to our old ruined houses again. Our total number amounted to thirty.

On the 25th, being Christmas day, prayers were read to the people as usual in the church of England. The captain this day received a present of tea and loaves of sugar from one of the queens, whose grandfather had been an English renegado.

In the afternoon of the 26th we received the disagreeable intelligence that the emperor would oblige all the English to work, like all the other Christian slaves, excepting the officers who were before him on the 21st. The next day this account was confirmed; for, at seven in the morning, an alcaid came and ordered all our people to work, excepting the sick. Upon our application, eight were allowed to stay at home every day to cook for the rest, and this office was performed by turns throughout the whole company. At four in the afternoon the people returned, some having been employed in carrying wood, some in turning up the ground with hoes, and others in picking weeds in the emperor's garden. Their victuals was prepared for them against their return.

On the 28th, all the people went to work as soon as they could see, and returned at four in the afternoon. Two of the soldiers received one hundred bastinadoes each, for behaving in a disrespectful manner while the emperor was looking at their work.

On the 30th, captain Barton received a kind message from the emperor, with permission to ride out or take a walk in his garden with his officers.

From this time the men continued in the same state of slavery till the arrival, in April, of captain Milbank, sent as an ambassador to the emperor. He concluded a treaty for the ransom of the crew of the Litchfield, together with the other English subjects in the emperor's power, and the sum stipulated to be paid for their release was one hundred and seventy thousand dollars. Our people accordingly set out for Sallee, attended by a bashaw and two soldiers on horseback. On the fourth day of their march they had a skirmish with some of the country Moors. The dispute began in consequence of some of our men in the rear stopping at a village to buy some milk, for which, after they had drank it, the Moors demanded an exorbitant price. This our men refused to give, on which the Moors had recourse to blows, which our people returned; and others coming to their assistance, they maintained a smart battle, till the enemy became too numerous. In the mean time some rode off to call the guard, who instantly came up with their drawn scimetars, and dealt round them pretty briskly. During this interval we were not idle, and had the pleasure to see the blood trickling down a good many of their faces. The guards seized the chief man of the village, and carried him before the bashaw, who was our conductor, and who, having heard the cause, dismissed him without farther punishment, in consideration of his having been well drubbed by us.

On the 22d of April we arrived at Sallee, and pitched our tents in an old castle, from whence we soon afterwards embarked on board the Gibraltar, which landed us at Gibraltar on the 27th of June. From that place the captain and crew were put on board the Marlborough store ship, prepared expressly for their reception, and arrived in England in the month of August, 1760.

LOSS OF THE PORTUGUESE VESSEL THE ST. JAMES,

Off the Coast of Africa, in 1586.

In the month of May, 1586, intelligence was received at Goa of the loss of the admiral's ship, the St. James. The account of this disaster stated, that after doubling the cape of Good Hope, the captain, conceiving he had neither rocks nor other dangers to dread, proceeded under full sail, without observing his charts, or at least not with the attention he ought. Having a favorable wind, he made much way in a short time, but was driven out of his course towards the rocks called Bassas de India, distant about fifty leagues from the island of Madagascar, and seventy from the continent.

Perceiving they were so near these rocks, and in imminent danger of striking upon them, several of the passengers, who had frequently traversed those seas, were much alarmed. They represented to the captain, that being in the midst of the rocks, it was extremely dangerous to suffer the ship to run under full sail, particularly during the night, and in a season when tempests were very frequent. The captain, regardless of their prudent remonstrances, exerted his authority, ordered the pilots to follow his commands, adding, that the king's commission entitled him to obedience, and that his opinion ought to be taken in preference. However, between eleven and twelve o'clock the same night the vessel was driven towards the rocks, and struck without a possibility of being got off. A confused cry of distress resounded, in every direction, from a multitude composed of above five hundred men and thirty women, who, having no other prospect before their eyes but inevitable destruction, bewailed their fate with the bitterest lamenta-

Loss of the St. James. *Page* 101.

tions. Every effort to save the ship proved ineffectual. The admiral, Fernando Mendoza, the captain, the first pilot, and ten or twelve other persons, instantly threw themselves into the boat, saying they would seek upon the rocks a proper place for collecting the wreck of the ship, with which they might afterwards construct a vessel large enough to convey the whole of the crew to the continent. With this view they actually landed on the rock, but being unable to find a spot proper for the execution of their design, they did not think proper to return to the ship, but resolved to steer towards the African coast. Some provisions which had been thrown in haste into the boat were distributed among them; they then directed their course towards the continent of Africa, where they arrived in safety, after a voyage of seventeen days, and enduring all the horrors of famine and tempestuous weather.

Those who remained on board, finding that the boat did not return, began to despair of saving their lives. To add to their distress, the vessel parted between the two decks, and the pinnace was much damaged by the repeated shocks she sustained from the fury of the waves. The workmen, though very expert, despaired of being able to repair her, when an Italian, named Cypriano Grimaldi, leaped into her, accompanied by ninety of the crew, and, assisted by most of those who had followed him, instantly fell to work to put her into a condition to keep the sea.

Those who could not get on board the pinnace beheld her bearing away from the wreck with tears and lamentations. Several who could swim threw themselves into the sea, in the hope of overtaking her; and some were on the point of getting on board, when their more fortunate comrades, fearing they should be sunk with the weight of all those who endeavored to obtain admittance, pushed them back into the sea, and with their sabres and hatchets cut, without mercy, the hands of such as would not quit their hold. It is impossible to describe the anguish of those who remained on the floating fragments of the wreck, and witnessed this barbarous scene

Seeing themselves cut off from every resource, their cries and lamentations would have melted the hardest heart. The situation of those in the pinnace was not much better; their great number, the want of provisions, their distance from the land, and the bad condition of the crazy bark that bore them, contributed to fill them with gloomy presentiments. Some of the most resolute, however, to prevent the anarchy and confusion which would have aggravated their misery, proposed to their companions to submit to the authority of a captain. To this they all agreed, and immediately chose a nobleman of Portuguese extraction, but born in India, to command them, investing him with absolute power. He instantly employed his authority, in causing the weakest, whom he merely pointed out with his finger, to be thrown overboard. In the number of these was a carpenter, who had assisted in repairing the pinnace; the only favor he requested was a little wine, after which he suffered himself to be thrown into the sea without uttering a word. Another, who was proscribed in the same manner, was saved by an uncommon exertion of fraternal affection. He was already seized and on the point of being sacrificed to imperious necessity, when his younger brother demanded a moment's delay. He observed that his brother was skilful in his profession, that his father and mother were very old, and his sisters not yet settled in life; that he could not be of that service to them which his brother might, and, as circumstances required the sacrifice of one of the two, he begged to die in his stead. His request was complied with, and he was accordingly thrown into the sea. But this courageous youth followed the bark upwards of six hours, making incessant efforts to get on board, sometimes on one side, and sometimes on the other, while those who had thrown him over endeavored to keep him off with their swords. But that which appeared likely to accelerate his end proved his preservation. The young man snatched at a sword, seized it by the blade, and neither the pain, nor the exertions made by him who held it, could make him quit his grasp. The others, admiring his resolution, and moved with the proof of fraternal affection which he had displayed, unanimously agreed to permit him to enter the pinnace. At length, after having endured hunger and thirst, and encountered the dangers of several tempests, they landed on the coast of Africa, on the twentieth day after their shipwreck, and there met with their companions who had escaped in the first boat.

The rest of the crew and passengers left on the wreck likewise attempted to reach the land. Collecting some loose rafters and planks, they formed a kind of raft, but were overwhelmed by the first sea, and all perished, excepting two who gained the shore. Those who had reached the coast of Africa had not arrived at the end of their sufferings; they had scarcely disembarked when they fell into the hands of the Caffres, a savage and inhuman people, who stripped and left them in the most deplorable state. However, mustering up their courage and the little strength they had left, they arrived at the place where the agent of the Portuguese, at Sofala and Mozambique, resided. By him they were received with the utmost humanity, and after reposing a few days, after their fatigues, they reached Mozambique, and repaired from thence to India. Only sixty survived out of all those who had embarked in the St. James; all the rest perished, either at sea, of fatigue, or hunger. Thus the imprudence of an individual occasioned the loss of a fine vessel, and the lives of above four hundred and fifty persons.

Upon the captain's return to Europe, the widows and orphans of the unfortunate sufferers raised such loud complaints against him that he was apprehended and put in prison; but he was soon afterwards released. The former catastrophe was not a sufficient lesson for this self-sufficient and obstinate man. He undertook the command of another vessel in 1588, and had nearly lost her in the same manner, and in the same place. Fortunately, at sunrise he discovered the rocks, towards which he was running with the same imprudence as in his former voyage. But on his return from India to Portugal he was lost, together with the vessel he was on board of; thus meeting with the just punishment of his culpable obstinacy and misconduct.

LOSS OF HIS MAJESTY'S SHIP CENTAUR,

Of Seventy-four Guns, September 23, 1782.

After the decisive engagement in the West Indies, on the glorious 12th of April, 1782, when the French fleet under count de Grasse was defeated by admiral Sir George Rodney, several of the captured ships, besides many others, were either lost or disabled, on their homeward-bound passage, with a large convoy. Among those lost was the Centaur, of seventy-four guns, whose commander, captain Inglefield, with the master and ten of the crew, experienced a most providential escape from the general fate.

The captain's narrative affords the best explanation of the manner and means by which this signal deliverance was effected. Those only who are personally involved in such a calamity can describe their sensations with full energy, and furnish, in such detail, those traits of the heart which never fail to interest.

The Centaur (says captain Inglefield) left Jamaica in rather a leaky condition, keeping two hand-pumps going, and when it blew fresh, sometimes a spell with a chain-pump was necessary. But I had no apprehension that the ship was not able to encounter a common gale of wind.

In the evening of the 16th of September, when the fatal gale came on, the ship was prepared for the worst weather usually met in those latitudes, the main-sail was reefed and set, the top-gallant masts struck, and the mizzen-yard lowered down, though at that time it did not blow very strong. Towards midnight it blew a gale of wind, and the ship made so much water that I was obliged to turn all hands up to spell the pumps. The leak still increasing, I had thoughts to try the ship before the sea. Happy I should have been, perhaps, had I in this been determined. The impropriety of leaving the convoy, except in the last extremity, and the hopes of the weather growing moderate, weighed against the opinion that it was right.

About two in the morning the wind lulled, and we flattered ourselves the gale was breaking. Soon after we had much thunder and lightning from the south-east, with rain, when it began to blow strong in gusts of wind, which obliged me to haul the main-sail up, the ship being then under bare poles. This was scarcely done, when a gust of wind, exceeding in violence any thing of the kind I had ever seen or had any conception of, laid the ship upon her beam ends. The water forsook the hold and appeared between decks, so as to fill the men's hammocks to leeward: the ship lay motionless, and to all appearance irrecoverably overset. The water increasing fast, forced through the cells of the ports, and scuttled in the ports from the pressure of the ship. I gave immediate directions to cut away the main and mizzen masts, hoping when the ship righted to wear her. The mizzen-mast went first, upon cutting one or two of the lanyards, without the smallest effect on the ship; the main-mast followed, upon cutting the lanyard of one shroud; and I had the disappointment to see the fore-mast and bowsprit follow. The ship upon this immediately righted, but with great violence; and the motion was so quick, that it was difficult for the people to work the pumps. Three guns broke loose upon the main-deck, and it was some time before they were secured. Several men being maimed in this attempt, every movable was destroyed, either from the shot thrown loose from the lockers, or the wreck of the deck. The officers, who had left their beds naked when the ship overset in the morning, had not an article of clothes to put on, nor could their friends supply them.

The masts had not been over the sides ten minutes before I was informed the tiller had broken short in the rudder-head; and before the chocks could be placed, the rudder itself was gone. Thus we were as much disastered as it was possible, lying at the mercy of the wind and sea: yet I had one comfort, that the pumps, if any thing, reduced the water in the hold; and as the morning came on (the 17th) the weather grew more moderate, the wind having shifted, in the gale, to north-west.

At daylight I saw two line-of-battle ships to leeward; one had lost her fore-mast and bowsprit, the other her main-mast. It was the general opinion on board the Centaur, that the former was the Canada, the other the Glorieux. The Ramilies was not in sight, nor more than fifteen sail of merchant ships.

About seven in the morning I saw another line-of-battle ship ahead of us, which I soon distinguished to be the Ville de Paris, with all her masts standing. I immediately gave orders to make the signal of distress, hoisting the ensign on the stump of the mizzen-mast, union downwards, and firing one of the forecastle guns. The ensign blew away soon after it was hoisted, and it was the only one we had remaining; but I had the satisfaction to see the Ville de Paris wear and stand towards us. Several of the merchant ships also approached us, and those that could hailed, and offered their assistance; but depending upon the king's ship, I only thanked them, desiring, if they joined admiral Graves, to acquaint him of our condition. I had not the smallest doubt but the Ville de Paris was coming to us, as she appeared to us not to have suffered in the least by the storm, and having seen her wear, we knew she was under government of her helm; at this time, also, it was so moderate that the merchantmen set their top-sails: but, approaching within two miles, she passed us to windward; this being observed by one of the merchant ships, she wore and came under our stern, offering to carry any message to her. I desired the master would acquaint captain Wilkinson that the Centaur had lost her rudder, as well as her masts; that she made a great deal of water, and that I desired he would remain with her until the weather grew moderate. I saw the merchantman approach afterwards near enough to speak to the Ville de Paris, but

I am afraid that her condition was much worse than it appeared to be, as she continued upon that tack. In the mean time all the quarter-deck guns were thrown overboard, and all but six, which had overset, off the main-deck. The ship, lying in the trough of the sea, labored prodigiously. I got over one of the small anchors, with a boom and several gun carriages, veering out from the head-door by a large hawser, to keep the ship's bow to the sea; but this, with a top-gallant sail upon the stump of the mizzen-mast, had not the desired effect.

As the evening came on it grew hazy, and blew strong in squalls. We lost sight of the Ville de Paris, but I thought it a certainty that we should see her the next morning. The night was passed in constant labor at the pump. Sometimes the wind lulled, and the water diminished; when it blew strong again, the sea rising, the water again increased.

Towards the morning of the 18th I was informed there was seven feet water upon the kelson; that one of the winches was broken; that the two spare ones would not fit, and that the hand-pumps were choked. These circumstances were sufficiently alarming; but upon opening the after-hold to get some rum up for the people, we found our condition much more so.

It will be necessary to mention, that the Centaur's after-hold was inclosed by a bulk-head at the after part of the well; here all the dry provisions and the ship's rum were stowed upon twenty chaldrons of coal, which unfortunately had been started on this part of the ship, and by them the pumps were continually choked. The chain-pumps were so much worn as to be of little use; and the leathers, which, had the well been clear, would have lasted twenty days, or more, were all consumed in eight. At this time it was observed that the water had not a passage to the well, for there was so much that it washed against the orlop-deck. All the rum, twenty-six puncheons, and all the provisions, of which there was sufficient for two months, in casks, were staved, having floated with violence from side to side until there was not a whole cask remaining: even the staves that were found upon clearing the hold were most of them broken in two pieces. In the fore-hold we had a prospect of perishing: should the ship swim, we had no water but what remained in the ground tier; and over this all the wet provisions, and butts filled with salt-water, were floating, and with so much motion that no man could with safety go into the hold. There was nothing left for us to try but bailing with buckets at the fore-hatchway and fish-room; and twelve large canvas buckets were immediately employed at each. On opening the fish-room we were so fortunate as to discover that two puncheons of rum, which belonged to me, had escaped. They were immediately got up, and served out at times in drams; and had it not been for this relief, and some lime-juice, the people would have dropped.

We soon found our account in bailing; the spare pump had been put down the fore-hatchway, and a pump shifted to the fish-room; but the motion of the ship had washed the coals so small, that they had reached every part of the ship, and the pumps were soon choked. However, the water by noon had considerably diminished by working the buckets; but there appeared no prospect of saving the ship, if the gale continued. The labor was too great to hold out without water; yet the people worked without a murmur, and indeed with cheerfulness.

At this time the weather was more moderate, and a couple of spars were got ready for shears to set up a jury fore-mast; but as the evening came on, the gale again increased. We had seen nothing this day but the ship that had lost her main-mast, and she appeared to be as much in want of assistance as ourselves, having fired guns of distress; and before night I was told her fore-mast was gone.

The Centaur labored so much, that I had scarcely a hope she could swim till morning. However, by great exertion of the chain-pumps and bailing, we held our own, but our sufferings for want of water were very great, and many of the people could not be restrained from drinking salt-water.

At daylight (the 19th) there was no vessel in sight; and flashes from guns having been seen in the night, we feared the ship that we had seen the preceding day had foundered. Towards ten o'clock in the forenoon the weather grew more moderate, the water diminished in the hold, and the people were encouraged to redouble their efforts to get the water low enough to break a cask of fresh water out of the ground tier; and some of the most resolute of the seamen were employed in the attempt. At noon we succeeded with one cask, which, though little, was a seasonable relief. All the officers, passengers, and boys, who were not of the profession of seamen, had been employed thrumming a sail, which was passed under the ship's bottom, and I thought it had some effect. The shears were raised for the fore-mast; the weather looked promising, the sea fell, and at night we were able to relieve at the pumps and bailing every two hours. By the morning of the 20th the fore-hold was cleared of the water, and we had the comfortable promise of a fine day. It proved so, and I was determined to make use of it with every possible exertion. I divided the ship's company, with the officers attending them, into parties, to raise the jury fore-mast; to heave over the lower-deck guns; to clear the wrecks of the fore and after holds; to prepare the machine for steering the ship, and to work the pumps. By night the after-hold was as clear as when the ship was launched; for, to our astonishment, there was not a shovel of coals remaining, twenty chaldrons having been pumped out since the commencement of the gale. What I have called the wreck of the hold, was the bulk-heads of the after hold, fish-room, and spirit-rooms. The standards of the cockpit, an immense quantity of staves and wood, and part of the lining of the ship, were thrown overboard, that if the water should again appear in the hold, we might have no impediment in bailing. All the guns were overboard, the fore-mast secured, and the machine, which was to be similar to that with which the Ipswich was steered, was in great forwardness; so that I was in hopes, the moderate weather continuing, that I should be able to steer the ship by noon the following day, and at least save the people on some of the Western Islands. Had we had any other ship in company with us, I should have thought it my duty to have quitted the Centaur this day.

This night the people got some rest by relieving the watches; but in the morning of the 21st we had the mortification to find that the weather again threatened, and by noon it blew a gale. The ship labored greatly, and the water appeared in the fore and after-hold, and increased. The carpenter also informed me that the leathers were nearly consumed; and likewise that the chains of the pumps, by constant exertion and the friction of the coals, were considered as nearly useless.

As we had now no other resource but bailing, I gave orders that scuttles should be cut through the decks to introduce more buckets into the hold; and all the sailmakers were employed, night and day, in making canvas buckets; and the orlop-deck having falled in on the larboard side, I ordered the sheet cable to be roused overboard. The wind at this time was at west, and being on the larboard tack, many schemes had been practised to wear the ship, that we might drive into a less boisterous latitude, as well as approach the Western Islands; but none succeeded: and having a weak carpenter's crew, they were hardly sufficient to attend the pumps; so that we could not make any progress with the steering machine. Another sail had been thrummed and got over, but we did not find its use; indeed there was no prospect but in a change of weather. A large leak had been discovered and stopped in the fore-hold and another in the lady's hole, but the ship appeared so weak from her laboring, that it was clear she could not last long. The after cock-pit had fallen in, the fore cock-pit the same, with all the store rooms down; the stern post was so loose, that as the ship rolled, the water rushed in on either side in great streams, which we could not stop.

Night came on, with the same dreary prospect as on the preceding, and was passed in continual efforts of labor. Morning came, (the 22d,) without our seeing any thing, or any change of weather, and the day was spent with the same struggles to keep the ship above water, pumping and bailing at the hatchways and scuttles. Towards night another of the chain pumps was rendered quite useless, by one of the rollers being displaced at the bottom of the pump, and this was without remedy, there being too much water in the well to get to it: we also had but six leathers remaining, so that the fate of the ship was not far off. Still the labor went on without any apparent despair, every officer taking his share of it, and the people were always cheerful and obedient.

During the night the water increased: but about seven in the morning of the 23d I was told that an unusual quantity of water appeared, all at once, in the fore-hold, which, upon my going forward to be convinced, I found but too true; the stowage of the hold ground-tier was all in motion, so that in a short time there was not a whole cask to be seen. We were convinced the ship had sprung a fresh leak. Another sail had been thrumming all night, and I was giving directions to place it over the bows, when I perceived the ship settling by the head, the lower deck bow-ports being even with the water.

At this period the carpenter acquainted me the well was staved in, destroyed by the wreck of the hold, and the chain pumps displaced and totally useless. There was nothing left but to redouble our efforts in bailing, but it became difficult to fill the buckets, from the quantity of staves, planks, anchor-stock, and yard-arm pieces, which were now washed from the wings, and floating from side to side with the motion of the ship. The people, till this period, had labored, as if determined to conquer their difficulties, without a murmur or without a tear; but now seeing their efforts useless, many of them burst into tears and wept like children.

I gave orders for the anchors, of which we had two remaining, to be thrown overboard, one of which (the spare anchor) had been most surprisingly hove in upon the forecastle and midships, when the ship had been upon her beam ends, and gone through the deck.

Every time that I visited the hatchway I observed the water increased, and at noon washed even with the orlop-deck: the carpenter assured me the ship could not swim long, and proposed making rafts to float the ship's company, whom it was not in my power to encourage any longer with a prospect of their safety. Some appeared perfectly resigned, went to their hammocks and desired their messmates to lash them in; others were lashing themselves to gratings and small rafts; but the most predominant idea was that of putting on their best and cleanest clothes.

The weather, about noon, had been something moderate, and as rafts had been mentioned by the carpenter, I thought it right to make the attempt, though I knew our booms could not float half the ship's company in fine weather; but we were in a situation to catch at a straw. I therefore called the ship's company together, told them my intention, recommending to them to remain regular and obedient to their officers. Preparations were immediately made to this purpose; the booms were cleared; the boats, of which we had three, viz. cutter, pinnace, and five-oared yawl, were got over the side; a bag of bread was ordered to be put in each, and any liquors that could be got at, for the purpose of supplying the rafts. I had intended myself to go in the five-oared yawl, and the coxswain was desired to get any thing from my steward that might be useful. Two men, captains of the tops, of the forecastle, or quartermasters, were placed in each of them, to prevent any person from forcing the boats, or getting into them until an arrangement was made. While these preparations were making, the ship was gradually sinking, the orlop-decks having been blown up by the water in the hold, and the cables floated to the gun-deck. The men had some time quitted their employment of bailing, and the ship was left to her fate.

In the afternoon the weather again threatened, and blew strongly in squalls; the sea ran high, and one of the boats (the yawl) was staved alongside and sunk. As the evening approached, the ship appeared little more than suspended in water. There was no certainty that she would swim from one minute to another; and the love of life, which I believe never showed itself later in the approach to death, began now to level all distinctions. It was impossible, indeed, for any man to deceive himself with a hope of being saved upon a raft in such a sea: besides that, the ship in sinking, it was probable, would carry every thing down with her in a vortex, to a certain distance.

It was near five o'clock, when, coming from my cabin, I observed a number of people looking very anxiously over the side; and looking over myself, I saw that several men had forced the pinnace, and that more were attempting to get in. I had immediate thoughts of securing this boat before she might be sunk by numbers. There appeared not more than a moment for consideration; to remain and perish with the ship's company, to whom I could not be of use any longer, or seize the opportunity, which seemed the only way of escaping, and leave the people, with whom I had been so well satisfied on a variety of occasions that I thought I could give my life to preserve them. This, indeed, was a painful conflict, such as, I believe, no man can describe, nor any have a just idea of who has not been in a similar situation.

The love of life prevailed. I called to Mr. Rainy, the master, the only officer upon deck, desired him to follow me, and immediately descended into the boat at the after part of the chains, but not without great difficulty got the boat clear of the ship, twice the number that the boat would carry pushing to get in, and many jumping into the water. Mr. Baylis, a young gentleman fifteen years of age, leaped from the chains, after the boat had got off, and was taken in. The boat falling astern, became exposed to the sea, and we endeavored to pull her bow round to keep her to the break of the sea, and to pass to windward of the ship; but in the attempt she was nearly filled, the sea ran too high, and the only probability of living was keeping her before the wind.

It was then that I became sensible how little, if any, better our condition was than that of those who remained in the ship; at best, it appeared to be only a prolongation of a miserable existence. We were, all together, twelve in number, in a leaky boat, with one of the gunwales staved, in nearly the middle of the Western ocean, without a compass, without quadrant, without sail, without great coat or cloak, all very thinly clothed, in a gale of wind, with a great sea running! It was now five o'clock in the evening, and in half an hour we lost sight of the ship. Before it was dark a blanket was discovered in the boat. This was immediately bent to one of the stretches, and under it, as a sail, we scudded all night, in expectation of being swallowed up by every wave, it being with great difficulty that we could sometimes clear the boat of the water before the return of the next great sea; all of us half drowned, and sitting, except those who bailed, at the bottom of the boat; and, without having really perished, I am sure no people ever endured more. In the morning the weather grew moderate, the wind having shifted to the southward, as we discovered by the sun. Having survived the night, we began to recollect ourselves, and to think of our future preservation.

When we quitted the ship the wind was at N. W. or N. N. W. Fayal had borne E. S. E. two hundred and fifty or two hundred and sixty leagues. Had the wind continued for five or six days, there was a probability that running before the sea we might have fallen in with some one of the Western-Islands. The change of wind was death to these hopes; for, should it come to blow, we knew there would be no preserving life but by running before the sea, which would carry us again to the northward, where we must soon afterwards perish.

Upon examining what we had to subsist on, I found a bag of bread, a small ham, a single piece of pork, two quart bottles of water, and a few of French cordials. The wind continued to the southward for eight or nine days, and providentially never blew so strong but that we could keep the side of the boat to the sea: but we were always most miserably wet and cold. We kept a sort of reckoning, but the sun and stars being somewhat hidden from us, for twenty-four hours, we had no very correct idea of our navigation. We judged, that we had nearly an E. N. E. course since the first night's run which had carried us to the S. E. and expected to see the island of Corvo. In this, however, we were disappointed, and we feared that the southerly wind had driven us far to the northward. Our prayers were now for a northerly wind. Our condition began to be truly miserable, both from hunger and cold: for on the fifth day we had discovered that our bread was nearly all spoiled by salt-water, and it was necessary to go on an allowance. One biscuit divided into twelve morsels for breakfast, and the same for dinner; the neck of a bottle broken off, with the cork in, served for a glass, and this, filled with water, was the allowance for twenty-four hours for each man. This was done without any partiality or distinction; but we must have perished ere this, had we not caught six quarts of rain water; and this we could not have been blessed with, had we not found in the boat a pair of sheets, which by accident had been put there. These were spread when it rained, and when thoroughly wet, wrung into the kidd, with which we bailed the boat. With this short allowance, which was rather tantalizing in our comfortless condition, we began to grow very feeble, and our clothes being continually wet, our bodies were, in many places, chafed into sores.

On the 15th day it fell calm, and soon after a breeze of wind sprung up from the N. N. W. and blew to a gale, so that we ran before the sea at the rate of five or six miles an hour under our blanket, till we judged we were to the southward of Fayal, and to the westward sixty leagues: but the wind blowing strong we could not attempt to steer for it. Our wishes were now for the wind to shift to the westward. This was the fifteenth day we had been in the boat, and we had only one day's bread, and one bottle of water remaining of a second supply of rain. Our sufferings were now as great as human strength could bear, but we were convinced that good spirits were a better support than great bodily strength for on this day Thomas Matthews, quartermaster, the stoutest man in the boat, perished from hunger and cold: on the day before he had complained of want of strength in his throat, as he expressed it, to swallow his morsel, and in the night drank salt-water, grew delirious, and died without a groan. As it became next to a certainty that we should all perish in the same manner in a day or two, it was somewhat comfortable to reflect, that dying of hunger was not so dreadful as our imaginations had represented. Others had complained of these symptoms in their throats; some had drank their own urine; and all but myself had drank salt-water.

As yet despair and gloom had been successfully prohibited; and, as the evenings closed in, the men had been encouraged by turns to sing a song, or relate a story, instead of supper; but this evening I found it impossible to raise either. As the night came on it fell calm, and about midnight a breeze of wind sprang up, we guessed from the westward by the swell, but there not being a star to be seen, we were afraid of running out of our way, and waited impatiently for the rising sun to be our compass.

As soon as the dawn appeared, we found the wind to be exactly as we had wished, at W. S. W. and immediately spread our sail, running before the sea at the rate of four miles an hour. Our last breakfast had been served with the bread and water remaining, when John Gregory, quartermaster, declared with much confidence that he saw land in the S. E. We had so often seen fog-banks, which had the appearance of land, that I did not trust myself to believe it, and cautioned the people, (who were extravagantly elated,) that they might not feel the effects of disappointment; till at length one of them broke out into a most immoderate swearing fit of joy, which I could not restrain, and declared he had never seen land in his life if what he now saw was not land.

We immediately shaped our course for it, though on my part with very little faith. The wind freshened; the boat went through the water at the rate of five or six miles an hour, and in two hours' time the land was plainly seen by every man in the boat, but at a very great distance, so that we did not reach it till ten at night. It must have been at least twenty leagues from us when first discovered; and I cannot help remarking, with much thankfulness, the providential favor shown to us in this instance.

In every part of the horizon, except where the land was discovered, there was so thick a haze that we could not have seen any thing for more than three or four leagues. Fayal, by our reckoning, bore E. by N. which course we were steering, and in a few hours, had not the sky opened for our preservation, we should have increased our distance from the land, got to the eastward, and of course missed all the island. As we approached the land our belief had strengthened that it was Fayal. The island of Pico, which might have revealed it to us, had the weather been perfectly clear, was at this time capped with clouds, and it was some time before we were quite satisfied, having traversed for two hours a great part of the island, where the steep and rocky shore refused us a landing. This circumstance was borne with much impatience, for we had flattered ourselves that we should meet with fresh water at the first part of the land we might approach; and being disappointed, the thirst of some had increased anxiety almost to a state of madness; so that we were near making the attempt to land in some places where the boat must have been dashed to pieces by the surf. At length we discovered a fishing canoe, which conducted us into the road of Fayal about midnight; but where the regulation of the port did not permit us to land till examined by the health officers; however, I did not think much of sleeping this night in the boat, our pilot having brought us some refreshments of bread, wine, and water. In the morning we were visited by Mr. Graham, the English consul, whose humane attention made very ample amends for the formality of the Portuguese. Indeed I can never sufficiently express the sense I have of his kindness and humanity, both to myself and people; for, I believe, it was the whole of his employment for several days to contrive the best means of restoring us to health and strength. It is true, I believe there never were more pitiable objects. Some of the stoutest men belonging to the Centaur were obliged to be supported through the streets of Fayal. Mr. Rainy, the master, and myself, were, I think, in better health than the rest; but I could not walk without being supported; and for several days, with the best and most comfortable provisions of diet and lodging, we grew rather worse than better.

LOSS OF THE SLOOP BETSY,

On the Coast of Dutch Guiana, August 5, 1756.

On the 1st of August, 1756, says captain Aubin, I set sail for Surinam, from Carlisle bay, in the island of Barbadoes. My sloop, of about eighty tons burthen, was built entirely of cedar, and freighted by Messrs. Roscoe and Nyles, merchants of Bridgetown. The cargo consisted of provisions of every kind, and horses. The Dutch colony being in want of a supply of those animals, passed a law that no English vessel should be permitted to enter there, if horses did not constitute part of her cargo. The Dutch were so rigid in enforcing this condition, that if the horses chanced to die on their passage, the master of the vessel was obliged to preserve the ears and hoofs of the animals, and to swear upon entering the port of Surinam, that when he embarked they were alive, and destined for that colony.

The coasts of Surinam, Berbice, Demarara, Oronoko, and all the adjacent parts, are low lands, and inundated by large rivers, which discharge themselves into the sea. The bottom all along this coast is composed of a kind of mud, or clay, in which the anchors sink to the depth of three or four fathoms, and upon which the keel sometimes strikes without stopping the vessel. The sloop being at anchor three leagues and a half from the shore in five fathoms water, the mouth of the Demarara river bearing S. S. W. and it being the rainy season, my crew drew up water from the sea for their use, which was just as sweet as good river water. The current occasioned by the trade winds, and the numerous rivers which fall into the sea, carried us at the rate of four miles an hour towards the west and north-west.

In the evening of the 4th of August, I was tacking about, between the latitude of ten and twelve degrees north, with a fresh breeze, which obliged me to reef my sails. At midnight, finding that the wind increased in proportion as the moon, then on the wane, rose above the horizon, and that my bark, which was deeply laden, labored excessively, I would not retire to rest till the weather became more moderate. I told my mate, whose name was Williams, to bring me a bottle of beer, and both sitting down, I upon a hen-coop, and Williams upon the deck, we began to tell stories to pass the time, according to the custom of mariners of every country. The vessel suddenly turned with her broadside to windward: I called to one of the seamen to put the helm a weather, but he replied it had been so for some time. I directed my mate to see if the cords were not entangled: he informed me that they were not. At this moment the vessel swung round with her head to the sea, and plunged; her head filled in such a manner that she could not rise above the surf, which broke over us to the height of the anchor stocks, and we were presently up to our necks in water; every thing in the cabin was washed away. Some of the crew, which consisted of nine men, were drowned in their hammocks, without a cry or groan. When the wave had passed, I took the hatchet that was hanging up near the fireplace, to cut away the shrouds to prevent the ship from upsetting, but in vain. She upset, and turned over again, with her masts and sails in the water; the horses rolled one over the other and were drowned, forming altogether a most melancholy spectacle.

I had but one small boat, about twelve or thirteen feet

long; she was fixed, with a cable coiled inside of her, between the pump and the side of the ship. Providentially for our preservation there was no occasion to lash her fast; but we at this time entertained no hope of seeing her again, as the large cable within her, together with the weight of the horses, and their stalls entangled one among another, prevented her from rising to the surface of the water.

In this dreadful situation, holding by the shrouds, and stripping off my clothes, I looked round me for some plank or empty box to preserve my life as long as it should please the Almighty, when I perceived my mate and two seamen hanging by a rope, and imploring God to receive their souls. I told them that the man who was not resigned to die when it pleased the Creator to call him out of the world was not fit to live. I advised them to undress as I had done, and to endeavor to seize the first object that could assist them in preserving their lives. Williams followed my advice, stripped himself quite naked, and betook himself to swimming, looking out for whatever he could find. A moment afterwards he cried out, "Here is the boat, keel uppermost!" I immediately swam to him, and found him holding the boat by the keel. We then set to work to turn her, but in vain; at length, however, Williams, who was the heaviest and strongest of the two, contrived to set his feet against the gunwale of the boat, laying hold of the keel with his hands, and with a violent effort nearly succeeded in overturning her. I being to windward, pushed and lifted her up with my shoulders on the opposite side. At length, with the assistance of the surf, we turned her over, but she was full of water. I got into her, and endeavored by the means of a rope belonging to the rigging to draw her to the mast of the vessel. In the intervals between the waves the mast always rose to the height of fifteen or twenty feet above the water. I passed the end of the rope fastened to the boat once round the head of the mast, keeping hold of the end; each time that the mast rose out of the water, it lifted up both the boat and me; I then let go the rope, and by this expedient the boat was three-fourths emptied; but having nothing to enable me to disengage her from the mast and shrouds, they fell down upon me, driving the boat and me again under water.

After repeated attempts to empty her, in which I was cruelly wounded and bruised, I began to haul the boat, filled with water, towards the vessel, by the shrouds; but the bark had sunk by this time to such a depth, that only a small part of her stern was to be seen, upon which my mate and two other seamen were holding fast by a rope. I threw myself into the water, with the rope of the boat in the mouth, and swam towards them to give them the end to lay hold of, hoping, by our united strength, that we should be able to haul the boat over the stern of the vessel; we exerted our utmost efforts, and at this moment I nearly had my thigh broken by a shock of the boat, being between her and the ship. At length we succeeded in hauling her over the stern, but had the misfortune to break a hole in her bottom in this manœuvre. As soon as my thigh was a little recovered from the blow, I jumped into her with one of the men, and stopped the leak with a piece of his coarse shirt. It was extremely fortunate for us that this man did not know how to swim; it will soon be seen what benefit we derived from his ignorance; had it not been for this we must all have perished. Being unable to swim, he had not stripped, and had thus preserved his coarse shirt, a knife that was in his pocket, and an enormous hat, in the Dutch fashion. The boat being fastened to the rigging, was no sooner cleared of the greatest part of the water than a dog of mine came to me, running along the gunwale; I took him in, thanking Providence for having thus sent provision for a time of necessity. A moment after the dog had entered, the rope broke with a jerk of the vessel, and I found myself drifting away. I called my mate and the other man, who swam to me: the former had fortunately found a small spare top-mast, which served us for a rudder. We assisted the two others to get into the boat, and soon lost sight of our ill-fated bark.

It was then four o'clock in the morning, as I judged by the dawn of day, which began to appear, so that about two hours had elapsed since we were obliged to abandon her. What prevented her from foundering sooner was my having taken on board about one hundred and fifty barrels of biscuit, as many or more casks of flour, and three hundred firkins of butter, all which substances float upon the water, and are soaked through but slowly and by degrees. As soon as we were clear of the wreck, we kept the boat before the wind as well as we could, and when it grew light I perceived several articles that had floated from the vessel. I perceived my box of clothes and linen, which had been carried out of the cabin by the violence of the waves. I felt an emotion of joy. The box contained some bottles of orange and lime water, a few pounds of chocolate, sugar, &c. Reaching over the gunwale of our boat we laid hold of the box, and used every effort to open it on the water, for we could not think of getting it into the boat, being of a size and weight sufficient to sink her. In spite of all our endeavors we could not force open the lid; we were obliged to leave it behind, with all the good things it contained, and to increase our distress we had by this effort almost filled our boat with water, and had more than once nearly sunk her.

We, however, had the good fortune to pick up thirteen onions; we saw many more, but were unable to reach them. These thirteen onions and my dog, without a single drop of fresh water, or any liquor whatever, were all that we had to subsist upon. We were, according to my computation, above fifty leagues from land, having neither mast, sails, nor oars, to direct us, nor any kind of articles besides the knife of the sailor who could not swim, his shirt, a piece of which we had already used to stop the leak in our boat, and his wide trousers. We this day cut the remainder of his shirt into strips, which we twisted for rigging, and then fell to work alternately to loosen the planks with which the boat was lined, cutting, by dint of time and patience, all round the heads of the nails that fastened them. Of these planks we made a kind of mast, which we tied to the foremast bench; a piece of board was substituted for a yard, to which we fastened the two parts of the trousers, which served for sails, and assisted us in keeping the boat before the wind, steering with the top-mast as mentioned before.

As the pieces of plank which we had detached from the inside of the boat were too short, and were not sufficient to go quite round the edge, when the sea ran very high, we were obliged, in order to prevent the waves from entering the boat, to lie down several times along the gunwale on each side, with our backs to the water, and thus with our bodies to repel the surf, while the other, with the Dutch hat, was incessantly employed in bailing out the water; besides which the boat continued to make water at the leak, which we were unable entirely to stop.

It was in this melancholy situation, and stark naked, that we kept the boat before the wind as well as we could. The night of the first day after our shipwreck arrived before we had well completed our sail; it grew dark, and we contrived to keep our boat running before the wind, at the rate of about a league an hour. The second day was more calm; we each eat an onion, at different times, and began to feel thirst. In the night of the second day the wind became violent and variable, and sometimes blowing from the north, which caused me great uneasiness, being obliged to steer south, in order to keep the boat before the wind, whereas we could only hope to be saved by proceeding from east to west.

The third day we began to suffer exceedingly, not only from hunger and thirst, but likewise from the heat of the sun, which scorched us in such a manner, that from the neck to the feet our skin was as red and as full of blisters as if we had been burned by a fire. I then seized my dog and plunged the knife in his throat. I cannot even now refrain from weeping at the thought of it; but at the moment I felt not the least compassion for him. We caught his blood in the hat, receiving in our hands and drinking what ran over: we afterwards drank in turn out of the hat, and felt ourselves refreshed. The fourth day the wind was extremely violent, and the sea ran very high, so that we were more than once on the point of perishing; it was on this day in particular that we were obliged to make a rampart of our bodies in order to repel the waves. About noon a ray of hope dawned upon us, but soon vanished.

We perceived a sloop, commanded by captain Southey, which, like my vessel, belonged to the island of Barbadoes, and was bound to Demarara; we could see the crew walking upon the deck, and shouted to them, but were never seen nor heard. Being obliged, by the violence of the gale, to keep our boat before the wind, for fear of foundering, we had passed her a great distance before she crossed us; she steered direct south, and we bearing away to the west. Captain Southey was one of my particular friends. This disappointment so discouraged my two seamen that they refused to endeavor any longer to save their lives. In spite of all I could say, one of them would do nothing, not even bail out the water which gained upon us; I had recourse to entreaties; fell at his knees, but he remained unmoved. My mate and I, at length, prevailed upon him, by threatening to kill him instantly with the top-mast, which we used to steer by, and to kill ourselves afterwards, to put a period to our misery. This menace made some impression on him, and he resumed his employment of bailing as before.

On this day I set the others the example of eating a piece of the dog with some onions; it was with difficulty that I swallowed a few mouthfuls; but in an hour I felt that this morsel of food had given me vigor. My mate, who was of a much stronger constitution, eat more, which gave me much pleasure; one of the two men likewise tasted it, but the other, whose name was Comings, either would not or could not swallow a morsel.

The fifth day was more calm, and the sea much smoother. At daybreak we perceived an enormous shark, as large as our boat, which followed us several hours, as a prey that was destined for him. We also found in our boat a flying-fish, which had dropped there during the night; we divided it into four parts, which we chewed to moisten our mouths. It was on this day that, when pressed with hunger and despair, my mate, Williams, had the generosity to exhort us to cut off a piece of his thigh to refresh ourselves with the blood, and to support life. In the night we had several showers, with some wind. We tried to get some rain water by wringing the trousers which served us for a sail, but when we caught it in our mouths it proved to be as salt as that of the sea; the trousers having been so often soaked with sea-water, that they, as well as the hat, were quite impregnated with salt. Thus we had no other resource but to open our mouths and catch the drops of rain upon our tongues, in order to cool them: after the shower was over we again fastened the trousers to the mast.

On the sixth day the two seamen, notwithstanding all my remonstrances, drank sea-water, which purged them so excessively that they fell into a kind of delirium, and were of no more service to Williams and me. Both he and I kept a nail in our mouths, and often sprinkled our heads with water to cool them. I perceived myself the better for these ablutions, and that my head was more easy. We tried several times to eat of the dog's flesh, with a morsel of onion; but I thought myself fortunate if I could get down three or four mouthfuls. My mate always eat rather more than I could.

The seventh day was fine, with a moderate breeze, and the sea perfectly calm. About noon the two men who had drank sea-water grew so weak that they began to talk wildly, like people who are light-headed, not knowing any longer whether they were at sea or on shore. My mate and I were so weak too that we could scarcely stand on our legs, or steer the boat in our turns, or bail the water from the boat, which made a great deal at the leak.

In the morning of the eighth day, John Comings died, and three hours afterwards George Simpson likewise expired. The same evening, at sunset, we had the inexpressible satisfaction of discovering the high lands on the west point of the island of Tobago. Hope gave us strength. We kept the head of the boat towards the land all night, with a light breeze, and a current which was in our favor. Williams and I were that night in an extraordinary situation, our two comrades lying dead before us, with the land in sight, having very little wind to approach it, and being assisted only by the current, which drove strongly to the westward. In the morning we were not, according to my computation, more than five or six leagues from the land. That happy day was the last of our sufferings at sea. We kept steering the boat the whole day towards the shore, though we were no longer able to stand. In the evening the wind lulled, and it fell calm; but about two o'clock in the morning the current cast us on the beach of the island of Tobago, at the foot of a high shore, between little Tobago and Man-of-War bay, which is the easternmost part of the island. The boat soon bilged with the shock; my unfortunate companion and I crawled to the shore, leaving the bodies of our two comrades in the boat, and the remainder of the dog, which was quite putrid.

We clambered, as well as we could, on all fours, along the high coast, which rose almost perpendicularly to the height of three or four hundred feet. A great quantity of leaves had dropped down to the place where we were from the numerous trees over our heads; these we collected, and lay down upon them to wait for daylight. When it began to dawn we sought about for water, and found some in the holes of the rocks, but it was brackish, and not fit to drink. We perceived on the rocks around us several kinds of shell-fish, some of which we broke open with a stone, and chewed them to moisten our mouths.

Between eight and nine o'clock we were perceived by a young Caraib, who was sometimes walking and at others swimming towards the boat. As soon as he had reached it he called his companions with loud shouts, making signs of the greatest compassion. His comrades instantly followed him, and swam towards us, having perceived us almost at the same time.

The oldest, who was about sixty, approached us, with the two youngest, whom we afterwards found to be his son and son-in-law. At the sight of us the tears flowed from their eyes: I endeavored by words and signs to make them comprehend that we had been nine days at sea, in want of every thing. They understood a few French words, and signified that they would fetch a boat to convey us to their hut. The old man took a handkerchief from his head and tied it round mine, and one of the young Caraibs gave Williams his straw hat; the other swam round the projecting rock and brought us a calabash of fresh water, some cakes of cassava, and a piece of broiled fish, but we could not eat. The two others took the two corpses out of the boat, and laid them upon the rock, after which all three of them hauled the boat out of the water. They then left us, with marks of the utmost compassion, and went to fetch their canoe.

About noon they returned in their canoe, to the number of six, and brought with them, in an earthen pot, some soup which we thought delicious. We took a little, but my stomach was so weak that I immediately cast it up again. Williams did not vomit at all. In less than two hours we arrived at Man-of-War bay, where the huts of the Caraibs are situated. They had only one hammock, in which they laid me, and the woman made us a very agreeable mess of herbs and broth of quatracas and pigeons. They bathed my wounds, which were full of worms, with a decoction of tobacco and other plants. Every morning the man lifted me out of the hammock, and carried me in his arms beneath a lemon tree, where he covered me with plantain leaves to screen me from the sun. There they anointed our bodies with a kind of oil to cure the blisters raised by the sun. Our compassionate hosts even had the generosity to give each of us a shirt and a pair of trousers, which they had procured from the ships that came from time to time to trade with them for turtles and tortoise shell.

After they had cleansed my wounds of the vermin, they kept me with my legs suspended in the air, and anointed them morning and evening with an oil extracted from the tail of a small crab, resembling what the English call the soldier-crab, because its shell is red. They take a certain quantity of these crabs, bruise the ends of their tails, and put them to digest in a large shell upon the fire. It was with this ointment that they healed my wounds, covering them with nothing but plantain leaves.

Thanks to the nourishing food procured us by the Caraibs, and their humane attention, I was able, in about three weeks, to support myself upon crutches, like a person recovering from a severe illness. The natives flocked from all parts of the island to see us, and never came empty handed; sometimes bringing eggs, and at others fowls, which were given with pleasure, and accepted with gratitude. We even had visiters from the island of Trinidad. I cut my name with a knife upon several boards, and gave them to different Caraibs, to show them to any ships which chance might conduct to the coast. We almost despaired of seeing any arrive, when a sloop from Oronoko, laden with mules and bound to St. Pierre, in the island of Martinique, touched at the sandy point on the west side of Tobago. The Indians showed the crew a plank upon which my name was carved, and acquainted them with our situation. Upon the arrival of this vessel at St. Pierre, those on board related the circumstance. Several merchants of my acquaintance, who traded under Dutch colors, happened to be there: they transmitted the information to my owners, Messrs. Roscoe and Nyles, who instantly despatched a small vessel in quest of us. After living about nine weeks with this benevolent and charitable tribe of savages, I embarked and left them, when my regret was equal to the joy and surprise I had experienced at meeting with them.

When we were ready to depart they furnished us with an abundant supply of bananas, figs, yams, fowls, fish, and fruits; particularly oranges and lemons. I had nothing to give them as an acknowledgment of their generous treatment but my boat, which they had repaired, and used for occasionally visiting their nests of turtles: being larger than their canoes, it was much more fit for that purpose. Of this I made them a present, and would have given them my blood. My friend, captain Young, assisted me to remunerate my benefactors. He gave me all the rum he had with him, being about seven or eight bottles, which I likewise presented to them. He also gave them several shirts and trousers, some knives, fish-hooks, sail-cloth for the boat, with needles and ropes.

At length, after two days spent in preparations for our departure, we were obliged to separate. They came down to the beach to the number of about thirty, men, women and children, and all appeared to feel the sincerest sorrow, especially the old man, who had acted like a father to me. When the vessel left the bay, the tears flowed from our eyes, which still continued fixed upon them. They remained standing in a line upon the shore till they lost sight of us. As we set sail about nine o'clock in the morning, steering north-east, and as Man-of-War bay is situated at the north-east point of the island, we were a long time in sight of each other. I still recollect the moment when they disappeared from my sight, and the profound regret which filled my heart. I feared that I should never again be so happy as I had been among them. I loved them, and will continue to love my dear Caraibs as long as I live; I would shed my blood for the first of those benevolent savages that might stand in need of my assistance, if chance should ever bring one of them to Europe, or my destiny should again conduct me to their island.

In three days we arrived at Barbadoes. I continued to have a violent oppression on my breast, which checked respiration, and was not yet able to go without crutches. We received from the whole island marks of the most tender interest, and the most generous compassion; the benevolence of the inhabitants was unbounded. The celebrated Dr. Hilery, the author of a treatise on the diseases peculiar to that island, came to see me, together with Dr. Lilihorn. They prescribed various remedies, but without effect. Both Williams and myself were unable to speak without the greatest difficulty. Williams remained at Barbadoes, but I, being more affected, and less robust, was advised to return to Europe. In compliance with their advice I went to London, where I was attended by doctors Reeves, Akenside, Schomberg, and the most celebrated physicians of that metropolis, who gave me all the assistance within the power of their art, from which I received scarcely any relief. At length, after I had been about a week in London, Dr. Alexander Russell, on his return from Bath, heard my case mentioned. He came to see me, and with his accustomed humanity promised to undertake my cure, without any fee; but he candidly acknowledged that it would be both tedious and expensive. I replied that the generosity of the inhabitants of Barbadoes had rendered me easy on that head, entreating him to prescribe for me, and thanking him for his obliging offers.

As he had practised for a long time at Aleppo, he had there seen great numbers afflicted with the same malady as myself, produced by long thirst in traversing the deserts of Africa. He ordered me to leave town to enjoy a more wholesome air. I took a lodging at Homerton, near Hackney; there he ordered me to be bathed every morning, confining me to asses' milk as my only food, excepting a few new-laid eggs, together with moderate exercise, and a ride on horseback every day. After about a month of this regimen he ordered a goat to be brought every morning to my bedside; about five o'clock I drank a glass of her milk, quite hot, and slept upon it. He then allowed me to take some light chicken broth, with a morsel of the wing. By means of this diet my malady was in a great degree removed in the space of about five months, and I was in a state to resume any occupation I pleased; but my constitution has ever since been extremely delicate, and my stomach in particular very weak.

LOSS OF THE BRIG TYRREL.

In addition to the many dreadful shipwrecks already narrated, the following, which is a circumstantial account given by T. Purnell, chief mate of the brig Tyrrel, Arthur Cochlan, commander, and the only person among the whole crew who had the good fortune to escape, claims our particular attention.

On Saturday, June 28th, 1759, they sailed from New York to Sandy Hook, and came to an anchor, waiting for the captain's coming down with a new boat, and some other articles. Accordingly he came on board early the succeeding morning, and the boat was cleared, hoisted in, stowed and lashed. At eight o'clock A. M. they weighed anchor, sailed out of Sandy Hook, and the same day, at noon, took their departure from the highland Neversink, and proceeded on their passage to Antigua. As soon as they made sail, the captain ordered the boat to be cast loose, in order that she might be painted, with the oars, rudder, and tiller, which job he (the captain) undertook to do himself.

At four P. M. they found the vessel made a little more water than usual; but as it did not cause much additional labor at the pump, nothing was thought of it. At eight, the leak did not seem to increase. At twelve, it began to blow hard in squalls, which caused the vessel to lie down very much, whereby it was apprehended she wanted more ballast. Thereupon the captain came on deck, being the starboard watch; and close-reefed both top-sails.

At four A. M. the weather moderated—let out both reefs. At eight it became still more moderate, and they made more sail, and set the top-gallant sails; the weather was still thick and hazy. There was no further observation taken at present, except that the vessel made more water. The captain was now chiefly employed in painting the boat, oars, rudder, and tiller.

On Monday, June 30th, at four P. M., the wind was at E. N. E., freshened very much, and blew so very hard as occasioned the brig to lie along in such a manner as caused general alarm. The captain was now earnestly entreated to put for New York, or steer for the capes of Virginia. At eight, took in top-gallant sail, and close reefed both top-sails, still making more weather. Afterwards the weather became still more moderate and fair, and they made more sail.

July 1st, at four A. M., it began to blow in squalls very hard; took in one reef in each top-sail, and continued so until eight A. M., the weather being still thick and hazy.—No observation.

The next day she made still more water, but as every watch pumped it out, this was little regarded. At four P. M. took a second reef in each top-sail, close reefed both, and down top-gallant yard; the gale still increasing.

At four A. M. the wind got round to north, and there was no likelihood of its abating. At eight, the captain, well satisfied that she was very crank and ought to have had more ballast, agreed to make for Bacon Island road, in North Carolina; and in the very act of wearing her, a sudden gust of wind laid her down on her beam ends, and she never rose again! At this time Mr. Purnell was lying in the cabin, with his clothes on, not having pulled them off since they left land. Having been rolled out of his bed, (on his chest,) with great difficulty he reached the round-house door. The first salutation he met with was from the step-ladder that went from the quarter-deck to the poop, which knocked him against the companion; (a lucky circumstance for those below, as, by laying the ladder against the companion, it served both him and the rest of the people who were in the steerage as a conveyance to windward;) having transported the two after guns forward to bring her more by the head, in order to make her hold a better wind: thus they got through the aftermost gun-port on the quarter-deck, and being all on her broadside, every movable rolled to leeward; and as the vessel overset, so did the boat, and turned bottom upwards. Her lashings being cast loose by order of the captain, and having no other prospect of saving their lives but by the boat, Purnell, with two others, and the cabin boy, who were excellent swimmers, plunged into the water, and with great difficulty righted her, when she was brimful, and washing with the water's edge. They then made fast the end of the main-sheet to the ring in her stern-post, and those who were in the fore-chains sent down the end of the boom-tackle, to which they made fast the boat's painter, and by which they lifted her a little out of the water, so that she swam about two or three inches free, but almost full. They then put the cabin boy into her, and gave him a bucket that happened to float by, and he bailed away as quick as he could, and soon after another person got in with another bucket, and in a short time got all the water out of her. They then put two long oars that were stowed in the larboard quarter of the Tyrrel into the boat, and pulled or rowed right to windward; for, as the wreck drifted, she made a dreadful appearance in the water; and Mr. Purnell and two of the people put off from the wreck, in search of the oars, rudder and tiller. After a long while they succeeded in picking them all up, one after another. They then returned to their wretched companions, who were all overjoyed to see them, having given them up for lost.

By this time night drew on very fast. While they were rowing in the boat, some small quantity of white biscuit (Mr. Purnell supposed about half a peck) floated in a small cask out of the round-house; but before it came to hand, it was so soaked with salt water that it was almost in a fluid state; and about double the quantity of common ship-biscuit likewise floated, which was in like manner soaked. This was all the provisions that they had; not a drop of fresh water could they get; neither could the carpenter get at any of the tools to scuttle her sides, for, could this have been accomplished, they might have saved plenty of provisions and water.

By this time it was almost dark. Having got one compass, it was determined to quit the wreck, and take their chance in the boat, which was nineteen feet six inches long, and six feet four inches broad: Mr. Purnell supposes it was now about nine o'clock: it was very dark. They had run three hundred and sixty miles by their dead reckoning, on a S. E. by E. course. The number in the boat was seventeen in all; the boat was very deep, and little hopes were entertained of either seeing land or surviving long. The wind got round to westward, which was the course they wanted to steer; but it began to blow and rain so very hard, that they were obliged to keep the boat before the wind and sea in order to preserve her above water. Soon after they had put off from the wreck the boat shipped two heavy seas, one after another, so that they were obliged to keep her before the wind and sea; for had she shipped another sea, she certainly would have swamped with them.

By sunrise the next morning, July 3d, they judged that they had been running E. S. E., which was contrary to their wishes. The wind dying away, the weather became very moderate. The compass which they had saved proved of no utility, one of the people having trod upon and broken it; it was accordingly thrown overboard. They now proposed to make a sail of frocks and trousers, but they had got neither needles nor sewing-twine: one of the people however had a needle in his knife, and another several fishing lines in his pockets, which were unlaid by some, and others were employed in ripping the frocks and trousers. By sunset they had provided a tolerable lugsail: having split one of the boat's thwarts, (which was of yellow deal,) with a very large knife which one of the crew had in his pocket, they made a yard and lashed it together by the strands of the fore-top-gallant halliards, that were thrown into the boat promiscuously. They also made a mast of one of the long oars, and set their sails with sheets and tacks made out of the strands of the top-gallant halliards. Their only guide was the north star. They had a tolerably good breeze all night; and the whole of the next day, July 4th, the weather continued very moderate, and the people were in as good spirits as their dreadful situation would permit.

July 5th, the wind and weather continued much the same, and they knew by the north star that they were standing in for land. The next day Mr. Purnell observed some of the men drinking salt water, and seeming rather fatigued. At this time they imagined the wind had got round to the southward, and they steered, as they thought, by the north star, to the north-west quarter; but on the 7th, the wind had got back to the northward and blew very fresh. They got their oars out the greatest part of the night; and the next day, the wind still dying away, the people labored alternately at the oars, without distinction. About noon the wind sprung up so that they lay on their oars, and, as they thought, steered about N. N. W., and continued so until about eight or nine o'clock in the morning of July 9th, when they all thought they were upon soundings, by the coldness of the water. They were in general in very good spirits. The weather continued still thick and hazy, and by the north star they found that they had been steering about north by west.

July 10.—The people had drank so much salt water, that it came from them as clear as it was before they drank it; and Mr. Purnell perceived that the second mate had lost a considerable share of his strength and spirits; and also, at noon, that the carpenter was delirious, his malady increasing every hour; about dusk he had almost overset the boat, by attempting to throw himself overboard, and otherwise behaving quite violently. As his strength, however, failed him, he became more manageable, and they got him to lie down in the middle of the boat, among some of the people. Mr. Purnell drank once a little salt water, but could not relish it; he preferred his own urine, which he drank occasionally as he made it. Soon after sunset the second mate lost his speech. Mr. Purnell desired him to lean his head on him: he died, without a groan or struggle, on the 11th of July, being the ninth day they were in the boat. In a few minutes after, the carpenter expired, almost in a similar manner. These melancholy scenes rendered the situation of the survivors more dreadful; it is impossible to describe their feelings. Despair became general; every man imagined his own dissolution was near. They all now went to prayers; some in the Welch language, some in Irish, and others in English; then, after a little deliberation, they stripped the two dead men and hove them overboard.

The weather being now very mild, and almost calm, they turned to, cleaned the boat, and resolved to make their sail larger out of the frocks and trousers of the two deceased men. Purnell got the captain to lie down with the rest of the people, the boatswain and one man excepted, who assisted him in making the sail larger, which they had completed by six or seven o'clock in the afternoon, having made a shroud out of the boat's painter, which served as a shifting back-stay. Purnell also fixed his red flannel waistcoat at the mast head, as a signal the most likely to be seen.

Soon after this some of them observed a sloop at a great distance, coming, as they thought, from the land. This roused every man's spirits: they got out their oars, at which they labored alternately, exerting all their remaining strength to come up with her; but night coming on, and the sloop getting a fresh breeze of wind, they lost sight of her, which occasioned a general consternation; however, the appearance of the north star, which they kept on their starboard bow, gave them hopes that they stood in for land. This night one William Wathing died; he was sixty-four years of age, and had been to sea fifty years: quite worn out with fatigue and hunger, he earnestly prayed, to the last moment, for a drop of water to cool his tongue. Early the next morning Hugh Williams also died, and in the course of the day, another of the crew; entirely exhausted, they both expired without a groan.

Early in the morning of July 13th, it began to blow very fresh, and increased so much that they were obliged to furl their sail, and keep their boat before the wind and sea, which drove them off soundings. In the evening their gunner died. The weather now becoming moderate, and the wind in the south-west quarter, they made sail, not one of them being able to row or pull an oar at any rate; they ran all this night with a fine breeze.

The next morning, July 14th, two more of the crew died, and in the evening they also lost the same number. They found they were on soundings again, and concluded the wind had got round to the north-west quarter. They stood in for the land all this night, and early on July 15th, two others died: the deceased were thrown overboard as soon as their breath had departed. The weather was now thick and hazy, and they were still certain that they were on soundings.

The cabin boy was seldom required to do any thing, and as his intellects at this time were very good, and his understanding clear, it was the opinion of Mr. Purnell that he would survive them all, but he prudently kept his thoughts to himself. The captain seemed likewise tolerably well, and to have kept up his spirits. On account of the haziness of the weather, they could not so well know how they steered in the day-time, as at night; for, whenever the north star appeared, they endeavored to keep it on their starboard bow, by which means they were certain of making the land some time or other. In the evening two more of the crew died; also, before sunrise, one Thomas Philpot, an old, experienced seaman, and very strong; he departed rather convulsed: having latterly lost the power of articulation, his meaning could not be comprehended. He was a native of Belfast, Ireland, and had no family. The survivors found it very difficult to heave his body overboard, as he was a very corpulent man.

About six or seven the next morning, July 16th, they stood in for land, according to the best of their judgment; the weather still thick and hazy. Purnell now prevailed upon the captain and boatswain of the boat to lie down in the fore part of the boat, to bring her more by the head, in order to make her hold a better wind. In the evening the cabin boy, who lately appeared so well, breathed his last, leaving behind the captain, the boatswain, and Mr. Purnell.

The next morning, July 17th, Purnell asked his two companions if they thought they could eat any of the boy's flesh; and having expressed an inclination to try, and the boy being quite cold, he cut the inside of his thigh, a little above his knee, and gave a piece to the captain and boatswain, reserving a small piece for himself; but so weak were their stomachs that none of them could swallow a morsel of it; the body was therefore thrown overboard.

Early in the morning of the 18th, Mr. Purnell found both of his companions dead and cold! Thus destitute, he began to think of his own dissolution; though feeble, his understanding was still clear, and his spirits as good as his forlorn situation would possibly admit. By the color and coldness of the water, he knew he was not far from land, and still maintained hopes of making it. The weather continued very foggy. He lay to all this night, which was very dark, with the boat's head to the northward.

In the morning of the 19th it began to rain; it cleared up in the afternoon, and the wind died away; still Purnell was convinced he was on soundings.

On the 20th, in the afternoon, he thought he saw land, and stood in for it; but night coming on, and it being now very dark, he lay to, fearing he might get on some rocks or shoals.

July 21st, the weather was very fine all the morning, but in the afternoon it became thick and hazy. Purnell's spirits still remained good, but his strength was almost exhausted: he still drank his own water occasionally.

On the 22d, he saw some barnacles on the boat's rudder, very similar to the spawn of an oyster, which filled him with great hopes of being near to land. He unshipped the rudder, and scraping them off with his knife, found they were of a salt fishy substance, and eat them; he was now so weak, and the boat having a great motion, that he found it a difficult task to ship the rudder.

At sunrise, July 23d, he became so sure that he saw land, that his spirits were considerably raised. In the middle of this day he got up, leaned his back against the mast, and received succor from the sun, having previously contrived to steer the boat in this position. The next day he saw, at a very great distance, some kind of a sail, which he judged was coming from the land, which he soon lost sight of. In the middle of the day he got up, and received warmth from the sun as before. He stood on all night for the land.

Very early in the morning of the 25th, after drinking his morning draught, to his inexpressible joy, he saw, while the sun was rising, a sail, and when the sun was up, found she was a two-mast vessel. He was, however, considerably perplexed, not knowing what to do, as she was a great distance astern and to the leeward. In order to watch her motion better, he tacked about. Soon after this he perceived she was standing on her starboard tack, which was the same he had been standing on for many hours. He saw she approached him very fast, and he lay to, for some time, till he believed she was within two miles of the boat, but still to leeward; therefore he thought it best to steer larger, when he found she was a topsail schooner, nearing him very fast. He continued to edge down towards her, until he had brought her about two points under his lee-bow, having it in his power to spring his luff, or bear away. By this time she was within half a mile, and he saw some of the people standing forward on her deck, and waving for him to come under their lee-bow. At the distance of about two hundred yards, they hove the schooner up in the wind, and kept her so until Purnell got alongside, when they threw him a rope, still keeping the schooner in the wind. They now interrogated him very closely; by the manner the boat and oars were painted, they imagined she belonged to a man-of-war, and that they had run away with her from some of his majesty's ships at Halifax, consequently that they would be liable to some punishment if they took him up: they also thought, as the captain and boatswain were lying dead in the boat, they might expose themselves to some contagious disorder. Thus they kept Purnell in suspense for some time. They told him they had made the land that morning from the mast-head, and that they were running along shore for Marblehead, to which place they belonged, and where they expected to be the next morning. At last they told him he might come on board; which, as he said, he could not do without assistance; when the captain ordered two of his men to help him. They conducted him aft on the quarter-deck, where they left him resting against the companion. They were now for casting the boat adrift, when Purnell told them she was not above a month old, built at New York, and if they would hoist her in, it would pay them well for their trouble. To this they agreed, and having thrown the two corpses overboard, and taken out the clothes that were left by the deceased, they hoisted her in and made sail.

Being now on board, Purnell asked for a little water; captain Castleman (for that was his name) ordered one of his sons (having two on board) to fetch him some; when he came with the water, his father looked to see how much he was bringing him, and thinking it too much, threw a part of it away, and desired him to give the remainder, which he drank, being the first fresh water he had tasted for twenty-three days. As he leaned all this time against the companion, he became very cold, and begged to go below: the captain ordered two men to help him down to the cabin, where they left him sitting on the cabin deck, leaning upon the lockers, all hands being now engaged in hoisting in and securing the boat. This done, all hands went down to breakfast, except the man at the helm. They made some soup for Purnell, which he thought very good, but at that time could eat but very little, and in consequence of his late draughts, he had broke out in many parts of his body, so that he was in great pain whenever he stirred. They made a bed for him out of an old sail, and behaved very attentive. While they were at breakfast a squall of wind came on, which called them all upon deck; during their absence, Purnell took up a stone bottle, and without smelling or tasting it, but thinking it was rum, took a hearty draught of it, and found it to be sweet oil; having placed it where he found it, he lay down.

They still ran along shore with the land in sight, and were in great hopes of getting into port that night, but the wind dying away, they did not get in till nine o'clock the next night. All this time Purnell remained like a child; some one or other was always with him, to give him whatever he wished to eat or drink.

As soon as they came to anchor, captain Castleman went on shore, and returned on board the next morning, with the owner, John Pickett, Esq. Soon after, they got Purnell into a boat and carried him on shore; but he was still so very feeble, that he was obliged to be supported by two men. Mr. Pickett took a very genteel lodging for him, and hired a nurse to attend him; he was immediately put to bed, and afterwards provided with a change of clothes. In the course of the day he was visited by every doctor in the town, who all gave him hopes of recovering; but told him it would be some time; for the stronger the constitution, (said they,) the longer it takes to recover its lost strength. Though treated with the utmost tenderness and humanity, it was three weeks before he was able to come down stairs. He stayed in Marblehead two months, during which he lived very comfortably, and gradually recovered his strength. The brig's boat and oars were sold for ninety-five dollars, which paid all his expenses, and procured him a passage to Boston. The nails of his fingers and toes withered away almost to nothing, and did not begin to grow for many months after.

LOSS OF THE FRENCH EAST INDIAMAN THE PRINCE, BY FIRE.

By one of the Lieutenants of that Ship.

THE French East India Company's ship, The Prince, commanded by M. Morin, and bound to Pondicherry, weighed anchor on the 19th of February, 1752, from the harbor of L'Orient. She had scarcely passed the island of St. Michael, when the wind shifting, it was found impossible to double the Turk bank. The utmost efforts, and the greatest precautions, could not prevent her from striking on the bank, in such a manner that the mouths of the guns were immersed in the water. We announced our misfortune by signals of distress, when M. de Godeheu, the commander of the port of L'Orient, came on board to animate the crew by his presence and his orders. All the chests, and other articles, of the greatest value, were removed safely into smaller vessels to lighten the ship; the whole night was occupied with the most laborious exertions. At length the tide, in the morning, relieved us from our dangerous situation, and enabled us to reach the road of Port Louis: we owed the preservation of the ship entirely to the prudent directions of M. de Godeheu, and the measures adopted in consequence. The ship had sprung several leaks, but fortunately our pumps kept the water under: half the cargo was taken out of the vessel, and in about a week we returned to L'Orient, where she was entirely unloaded. She was then careened and caulked afresh. These precautions seemed to promise a successful voyage, and the misfortune we had already experienced showed the strength of the vessel, which fire alone appeared capable of destroying.

On the 10th of June, 1752, a favorable wind carried

us out of the port, but after a fortunate navigation we met with a disaster of which the strongest expressions can convey but a faint idea. In this narrative I shall confine myself to a brief detail, as it is impossible to recollect all the circumstances.

The 26th of July, 1752, being in the latitude of eight degrees thirty minutes south, and in longitude five degrees west, the wind being S. W. just at the moment of taking the observation of the meridian, I had repaired to the quarter, where I was going to command, when a man informed me that a smoke was seen to issue from the pannel of the greater hatchway.

Upon this information the first lieutenant, who kept the keys of the hold, opened all the hatchways, to discover the cause of an accident, the slightest suspicion of which frequently causes the most intrepid to tremble. The captain, who was at dinner in the great cabin, went upon deck and gave orders for extinguishing the fire. I had already directed several sails to be thrown overboard, and the hatchways to be covered with them, hoping, by these means, to prevent the air from penetrating into the hold. I had even proposed, for the greater security, to let in the water between decks, to the height of a foot; but the air, which had already obtained a free passage through the opening of the hatchways, produced a very thick smoke, that issued forth in abundance, and the fire continued gradually to gain ground.

The captain ordered sixty or eighty of the soldiers under arms to restrain the crew, and prevent the confusion likely to ensue in such a critical moment. These precautions were seconded by M. de la Touche, with his usual fortitude and prudence. That hero deserved a better opportunity of signalizing himself, and had destined his soldiers for other operations more useful to his country.

All hands were now employed in getting water; not only the buckets, but likewise all the pumps were kept at work, and pipes were carried from them into the hold; even the water in the jars was emptied out. The rapidity of the fire, however, baffled our efforts and augmented the general consternation.

The captain had already ordered the yawl to be hoisted overboard, merely because it was in the way; four men, among whom was the boatswain, took possession of it. They had no oars, but called out for some, when three sailors jumped overboard and carried them what they stood so much in need of. These fortunate fugitives were required to return; they cried out that they had no rudder, and desired a rope to be thrown them; perceiving that the progress of the flames left them no other resource, they endeavored to remove to a distance from the ship, which passed them in consequence of a breeze that sprang up.

All hands were still busy on board; the impossibility of escaping seemed to increase the courage of the men. The master boldly ventured down into the hold, but the heat obliged him to return; he would have been burned if a great quantity of water had not been thrown over him. Immediately afterwards, the flames were seen to issue with impetuosity from the great pannel. The captain ordered the boats overboard, but fear had exhausted the strength of the most intrepid. The jolly-boat was fastened at a certain height, and preparations were made for hoisting her over; but, to complete our misfortunes, the fire, which increased every moment, ascended the main-mast with such violence and rapidity as to burn the tackle; the boat pitching upon the starboard guns, fell bottom upwards, and we lost all hopes of raising her again.

We now perceived that we had nothing to hope from human aid, but only from the mercy of the Almighty. Dejection filled every mind; the consternation became general; nothing but sighs and groans were heard; even the animals we had on board uttered the most dreadful cries. Every one began to raise his heart and hands towards heaven; and in the certainty of a speedy death each was occupied only with the melancholy alternative between the two elements ready to devour us.

The chaplain, who was on the quarter-deck, gave the

general absolution, and went into the gallery to impart the same to the unhappy wretches who had already committed themselves to the mercy of the waves. What a horrid spectacle! Each was occupied only in throwing overboard whatever promised a momentary preservation; coops, yards, spars, every thing that came to hand was seized in despair and disposed of in the same manner. The confusion was extreme; some seemed to anticipate death by jumping into the sea, others, by swimming, gained the fragments of the vessel; while the shrouds, the yards, and ropes, along the side of the ship were covered with the crew who were suspended from them, as if hesitating between two extremes, equally imminent and equally terrible.

Uncertain for what fate Providence intended me, I saw a father snatch his son from the flames, embrace him, throw him into the sea then following himself, they perished in each other's embrace. I had ordered the helm to be turned to starboard; the vessel heeled, and this manœuvre preserved us for some time on that side, while the fire raged on the larboard side from stem to stern.

Till this moment, I had been so engaged that my thoughts were directed only to the preservation of the ship; now, however, the horrors of a twofold death presented themselves; but through the kindness of heaven, my fortitude never forsook me. I looked round and found myself alone upon the deck. I went into the round-house, where I met M. de la Touche, who regarded death with the same heroism that procured him success in India. "Farewell, my brother and my friend," said he, embracing me—"Why, where are you going?" replied I. "I am going, (said he,) to comfort my friend Morin." He spoke of the captain, who was overwhelmed with grief at the melancholy fate of his female cousins, who were passengers on board his ship, and whom he had persuaded to trust themselves to sea in hen-coops, after having hastily stripped off their clothes, while some of the sailors, swimming with one hand, endeavored to support them with the other.

The yards and masts were covered with men struggling with the waves around the vessel; many of them perished every moment by the balls discharged by the guns in consequence of the flames; a third species of death, that augmented the horrors by which we were surrounded. With a heart oppressed with anguish, I turned my eyes away from the sea. A moment afterwards I entered the starboard gallery, and saw the flames rushing with a horrid noise through the windows of the great cabin and the round-house. The fire approached, and was ready to consume me; my presence was then entirely useless for the preservation of the vessel, or the relief of my fellow sufferers.

In this dreadful situation I thought it my duty to prolong my life a few hours, in order to devote them to my God. I stripped off my clothes with the intention of rolling down a yard, one end of which touched the water; but it was so covered with unfortunate wretches, whom the fear of drowning kept in that situation, that I tumbled over them and fell into the sea, recommending myself to the mercy of Providence. A stout soldier who was drowning caught hold of me in this extremity; I employed every exertion to disengage myself from him, but without effect. I suffered myself to sink under the water, but he did not quit his hold; I plunged a second time, and he still held me firmly in his grasp; he was incapable of reflecting that my death would rather hasten his own than be of service to him. At length, after struggling a considerable time, his strength was exhausted in consequence of the quantity of water he had swallowed, and perceiving that I was sinking the third time, and fearing lest I should drag him to the bottom along with me, he loosed his hold. That he might not catch me again I dived, and rose a considerable distance from the spot.

This first adventure rendered me more cautious in future; I even shunned the dead bodies, which were so numerous, that, to make a free passage, I was obliged to push them aside with one hand, while I kept myself above water with the other. I imagined that each of them was a man who would assuredly seize and involve me in his own destruction. My strength began to fail, and I was convinced of the necessity of resting, when I met a piece of the flag staff. To secure it I put my arm through the noose of the rope, and swam as well as I was able; I perceived a yard floating before me, when I approached and seized it by the end. At the other extremity I saw a young man, scarcely able to support himself, and speedily relinquished this feeble assistance that announced a certain death. The sprit-sail yard next appeared in sight; it was covered with people, and I durst not take a place upon it without asking permission, which my unfortunate companions cheerfully granted. Some were quite naked, and others in their shirts; they expressed their pity at my situation, and their misfortune put my sensibility to the severest test.

M. Morin and M. de la Touche, both so worthy of a better fate, never quitted the vessel, and were doubtless buried in its ruins. Whichever way I turned my eyes, the most dismal sights presented themselves. The main-mast, burnt away at the bottom, fell overboard, killing some, and affording to others a precarious resource. This mast I observed covered with people, and abandoned to the impulse of the waves; at the same moment I perceived two sailors upon a hen-coop with some planks, and cried out to them, "My lads, bring the planks, and swim to me." They approached me, accompanied by several others; and each taking a plank, which we used as oars, we paddled along upon the yard, and joined those who had taken possession of the main-mast.

So many changes of situation presented only new spectacles of horror. I fortunately here met with our chaplain, who gave me absolution. We were in number about eighty persons, who were incessantly threatened with destruction by the balls from the ship's guns. I saw likewise on the mast two young ladies, by whose piety I was much edified; there were six females on board, and the other four were, in all probability, already drowned or burned. Our chaplain, in this dreadful situation, melted the most obdurate hearts by his discourse and the example he gave of patience and resignation. Seeing him slip from the mast and fall into the sea, as I was behind him, I lifted him up again. "Let me go, (said he,) I am full of water, and it is only a prolongation of my sufferings." "No, my friend, (said I,) we will die together when my strength forsakes me." In his pious company I awaited death with perfect resignation. I remained in this situation three hours, and saw one of the ladies fall off the mast with fatigue, and perish; she was too far distant for me to give her any assistance.

When I least expected it, I perceived the yawl close to us; it was then five o'clock, P. M. I cried out to the men in her that I was their lieutenant, and begged permission to share our misfortune with them. They gave me leave to come on board, upon condition that I would swim to them. It was their interest to have a conductor, in order to discover land; and for this reason my company was too necessary for them to refuse my request. The condition they imposed upon me was perfectly reasonable; they acted prudently not to approach, as the others would have been equally anxious to enter their little bark; and we should all have been buried together in a watery grave. Mustering, therefore, all my strength, I was so fortunate as to reach the boat. Soon afterwards I observed the pilot and master, whom I had left on the main-mast, follow my example; they swam to the yawl, and we took them in. This little bark was the means of saving the ten persons who alone escaped, out of nearly three hundred.

The flames still continued to consume our ship, from which we were not more than half a league distant; our too great proximity might prove pernicious, and we, therefore, proceeded a little to windward. Not long after, the fire communicated to the powder-room, and it is impossible to describe the noise with which our vessel blew up. A thick cloud intercepted the light of the sun; amidst this horrible darkness we could perceive nothing but large pieces of flaming wood projected into the air, and whose fall threatened to dash to pieces

Loss of the Prince by Fire. *Page* 148.

numbers of unhappy wretches still struggling with the agonies of death. We, ourselves, were not quite out of danger; it was not impossible but that one of the flaming fragments might reach us, and precipitate our frail vessel to the bottom. The Almighty, however, preserved us from that misfortune; but what a spectacle now presented itself! The vessel had disappeared; its fragments covered the sea to a great distance, and floated in all directions with our unfortunate companions, whose despair and whose lives, had been terminated together by their fall. We saw some completely suffocated, others mangled, half burned, and still preserving sufficient life to be sensible of the accumulated horrors of their fate.

Through the mercy of heaven, I retained my fortitude, and proposed to make towards the fragments of the wreck to seek provisions, and to pick up any other articles we might want. We were totally unprovided, and were in danger of perishing with famine; a death more tedious and more painful than that of our companions. We found several barrels, in which we hoped to find a resource against this pressing necessity, but discovered to our mortification that it was part of the powder which had been thrown overboard during the conflagration.

Night approached; but we providentially found a cask of brandy, about fifteen pounds of salt pork, a piece of scarlet cloth, twenty yards of linen, a dozen of pipe staves, and a few ropes. It grew dark, and we could not wait till daylight in our present situation, without exposing ourselves a hundred times to destruction among the fragments of the wreck, from which we had not yet been able to disengage ourselves. We therefore rowed away from them as speedily as possible, in order to attend to the equipment of our new vessel. Every one fell to work with the utmost assiduity; we employed every thing, and took off the inner sheathing of our boat for the sake of the planks and nails; we drew from the linen what thread we wanted; fortunately one of the sailors had two needles; our scarlet cloth served us for a sail, an oar for a mast, and a plank for a rudder.

Notwithstanding the darkness, our equipment was in a short time as complete as circumstances would permit. The only difficulty that remained was, how to direct our course; we had neither charts nor instruments, and were nearly two hundred leagues from land. We resigned ourselves to the mercy of the Almighty, whose assistance we implored in fervent prayers.

At length we raised our sail, and a favorable wind removed us forever from the floating corpses of our unfortunate companions. In this manner we proceeded eight days and eight nights, without perceiving land, exposed stark naked to the burning rays of the sun by day, and to intense cold by night. The sixth day, a shower of rain inspired us with the hope of some relief from the thirst by which we were tormented: we endeavored to catch the little water that fell in our mouths and hands. We sucked our sail, but having been before soaked in sea-water, it communicated the bitter taste of the latter to the rain which it received. If, however, the rain had been more violent, it might have abated the wind that impelled us, and a calm would have been attended with inevitable destruction.

That we might steer our course with the greater certainty, we consulted, every day, the rising and setting of the sun and moon; and the stars showed us what wind we ought to take. A very small piece of salt pork furnished us one meal in the twenty-four hours: and from even this we were obliged to desist on the fourth day, on account of the irritation of the blood which it occasioned. Our only beverage was a glass of brandy, from time to time; but that liquor burned our stomachs without allaying our thirst. We saw abundance of flying-fish, but the impossibility of catching them rendered our misery still more acute; we were, therefore, obliged to be contented with our provisions. The uncertainty with respect to our fate, the want of food, and the agitation of the sea, combined to deprive us of rest, and almost plunged us into despair. Nature seemed to have abandoned her functions; a feeble ray of hope alone cheered our minds and prevented us from envying the fate of our deceased companions.

I passed the eighth night at the helm: I remained at my post more than ten hours, frequently desiring to be relieved, till at length I sank down with fatigue. My miserable comrades were equally exhausted, and despair began to take possession of our souls. At last, when just perishing with fatigue, misery, hunger, and thirst, we discovered land, by the first rays of the sun, on Wednesday, the 3d of August, 1752. Only those who have experienced similar misfortunes can form an adequate conception of the change which this discovery produced in our minds. Our strength returned, and we took precautions not to be carried away by the currents. At two P. M. we reached the coast of Brazil, and entered the bay of Tresson, in latitude six degrees.

Our first care, upon setting foot on shore, was to thank the Almighty for his favors; we threw ourselves upon the ground, and, in the transports of our joy, rolled ourselves in the sand. Our appearance was truly frightful, our figures preserved nothing human that did not more forcibly announce our misfortunes. Some were perfectly naked, others had nothing but shirts that were rotten and torn to rags, and I had fastened round my waist a piece of scarlet cloth, in order to appear at the head of my companions. We had not yet, however, arrived at the end of all our hardships; although rescued from the greatest of our dangers, that of an uncertain navigation, we were still tormented by hunger and thirst, and in cruel suspense, whether we should find this coast inhabited by men susceptible of sentiments of compassion.

We were deliberating which way we should direct our course, when about fifty Portuguese, most of whom were armed, advanced towards us, and inquired the reason of our landing. The recital of our misfortunes was a sufficient answer, at once announced our wants, and strongly claimed the sacred rights of hospitality. Their treasures were not the object of our desire, the necessaries of life were all that we wanted. Touched by our misfortunes, they blessed the power that had preserved us, and hastened to conduct us to their habitations. Upon the way we came to a river, into which all my companions ran to throw themselves, in order to allay their thirst; they rolled in the water with extreme delight; and bathing was in the sequel one of the remedies of which we made the most frequent use, and which, at the same time, contributed most to the restoration of our health.

The principal person of the place came and conducted us to his house, about half a league distant from the place of our landing. Our charitable host gave us linen shirts and trousers, and boiled some fish, the water of which served us for broth, and seemed delicious. After this frugal repast, though sleep was equally necessary, yet we prepared to render solemn thanks to the Almighty. Hearing that, at the distance of half a league, there was a church dedicated to St. Michael, we repaired thither, singing praises to the Lord, while we presented the homage of our gratitude to Him to whom we were so evidently indebted for our preservation. The badness of the road had fatigued us so much that we were obliged to rest in the village; our misfortunes, together with such an edifying spectacle, drew all the inhabitants around us, and every one hastened to fetch us refreshments. After resting a short time, we returned to our kind host, who, at night, furnished us with another repast of fresh fish. As we wanted more invigorating food, we purchased an ox, which we had in exchange for twenty-five quarts of brandy.

We had to go to Paraibo, a journey of fifteen leagues, barefoot, and without any hope of meeting with good provisions on the way; we therefore took the precaution of smoke-drying our meat, and added to it a provision of flour. After resting three days, we departed under an escort of three soldiers. We proceeded seven leagues the first day, and passed the night at the house of a man, who received us kindly. The next evening, a sergeant, accompanied by twenty-nine soldiers, came to meet us for the purpose of conducting and presenting us to the commandant of the fortress; that worthy officer received us graciously, gave us an entertainment, and a boat to go to Paraibo. It was midnight when we arrived at that town; a Portuguese captain was waiting to present us to the governor, who gave us a gracious reception, and furnished us with all the comforts of life. We there reposed for three days, but being desirous of reaching Fernambuc to take advantage of a Portuguese fleet that was expected to sail every day, in order to return to Europe, the governor ordered a corporal to conduct us thither. My feet were so lacerated that I could scarcely stand, and a horse was therefore provided for me.

At length after a journey of four days, we entered the town of Fernambuc. My first business was to go, with my people, to present myself to the general, Joseph de Correa, who condescended to give me an audience; after which Don Francisco Miguel, a captain of a king's ship, took us in his boat to procure us the advantage of saluting the admiral of the fleet, Don Juan d'Acosta de Porito. During the fifty days that we remained at Fernambuc that gentleman never ceased to load me with new favors and civilities. His generosity extended to all my companions in misfortune, to some of whom he even gave appointments in the vessels of his fleet.

On the fifth of October we set sail, and arrived without any accident, at Lisbon, on the 17th of December. On the second of January, our consul, M. du Vernay, procured me a passage in a vessel bound to Morlaix. The master and myself went on board together, the rest of my companions being distributed among other ships. I arrived at Morlaix on the 2d of February. My fatigues obliged me to take a few days rest in that place, from whence I repaired on the 10th to l'Orient, overwhelmed with poverty, having lost all that I possessed in the world, after a service of twenty-eight years, and with my health greatly impaired by the hardships I had endured.

LOSS OF HIS MAJESTY'S SHIP PHŒNIX,

Off the Island of Cuba, in the year 1780.

THE Phœnix, of forty-four guns, captain Sir Hyde Parker, was lost in a hurricane, off Cuba, in the year 1780. The same hurricane destroyed the Thunderer, seventy-four; Stirling Castle, sixty-four; La Blanche, forty-two; Laurel, twenty-eight; Andromeda, twenty-eight; Deal Castle, twenty-four; Scarborough, twenty; Beaver's Prize, sixteen; Barbadoes, fourteen; Cameleon, fourteen; Endeavor, fourteen; and Victor, ten guns. Lieutenant Archer was first lieutenant of the Phœnix at the time she was lost. His narrative in a letter to his mother contains a most correct and animated account of one of the most awful events in the service. It is so simple and natural as to make the reader feel himself on board the Phœnix. Every circumstance is detailed with feeling, and powerful appeals are continually made to the heart. It must likewise afford considerable pleasure to observe the devout spirit of a seaman frequently bursting forth, and imparting sublimity to the relation.

At sea, June 30, 1780.

MY DEAREST MADAM,

I am now going to give you an account of our last cruise in the Phœnix; and must premise, that should any one see it beside yourself, they must put this construction on it—that it was originally intended for the eyes of a mother, and a mother only, as, upon that supposition, my feelings may be tolerated. You will also meet with a number of sea terms, which, if you don't understand, why, I cannot help you, as I am unable to give a sea description in any other words.

To begin then:—On the 2d of August, 1780, we weighed and sailed for Port Royal, bound from Pensacola, having two store-ships under convoy, and to see safe in; then cruise off the Havannah, and in the gulf of Mexico, for six weeks. In a few days we made the two sandy islands, that look as if they had just risen out of the sea, or fallen from the sky; inhabited nevertheless, by upwards of three hundred English, who get their bread by catching turtles and parrots, and raising vegetables, which they exchange with ships that pass, for clothing and a few of the luxuries of life, as rum, &c.

About the 12th we arrived at Pensacola, without any thing remarkable happening, except our catching a vast quantity of fish, sharks, dolphins, and bonettos. On the 13th sailed singly, and on the 14th had a very heavy gale of wind at north, right off the land, so that we soon left the sweet place, Pensacola, a distance astern. We then looked into the Havannah, saw a number of ships there, and knowing that some of them were bound round the bay, we cruised in the track: a fortnight, however, passed, and not a single ship hove in sight to cheer our spirits. We then took a turn or two round the gulf, but not near enough to be seen from the shore. Vera Cruz we expected would have made us happy, but the same luck still continued; day followed day, and no sail. The dollar bag began to grow a little bulky, for every one had lost two or three times, and no one had won: (this was a small gambling party entered into by Sir Hyde and ourselves; every one put a dollar into a bag, and fixed on a day when we should see a sail, but no two persons were to name the same day, and whoever guessed right first was to have the bag.)

Being now tired of our situation, and glad the cruise was almost out, for we found the navigation very dangerous, owing to unaccountable currents; so shaped our course for cape Antonio. The next day the man at the mast-head, at about one o'clock in the afternoon, called out: "A sail upon the weather bow! Ha! Ha! Mr. Spaniard, I think we have you at last. Turn out all hands! make sail. All hands! give chase!" There was scarcely any occasion for this order, for the sound of a sail being in sight flew like wildfire through the ship, and every sail was set, in an instant, almost before the orders were given. A lieutenant at the mast-head, with a spy glass, "What is she?" "A large ship studding athwart right before the wind. P-o-r-t! Keep her away! set the studding sails ready!" Up comes the little doctor, rubbing his hands; "Ha! Ha! I have won the bag." "The devil take you and the bag; look, what's ahead will fill all our bags." Mast-head again; "Two more sail on the larboard beam!" "Archer, go up and see what you can make of them." "Upon deck there; I see a whole fleet of twenty sail coming right before the wind." "Confound the luck of it; this is some convoy or other, but we must try if we can pick some of them out." "Haul down the studding sails! Luff! bring her to the wind! Let us see what we can make of them."

About five we got pretty near them, and found them to be twenty-six sail of Spanish merchantmen, under convoy of three line-of-battle ships, one of which chased us; but when she found we were playing with her (for the old Phœnix had heels) she left chase, and joined the convoy; which they drew up into a lump, and placed themselves at the outside; but we still kept smelling about till after dark. O, for the Hector, the Albion, and a frigate, and we should take the whole fleet and convoy, worth some millions! About eight o'clock perceived three sail at some distance from the fleet; dashed in between them and gave chase, and were happy to find they steered from the fleet. About twelve, came up with a large ship of twenty-six guns. "Archer, every man to his quarters! run the lower deck guns out, and light the ship up: show this fellow our force; it may prevent his firing into us and killing a man or two." No sooner said than done. "Hoa, the ship ahoy! lower your sails, and bring to instantly, or I'll sink you." Clatter, clatter, went the blocks, and away flew all their sails in proper confusion. "What ship is that?" "The Polly." "Whence came you!" "From Jamaica." "Where are you bound?" "To New York." "What ship is that?" "The Phœnix." Huzza, three times by the whole ship's company. An old grum fellow of a sailor standing close by me: "O, d—n your three cheers, we took you to be something else." Upon examination we found it to be as he reported, and that they had fallen in with the Spanish fleet that morning, and were chased the whole day, and that nothing saved them but our stepping in between; for the Spaniards took us for three consorts, and the Polly took the Phœnix for a Spanish frigate, till we hailed them. The other vessels in company were likewise bound to New York. Thus was I, from being worth thousands in idea, reduced to the old four shillings six-pence again; for the little doctor made the most prize money of us all that day, by winning the bag, which contained between thirty and forty dollars; but this is nothing to what we sailors sometimes undergo.

After parting company, we steered S. S. E. to go round Antonio, and so to Jamaica, (our cruise being out,) with our fingers in our mouths, and all of us as green as you please. It happened to be my middle watch, and about three o'clock, when the man upon the forecastle bawls out "Breakers ahead, and land upon the lee bow;" I looked out, and it was so, sure enough. "Ready about, put the helm down! Helm a lee!" Sir Hyde hearing me put the ship about, jumped upon deck. "Archer, what's the matter? You are putting the ship about without my orders!" Sir, 'tis time to go about; the ship is almost ashore, there is the land. "Good God, so it is! Will the ship stay?" Yes, sir, I believe she will, if we don't make any confusion; she is all aback —forward now? "Well, (says he,) work the ship, I will not speak a single word." The ship stayed very well. Then heave the lead! see what water we have! "Three fathom." Keep the ship away, W. N. W. "By the mark three." "This won't do, Archer." No, sir, we had better haul more to the northward; we came

S. S. E. and had better steer N. N. W. "Steady, and a quarter three." This may do, we deepen a little. "By the deep four." Very well, my lad, heave quick. "Five fathom." That's a fine fellow! another cast nimbly. "Quarter less eight." That will do, come, we shall get clear bye and bye. "Mark under water five." What's that? "Only five fathom, sir." Turn all hands up, bring the ship to an anchor, boy. Are the anchors clear? "In a moment, sir,—All clear." What water have you in the chains now? "Eight, half nine." Keep fast the anchors till I call you. "Aye, aye, sir, all fast." "I have no ground with this line." How many fathoms have you out? pass along the deep sea-line! "Aye, aye, sir,." Heave away, watch! watch! bear away, veer away. "No ground, sir, with a hundred fathom." That 's clever, come, Madame Phœnix, there is another squeak in you yet—all down but the watch; secure the anchors again; heave the main-top-sail to the mast; luff, and bring her to the wind!

I told you, Madam, you should have a little sea-jargon: if you can understand half of what is already said, I wonder at it, though it is nothing to what is to come yet, when the old hurricane begins. As soon as the ship was a little to rights, and all quiet again, Sir Hyde came to me in the most friendly manner, the tears almost starting from his eyes—"Archer, we ought all to be much obliged to you for the safety of the ship, and perhaps of ourselves. I am particularly so; nothing but that instantaneous presence of mind and calmness saved her; another ship's length and we should have been fast on shore; had you been the least diffident, or made the least confusion, so as to make the ship baulk in her stays, she must have been inevitably lost." Sir, you are very good, but I have done nothing that I suppose any body else would not have done, in the same situation. I did not turn all the hands up, knowing the watch able to work the ship; besides, had it spread immediately about the ship that she was almost ashore, it might have created a confusion that was better avoided. "Well," says he, "'tis well indeed."

At daylight we found that the current had set us between the Colladora rocks and cape Antonio, and that we could not have got out any other way than we did; there was a chance, but Providence is the best pilot. We had sunset that day twenty leagues to the S. E. of our reckoning by the current.

After getting clear of this scrape, we thought ourselves fortunate, and made sail for Jamaica, but misfortune seemed to follow misfortune. The next night, my watch upon deck too, we were overtaken by a squall, like a hurricane while it lasted; for though I saw it coming, and prepared for it, yet, when it took the ship, it roared, and laid her down so, that I thought she would never get up again. However, by keeping her away, and clueing up every thing, she righted. The remainder of the night we had very heavy squalls, and in the morning found the main-mast sprung half the way through: one hundred and twenty-three leagues to the leeward of Jamaica, the hurricane months coming on, the head of the main-mast almost off, and at a short allowance; well, we must make the best of it. The main-mast was well fished, but we were obliged to be very tender of carrying the sail.

Nothing remarkable happened for ten days afterwards, when we chased a Yankee man-of-war for six hours, but could not get near enough to her before it was dark, to keep sight of her; so that we lost her because unable to carry any sail on the main-mast. In about twelve days more made the island of Jamaica, having weathered all the squalls, and put into Montego bay for water; so that we had a strong party for kicking up a dust on shore, having found three men-of-war lying there. Dancing, &c. &c., till two o'clock every morning; little thinking what was to happen in four days' time: for out of the four men-of-war that were there, not one was in being at the end of that time, and not a soul alive but those left of our crew. Many of the houses where we had been so merry, were so completely destroyed, that scarcely a vestige remained to mark where they stood.

Thy works are wonderful, O God! praised be thy holy name!

September the 30th, weighed; bound for Port Royal, round the eastward of the island; the Barbadoes and Victor had sailed the day before, and the Scarborough was to sail the next. Moderate weather until October the 2d. Spoke the Barbadoes off Port Antonio in the evening. At eleven at night it began to snuffle, with a monstrous heavy bill from the eastward. Close reefed the top-sails. Sir Hyde sent for me: "What sort of weather have we, Archer!" It blows a little, and has a very ugly look; if in any other quarter but this, I should say we were going to have a gale of wind. "Aye, it looks so very often here when there is no wind at all; however, don't hoist the top-sails till it clears a little, there is no trusting any country." At twelve I was relieved; the weather had the same rough look: however, they made sail upon her, but had a very dirty night. At eight in the morning I came up again, found it blowing hard from the E. N. E. with close reefed top-sails upon the ship, and heavy squalls at times. Sir Hyde came upon deck: "Well, Archer, what do you think of it?" O, sir, 'tis only a touch of the times, we shall have an observation at twelve o'clock; the clouds are beginning to break; it will clear up at noon, or else blow very hard afterwards. "I wish it would clear up, but I doubt it much. I was once in a hurricane in the East Indies, and the beginning of it had much the same appearance as this. So take in the top-sails, we have plenty of sea-room."

At twelve, the gale still increasing, wore ship, to keep as near mid-channel, between Jamaica and Cuba, as possible; at one the gale increasing still; at two harder! Reefed the courses, and furled them; brought to under a foul mizzen stay-sail, head to the northward. In the evening no sign of the weather taking off, but every appearance of the storm increasing, prepared for a proper gale of wind; secured all the sails with spare gaskets; good rolling tackles upon the yards; squared the booms; saw the boats all made fast; new lashed the guns double breeched the lower deckers; saw that the carpenters had the tarpaulins and battens all ready for the hatchways; got the top-gallant-mast down upon the deck; jib-boom and sprit-sail-yard fore and aft; in fact, did every thing we could think of to make a snug ship.

The poor devils of birds now began to find the uproar in the elements, for numbers, both of sea and land kinds, came on board of us. I took notice of some, which happening to be to leeward, turned to windward, like a ship, tack and tack; for they could not fly against it. When they came over the ship they dashed themselves down upon the deck, without attempting to stir till picked up, and when let go again, they would not leave the ship, but endeavored to hide themselves from the wind.

At eight o'clock a hurricane; the sea roaring, but the wind still steady to a point; did not ship a spoonful of water. However, got the hatchways all secured, expecting what would be the consequence, should the wind shift; placed the carpenters by the main-mast, with broad axes, knowing, from experience, that at the moment you may want to cut it away to save the ship, an axe may not be found. Went to supper: bread, cheese, and porter. The purser frightened out of his wits about his bread bags; the two marine officers as white as sheets, not understanding the ship's working so much, and the noise of the lower deck guns; which, by this time, made a pretty screeching to the people not used to it; it seemed as if the whole ship's side was going at each roll. Wooden, our carpenter, was all this time smoking his pipe and laughing at the doctor; the second lieutenant upon deck, and the third in his hammock.

At ten o'clock I thought to get a little sleep; came to look into my cot; it was full of water; for every seam, by the straining of the ship, had begun to leak. Stretched myself, therefore, upon deck, between two chests, and left orders to be called, should the least thing happen. At twelve a midshipman came to me: "Mr. Archer, we are just going to wear ship, sir!" O, very well, I'll be up directly; what sort of weather have you got? "It blows a hurricane." Went upon deck, found Sir Hyde there. "It blows damn'd hard, Archer." It does indeed, sir. "I don't know that I ever remember its blowing so hard before; but the ship makes a very good weather of it upon this tack as she bows the sea; but we must wear her, as the wind has shifted to the S. E. and we are drawing right upon Cuba; so do you go forward, and have some hands stand by; loose the lee yard-arm of the fore-sail, and when she is right before the wind, whip the clue garnet close up, and roll up the sail." Sir! there is no canvas can stand against this a moment; if we attempt to loose him, he will fly into ribands in an instant, and we may lose three or four of our people; she'll wear by manning the fore shrouds. "O, I don't think she will." I'll answer for it, sir; I have seen it tried several times on the coast of America with success. "Well, try it; if she does not wear, we can only loose the fore-sail afterwards." This was a great condescension from such a man as Sir Hyde. However, by sending about two hundred people into the fore-rigging, after a hard struggle, she wore; found she did not make so good weather on this tack as on the other; for as the sea began to run across, she had not time to rise from one sea, before another dashed against her. Began to think we should lose our masts, as the ship lay very much along, by the pressure of the wind constantly upon the yards and masts alone: for the poor mizzen-stay-sail had gone in shreds long before, and the sails began to fly from the yards through the gaskets into coach whips. My God! to think that the wind could have such force.

Sir Hyde now sent me to see what was the matter between decks, as there was a good deal of noise. As soon as I was below, one of the Marine officers calls out: "Good God! Mr. Archer, we are sinking, the water is up to the bottom of my cot." Pooh, pooh! as long as it is not over your mouth, you are well off; what the devil do you make this noise for? I found there was some water between decks, but nothing to be alarmed at: scuttled the deck, and it ran into the well; found she made a good deal of water through the sides and decks; turned the watch below to the pumps, though only two feet of water in the well; but expected to be kept constantly at work now, as the ship labored much, with scarcely a part of her above water but the quarter-deck, and that but seldom. "Come, pump away, my boys. Carpenters, get the weather chain-pump rigged." "All ready, sir. Then man it, and keep both pumps going."

At two o'clock the chain pump was choked; set the carpenters at work to clear it; the two head pumps at work upon deck: the ship gained upon us while our chain-pumps were idle; in a quarter of an hour they were at work again, and we began to gain upon her. While I was standing at the pumps, cheering the people, the carpenter's mate came running to me with a face as long as my arm: "O, sir! the ship has sprung a leak in the gunner's room." Go, then, and tell the carpenter to come to me, but do not speak a word to any one else. Mr. Goodinoh, I am told there is a leak in the gunner's room; go and see what is the matter, but do not alarm any body, and come and make your report privately to me. In a short time he returned; "Sir, there is nothing there, it is only the water washing up between the timbers, that this booby has taken for a leak." O, very well; go upon deck and see if you can keep any of the water from washing down below. Sir, I have had four people constantly keeping the hatchways secure, but there is such a weight of water upon the deck that nobody can stand it when the ship rolls. The gunner soon afterwards came to me, saying, "Mr. Archer, I should be glad if you would step this way into the magazine for a moment." I thought some damned thing was the matter, and ran directly. Well, what is the matter here? He answered, "The ground tier of powder is spoiled, and I want to show you that it is not out of carelessness in me in stowing it, for no powder in the world could be better stowed. Now, sir, what am I to do? If you do not speak to Sir Hyde, he will be angry with me." I could not forbear smiling to see how easy he took the danger of the ship, and said to him, let us shake off this gale of wind first, and talk of the damaged powder afterwards.

At four, we had gained upon the ship a little, and I went upon deck, it being my watch. The second lieutenant relieved me at the pumps. Who can attempt to describe the appearance of things upon deck? If I was to write forever, I could not give you an idea of it—a total darkness all above; the sea on fire, running as it were in Alps, or Peaks of Teneriffe; (mountains are too common an idea;) the wind roaring louder than thunder, (absolutely no flight of imagination,) the whole made more terrible, if possible, by a very uncommon kind of blue lightning; the poor ship was very much pressed, yet doing what she could, shaking her sides, and groaning at every stroke. Sir Hyde upon deck, lashed to windward! I soon lashed myself alongside of him, and told him the situation of things below, saying the ship did not make more water than might be expected in such weather, and that I was only afraid of a gun breaking loose. "I am not in the least afraid of that; I have commanded her six years, and have had many a gale of wind in her; so that her iron work, which always gives way first, is pretty well tried. Hold fast! that was an ugly sea; we must lower the yards, I believe, Archer; the ship is much pressed." If we attempt it, sir, we shall lose them, for a man aloft can do nothing; besides, their being down would ease the ship very little; the main-mast is a sprung mast; I wish it was overboard without carrying any thing else along with it; but that can soon be done, the gale cannot last forever; 'it will soon be daylight now. Found by the master's watch that it was five o'clock, though but a little after four by ours: glad it was so near daylight, and looked for it with much anxiety. Cuba, thou art much in our way! Another ugly sea; sent a midshipman to bring news from the pumps; the ship was gaining on them very much, for they had broken one of their chains, but it was almost mended again. News from the pump again. "She still gains! a heavy lee!" Back water from the leeward, half way up the quarter deck; filled one of the cutters upon the booms, and tore her all to pieces; the ship lying almost on her beam-ends, and not attempting to right again. Word from below that the ship still gained on them, as they could not stand to the pumps, she lay so much along. I said to Sir Hyde:—This is no time, sir, to think of saving the masts; shall we cut the main-mast away? "Aye! as fast as you can." I accordingly went into the weather chains with a pole ax, to cut away the lanyards; the boatswain went to leeward, and the carpenters stood by the mast. We were all ready, and a very violent sea broke right on board of us, carried every thing upon deck away, filled the ship with water, the main and mizzen-masts went, the ship righted, but was in the last struggle of sinking under us.

As soon as we could shake our heads above water, Sir Hyde exclaimed, "We are gone, at last, Archer! foundered at sea!" Yes, sir, farewell, and the Lord have mercy upon us! I then turned about to look at the ship; and thought she was struggling to get rid of some of the water; but all in vain, she was almost full below. "Almighty God! I thank thee, that now I am leaving this world, which I have always considered as only a passage to a better, I die with a full hope of thy mercies through the merits of Jesus Christ, thy Son, our Savior!"

I then felt sorry that I could swim, as by that means I might be a quarter of an hour longer dying than a man who could not, and it is impossible to divest ourselves of a wish to preserve life. At the end of these reflections I thought I heard the ship thump and grinding under our feet; it was so. Sir, the ship is ashore! "What do you say?" The ship is ashore, and we may save ourselves yet! By this time the quarter-deck was full of men who had come up from below; and the Lord have mercy upon us, flying about from all quarters. The ship now made every body sensible that she was ashore, for every stroke threatened a total dissolution of her whole frame; found she was stern ashore, and the bow broke the sea a good deal, though it was washing clean over at every stroke. Sir Hyde cried out: "Keep to the quarter-deck, my lads, when she goes to pieces, it is your best chance!" Providentially got the fore-mast cut away, that she might not pay round broadside. Lost five men cutting away the foremast, by the breaking of a sea on board just as the mast went. That was nothing; every one expected it would be his own fate next; looked for daybreak with the greatest impatience. At last it came; but what a scene did it show us! The ship upon a bed of rocks, mountains of them on one side, and Cordilleras of water on the other; our poor ship grinding and crying out at every stroke between them; going away by piece-meal. However, to show the unaccountable workings of Providence, that which often appears to be the greatest evil, proves to be the greatest good! That unmerciful sea lifted and beat us up so high among the rocks, that at last the ship scarcely moved. She was very strong, and did not go to pieces at the first thumping, though her decks tumbled in. We found afterwards that she had beat over a ledge of rocks, almost a quarter of a mile in extent beyond us, where if she had struck, every soul of us must have perished.

I now began to think of getting on shore, so stripped off my coat and shoes for a swim, and looked for a line to carry the end with me. Luckily could not find one, which gave me time for recollection: "This won't do for me, to be the first man out of the ship, and first lieutenant; we may get to England again, and people may think I paid a great deal of attention to myself, and did not care for any body else. No, that won't do; instead of being the first, I'll see every man, sick and well, out of her before me."

I now thought there was no probability of the ship's soon going to pieces, therefore had not a thought of instant death; took a look round with a kind of philosophic eye, to see how the same situation affected my companions, and was surprised to find the most swaggering, swearing bullies in fine weather, now the most pitiful wretches on earth, when death appeared before

Loss of the Phoenix. *Page* 167.

them. However, two got safe; by which means, with a line, we got a hawser on shore, and made fast to the rocks, upon which many ventured and arrived safely. There were some sick and wounded on board, who could not avail themselves of this method; we therefore got a spare top-sail-yard from the chains and placed one end ashore and the other on the cabin window, so that most of the sick got ashore this way.

As I had determined, so I was the last man out of the ship; this was about ten o'clock. The gale now began to break. Sir Hyde came to me, and taking me by the hand was so affected that he was scarcely able to speak. "Archer, I am happy beyond expression to see you on the shore; but look at our poor Phœnix!" I turned about, but could not say a single word, being too full: my mind had been too intensely occupied before; but every thing now rushed upon me at once, so that I could not contain myself, and I indulged for a full quarter of an hour.

By twelve it was pretty moderate; got some nails on shore and made tents; found great quantities of fish driven up by the sea into holes of the rocks; knocked up a fire, and had a most comfortable dinner. In the afternoon made a stage from the cabin windows to the rocks, and got out some provisions and water, lest the ship should go to pieces, in which case we must all have perished of hunger and thirst; for we were upon a desolate part of the coast, and under a rocky mountain, that could not supply us with a single drop of water.

Slept comfortably this night, and the next day; the idea of death vanishing by degrees, the prospect of being prisoners, during the war, at the Havannah, and walking three hundred miles to it through the woods, was rather unpleasant. However, to save life for the present, we employed this day in getting more provisions and water on shore, which was not an easy matter, on account of decks, guns, and rubbish, and ten feet water that lay over them. In the evening I proposed to Sir Hyde to repair the remains of the only boat left, and to venture in her to Jamaica myself; and in case I arrived safe, to bring vessels to take them all off; a proposal worthy of consideration. It was next day agreed to; therefore, got the cutter on shore, and set the carpenters to work on her; in two days she was ready, and at four o'clock in the afternoon, I embarked with four volunteers and a fortnight's provision; hoisted English colors as we put off from shore, and received three cheers from the lads left behind; and set sail with a light heart; having not the least doubt, that, with God's assistance, we should come and bring them all off. Had a very squally night, and a very leaky boat, so as to keep two buckets constantly baling. Steered her, myself, the whole night by the stars, and in the morning saw the coast of Jamaica, distant twelve leagues. At eight in the evening, arrived at Montego bay.

I must now begin to leave off, particularly as I have but half an hour to conclude; else my pretty little short letter will lose its passage, which I should not like, after being ten days, at different times, writing it; beating up with the convoy to the northward, which is a reason that this epistle will never read well; for I never sat down with a proper disposition to go on with it; but as I knew something of the kind would please you, I was resolved to finish it: yet it will not bear an overhaul; so do not expose your son's nonsense.

But to proceed—I instantly sent off an express to the Admiral, another to the Porcupine man-of-war, and went myself to Martha Bray to get vessels; for all their vessels here, as well as many of their horses, were gone to *Moco.* Got three small vessels, and set out back again to Cuba, where I arrived the fourth day after leaving my companions. I thought the ship's crew would have devoured me on my landing; they presently whisked me up on their shoulders, and carried me to the tent; where Sir Hyde was.

I must omit many little occurrences that happened on shore, for want of time; but I shall have a number of stories to tell, when I get alongside of you; and the next time I visit you, I shall not be in such a hurry to quit you as I was the last, for then I hoped my nest would have been pretty well feathered:—But my tale is forgotten.

I found the Porcupine had arrived that day, and the lads had built a boat almost ready for launching, that would hold fifty of them, which was intended for another trial, in case I had foundered. Next day, embarked all our people that were left, amounting to two hundred and fifty; for some had died of the wounds they received in getting on shore; others of drinking rum, and others had straggled into the country. All our vessels were so full of people, that we could not take away the few clothes that were saved from the wreck; but that was a trifle since we had preserved our lives and liberty. To make short of my story, we all arrived safe at Montego bay, and shortly after at Port Royal, in the Janus, which was sent on purpose for us, and were all honorably acquitted for the loss of the ship. I was made admiral's aid de camp, and a little time afterwards sent down to St. Juan as a captain of the Resource, to bring what were left of the poor devils to Blue Fields, on the Musquito shore, and then to Jamaica, where they arrived after three months absence, and without a prize, though I looked out hard off Porto Bello and Carthagena. Found, in my absence, that I had been appointed captain of the Tobago, where I remain his majesty's most true and faithful servant, and my dear mother's most dutiful son. ——— ARCHER.

LOSS OF HIS MAJESTY'S SHIP LA TRIBUNE,

Off Halifax, (Nova Scotia,) November, 1797.

La Tribune was one of the finest frigates in his majesty's navy; mounted forty-four guns, and had recently been taken from the French by captain Williams, in the Unicorn frigate. She was commanded by captain S. Barker; on the 22d of September, 1797, sailed from Torbay, as convoy to the Quebec and Newfoundland fleets.

In latitude forty-nine degrees, fourteen minutes, longitude seventeen degrees twenty-two minutes she fell in with and spoke his majesty's ship Experiment, from Halifax; and lost sight of all her convoy on the 10th of October, in latitude seventy-four degrees sixteen minutes, longitude thirty-two degrees eleven minutes.

About eight o'clock in the morning of the following Thursday, they came in sight of the harbor of Halifax, and approached it very fast, with an E. S. E. wind, when captain Barker proposed to the master to lay the ship to, till they could procure a pilot. The master replied, that he had beat a forty-four gun ship into the harbor, that he had frequently been there, and there was no occasion for a pilot, as the wind was favorable. Confiding in these assurances, captain Barker went into his cabin, where he was employed in arranging some papers which he intended to take on shore with him. In the mean time, the master, placing great dependence on the judgment of a negro, named John Cosey, who had formerly belonged to Halifax, took upon himself the pilotage of the ship. By twelve o'clock, the ship had approached so near Thrum Cap shoals, that the master became alarmed, and sent for Mr. Galvin, master's mate, who was sick below. On his coming upon deck, he heard the man in the chains sing out, "by the mark five!" the black man forward at the same time crying, "steady!" Galvin got on one of the carronades to observe the situation of the ship; the master ran, in great agitation, to the wheel, and took it from the man who was steering, with the intention of wearing the ship; but before this could be effected, or Galvin was able to give an opinion, she struck. Captain Barker immediately went on deck and reproached the master with having lost the ship. Seeing Galvin likewise on deck, he addressed him, and said, "that, knowing he had formerly sailed out of the harbor, he was surprised he could stand by and see the master run the ship on shore;" to which Galvin replied, "that he had not been on deck long enough to give an opinion."

Signals of distress were instantly made, and answered by military posts and ships in the harbor, from which, as well as the dock-yard, boats immediatety put off to the relief of the Tribune. The military boats, and one of those from the dock yard, with Mr. Rackum, boatswain of the Ordinary, reached the ship, but the wind was so much against the others, that, in spite of all their exertions, they were unable to get on board. The ship was immediately lightened, by throwing overboard all her guns, excepting one retained for signals, and every other heavy article, so that about half past eight o'clock in the evening, the ship began to heave, and at nine, got off the shoals. She had lost her rudder about three hours before, and it was now found, on examination, that she had seven feet of water in her hold. The chain-pumps were immediately manned, and such exertions were made, that they seemed to gain on the leaks. By the advice of Mr. Rackum, the captain ordered the best bower anchor to be let go, but this did not bring her up. He then ordered the cable to be cut; and the jib and fore top-mast stay-sail were hoisted to steer by. During this interval a violent gale, which had come on at S. E., kept increasing, and carrying the ship to the western shore. The small bower anchor was soon afterwards let go: at which time they found themselves in thirteen fathom water, and the mizzen-mast was then cut away.

It was now ten o'clock, and as the water gained fast upon them, the crew had but little hope left of saving either the ship or their lives. At this critical period, lieutenant Campbell quitted the ship, and lieutenant North was taken into the boat, out of one of the ports. From the moment at which the former left the vessel, all hopes of safety had vanished; the ship was sinking fast, the storm was increasing with redoubled violence, and the rocky shore which they were approaching, resounding with the tremendous noise of the rolling billows, presented nothing to those who might survive the loss of the ship, but the expectation of a more painful death, by being dashed against precipices, which, even in the calmest day, it is impossible to ascend. Dunlap, one of the survivors, declared, that about half past ten, as nearly as he could conjecture, one of the men who had been below, came to him on the forecastle, and told him it was all over. A few minutes afterwards, the ship took a lurch, like a boat nearly filled with water and going down; on which Dunlap immediately began to ascend the fore-shrouds, and at the same moment casting his eyes towards the quarter-deck, he saw captain Barker standing by the gangway, and looking into the water, and directly afterwards he heard him call for the jolly-boat. He then saw the lieutenant of marines running towards the taffrel, to look, as he supposed, for the jolly-boat, which had been previously let down with men in her; but the ship instantly took a second lurch and sank to the bottom, after which neither the captain nor any of the other officers were again seen.

The scene, before sufficiently distressing, now became peculiarly awful. More than two hundred and forty men, besides several women and children, were floating on the waves, making the last effort to preserve life. Dunlap, who has been already mentioned, gained the fore-top. Mr. Galvin, the master's mate, with incredible difficulty, got into the main-top. He was below, when the ship sank, directing the men at the chain-pump, but was washed up the hatchway, thrown into the waist, and from thence into the water, and his feet, as he plunged, struck against a rock. On ascending he swam to gain the main-shrouds, when three men suddenly seized hold of him. He now gave himself up for lost; but to disengage himself from them he made a dive into the water, which caused them to quit their grasp. On rising again he swam to the shrouds, and having reached the main-top, seated himself on an arm chest which was lashed to the mast.

From the observations of Galvin, in the main-top, and Dunlap, in the fore-top, it appears that nearly one hundred persons were hanging for a considerable time, to the shrouds, the tops, and other parts of the wreck. From the length of the night, and the severity of the storm, nature, however, became exhausted, and during the

Loss of the La Tribune. *Page* 172.

whole night, they kept dropping off and disappearing. The cries and groans of the unhappy sufferers, from the bruises many of them had received, and their hopes of deliverance beginning to fail, were continued through the night; but as morning approached, in consequence of the few who then survived, they became extremely feeble.

About twelve o'clock, the main-mast gave way; at that time there were, on the main-top and shrouds, about forty persons. By the fall of the mast the whole of these unhappy wretches were again plunged into the water, and ten only regained the top, which rested on the main yard, and the whole remained fast to the ship by some of the rigging. Of the ten, who thus reached the top, four only were alive when morning appeared. Ten were at that time alive on the fore-top, but three were so exhausted, and so helpless, that they were washed away before any relief arrived; three others perished, and thus only four were, at last, left alive on the fore-top.

The place, where the ship went down, was barely three times her length to the southward of the entrance into Herring Cove. The inhabitants came down in the night, to the point opposite to which the ship sank, kept up large fires, and were so near as to converse with the people on the wreck.

The first exertion that was made for their relief was by a boy thirteen years old, from Herring Cove, who ventured off in a small skiff by himself about eleven o'clock, the next day. This youth, with great labor and extreme risk to himself, boldly approached the wreck, and backed in his little boat so near to the fore-top, as to take off two of the men, for the boat could not, with safety, hold any more. And here a trait of generous magnanimity was exhibited, which ought not to pass unnoticed. Dunlap and another man, named Monro, had, throughout this disastrous night, preserved their strength and spirits in a greater degree, than their unfortunate companions, whom they endeavored to cheer and encourage when they found their spirits sinking.

Upon the arrival of the boat, these two might have stepped into it, and thus have terminated their own sufferings; for their two companions, though alive, were unable to stir; they lay exhausted on the top, wishing not to be disturbed, and seemed desirous to perish in that situation. These generous fellows hesitated not a moment to remain, themselves, on the wreck, and to save their unfortunate companions, against their will. They lifted them up, and with the greatest exertion placed them in the little skiff; the *manly boy* rowed them triumphantly to the Cove, and immediately had them conveyed to a comfortable habitation. After shaming, by his example, older persons, who had larger boats, he again put off with his skiff, but with all his efforts, he could not then approach the wreck. His example, however, was soon followed by four of the crew, who had escaped in the Tribune's jolly-boat, and by some of the boats in the Cove. With their joint exertions, the eight men were preserved, and these, with the four who had saved themselves in the jolly-boat, were the whole of the survivors of this fine ship's company.

A circumstance occurred, in which that cool thoughtlessness of danger, which so often distinguishes the British tars, was displayed in such a striking manner, that it would be inexcusable to omit it. Daniel Monro, as we have already seen, had gained the fore-top. He suddenly disappeared, and it was concluded he had been washed away, like many others. After being absent from the top about two hours, he, to the surprise of Dunlap, who was likewise on the fore-top, raised his head through the lubber-hole. Dunlap inquiring where he had been, he told him he had been cruising for a better birth; that after swiming about the wreck a considerable time, he had returned to the fore-shrouds, and crawling in on the cat-harpings, had actually been sleeping there more than an hour, and appeared greatly refreshed.

AN EXTRAORDINARY FAMINE IN THE AMERICAN SHIP PEGGY,

On her return from the Azores to New York, in 1765.

FAMINE frequently leads men to the commission of the most horrible excesses: insensible, on such occasions, to the appeals of nature and reason, man assumes the character of a beast of prey; he is deaf to every representation, and coolly meditates the death of his fellow-creature.

One of these scenes, so afflicting to humanity, was, in the year 1765, exhibited in the brigantine the Peggy, David Harrison, commander, freighted by certain merchants of New York, and bound to the Azores. She arrived without accident at Fayal, one of those islands, and having disposed of her cargo, took on board a lading of wine and spirits. On the 24th of October, of the same year, she set sail on her return to New York.

On the 29th, the wind, which had till then been favorable, suddenly shifted. Violent storms, which succeeded each other, almost without interruption, during the month of November, did much damage to the vessel. In spite of all the exertions of the crew, and the experience of the captain, the masts went by the board, and all the sails, excepting one, were torn to rags: and, to add to their distress, several leaks were discovered in the hold.

At the beginning of December, the wind abated a little, but the vessel was driven out of her course; and, destitute of masts, sails, and rigging, she was perfectly unmanageable, and drifted to and fro, at the mercy of the waves. This, however, was the smallest evil; another of a much more alarming nature soon manifested itself.

Upon examining the state of the provisions, they were found to be almost totally exhausted. In this deplorable situation, the crew had no hope of relief, but from chance.

A few days after this unpleasant discovery, two vessels were descried early one morning, and a transient ray of hope cheered the unfortunate crew of the Peggy. The sea ran so high as to prevent captain Harrison from approaching the ships, which were soon out of sight. The disappointed seamen, who were in want of every thing, then fell upon the wine and brandy, with which the ship was laden. They allotted to the captain two small jars of water, each containing about a gallon, being the remainder of their stock. Some days elapsed, during which the men, in some measure, appeased the painful cravings of hunger, by incessant intoxication.

On the fourth day, a ship was observed bearing towards them, in full sail: no time was lost in making signals of distress, and the crew had the inexpressible satisfaction to perceive that they were answered. The sea was sufficiently calm to permit the two vessels to approach each other. The strangers seemed much affected by the account of their sufferings and misfortunes, and promised them a certain quantity of biscuit; but it was not immediately sent on board, the captain alleging, as an excuse for the delay, that he had just begun a nautical observation, which he was desirous to finish. However unreasonable such a pretext appeared, under the present circumstances, the famished crew of the Peggy was obliged to submit. The time mentioned by the captain had nearly expired, when, to their extreme mortification, the latter, regardless of his promise, crowded all his sails and bore away. No language is adequate to describe the despair and consternation which then overwhelmed the crew. Enraged, and destitute of hope they fell upon whatever they had spared till then. The only animals that remained on board were a couple of pigeons and a cat, which were devoured in an instant. The only favor they showed the captain was, to reserve for him the head of the cat. He afterwards declared, that however disgusting it would have been on any other occasion, he thought it, at that moment, a treat exquisitely delicious. The unfortunate men then supported their existence by living on oil, candles, and leather, and these were entirely consumed by the 28th of December.

From that day until the 13th of January, it is impossible to tell, in what manner they subsisted. Captain Harrison had been for some time unable to leave his cabin, being confined to his bed by a severe fit of the gout. On the last mentioned day, the sailors went to him in a body, with the mate at their head; the latter acted as spokesman, and after an affecting representation of the deplorable state to which they were reduced, declared that it was necessary to sacrifice one, in order to save the rest; adding, that their resolution was irrevocably fixed, and that they intended to cast lots for the victim.

The captain, a tender and humane man, could not hear such a barbarous proposition without shuddering; he represented to them that they were men, and ought to regard each other as brethren; that by such an assassination, they would forever consign themselves to universal execration, and commanded them, with all his authority, to relinquish the idea of committing such an atrocious crime. The captain was silent; but he had spoken to deaf men. They all with one voice replied, that it was indifferent to them, whether he approved of their resolution or not; that they had only acquainted him with it, out of respect, and because he would run the same risk as themselves; adding that, in the general misfortune, all command and distinction were at an end. With these words, they left him, and went upon deck, where the lots were drawn.

A negro, who was on board and belonged to captain Harrison, was the victim. It is more than probable, that the lot had been consulted only for the sake of form, and that the wretched black was proscribed, the moment the sailors first formed their resolution. They instantly sacrificed him. One of the crew tore out his liver and devoured it, without having the patience to dress it by broiling, or in any other manner. He was soon afterwards taken ill, and died the following day in convulsions, and with all the symptoms of madness. Some of his comrades proposed to keep his body to live upon, after the negro was consumed; but this advice was rejected by the majority, doubtless on account of the malady which had carried him off. He was, therefore, thrown overboard, and consigned to the deep.

The captain, in the intervals, when he was the least tormented by the gout, was not more exempt from the attacks of hunger, than the rest of the crew, but he resisted all the persuasions of his men to partake of their horrid repast. He contented himself with the water which had been assigned to him, mixing with it a small quantity of spirits, and this was the only sustenance he took during the whole period of his distress.

The body of the negro, equally divided, and eaten with the greatest economy, lasted till the 26th of January. On the 29th, the famished crew deliberated upon selecting a second victim. They again came to inform the captain of their intention, and he appeared to give his consent, fearing lest the enraged sailors might have recourse to the lot without him. They left it with him to fix upon any method that he should think proper. The captain, summoning all his strength, wrote upon small pieces of paper, the name of each man who was then on board the brigantine, folded them up, put them into a hat, and shook them well together. The crew, meanwhile, preserved an awful silence; each eye was fixed, and each mouth was open, while terror was strongly impressed upon every countenance. With a trembling hand, one of them drew, from the hat, the fatal billet, which he delivered to the captain, who opened it and read aloud the name of DAVID FLATT. The unfortunate man, on whom the lot had fallen, appeared perfectly resigned to his fate:—"My friends, (said he to his companions,) the only favor I request of you, is, not to keep me long in pain; dispatch me as speedily as you did the negro." Then turning to the man who had performed the first execution, he added:—"It is you, I choose to give me the mortal blow." He requested an hour to prepare himself for death, to which his comrades could only reply with tears. Meanwhile, compassion, and the remonstrances of the captain, prevailed over the hunger of the most hard-hearted. They unanimously resolved to defer the sacrifice till eleven o'clock the following morning. Such a short reprieve afforded very little consolation to FLATT.

The certainty of dying the next day made such a deep impression upon the mind, that his body, which, for above a month, had withstood the almost total privation of nourishment, sank beneath it. He was seized with a violent fever, and his state was so much aggravated by a delirium, with which it was accompanied, that some of the sailors proposed to kill him immediately, in order to terminate his sufferings. The majority, however, adhered to the resolution which had been taken, of waiting till the following morning.

At ten o'clock in the morning of the 30th of January, a large fire was already made to dress the limbs of the unfortunate victim, when a sail was descried, at a distance. A favorable wind drove her towards the Peggy, and she proved to be the Susan, returning from Virginia, and bound to London.

The captain could not refrain from tears at the affecting account of the sufferings endured by the famished crew. He lost no time in affording them relief, supplying them immediately with provisions and rigging, and offered to convoy the Peggy to London. The distance from New York, their proximity to the English coast, together with the miserable state of the brigantine, induced the two captains to proceed to England. The voyage was prosperous; only two men died; all the others gradually recovered their strength. Flatt himself was restored to perfect health, after having been so near the gates of death.

THE WRECKED SEAMEN.

The annexed thrilling sketch is extracted from the "Life of a Sailor, by a Captain in the British Navy." It relates to the exposures of the crew of the Magpie, who had taken to the boat, after their shipwreck on the coast of Cuba. The boat was upset,—the storm continues:—

"Even in this moment of peril, the discipline of the navy assumed its command. At the order from the lieutenant for the men on the keel to relinquish their position they instantly obeyed, the boat was turned over and once more the expedient was tried, but quite in vain; for no sooner had the two men begun to bale with a couple of hats, and the safety of the crew to appear within the bounds of probability, than one man declared he saw the fin of a shark. No language can convey an idea of the panic which seized the struggling seamen; a shark is at all times an object of horror to a sailor; and those who have seen the destructive jaws of this voracious fish, and their immense and almost incredible power, their love of blood, and their bold daring to obtain it, alone can form an idea of the sensations produced in a swimmer by the cry of "a shark! a shark!" Every man now struggled to obtain a moment's safety. Well they knew that one drop of blood would have been scented by the everlasting pilot-fish, the jackalls of the shark; and that their destruction was inevitable, if one only of these monsters should discover this rich repast, or be led to its food by the little rapid hunter of its prey. All discipline was now unavailing, the boat again turned keel up; one man only gained his security, to be pushed from it by others, and thus their strength began to fail from long continued exertion. However, as the enemy so much dreaded did not make its appearance, Smith once more urged them to endeavor to save themselves by the only means left, that of the boat; but as he knew, that he would only increase their alarm by endeavoring to persuade them that sharks did not abound in these parts, he used the wisest plan of desiring those who held on by the gun-wale, to keep splashing in the water with their legs in order to frighten the monsters at which they were so alarmed. Once more had hope begun to dawn:—the boat was clear to her thwarts, and four men were in her, hard at work; a little forbearance and a little obedience, and they were safe. At this moment, when those in the water urged their messmates in the boat to continue baling with unremitted exertion, a noise was heard close to them, and about fifteen sharks came right in amongst them. The panic was ten times more dreadful than before; the boat was again upset by the simultaneous endeavor to escape the danger; and the twenty-two sailors were again devoted to destruction. At first, the sharks did not seem inclined to seize their prey, but swam in amongst the men, playing in the water, sometimes leaping about and rubbing against their victims. This was of short duration; a loud shriek from one of the men announced his sudden pain; a shark had seized him by the leg, and severed it entirely from the body. No sooner had the blood been tasted than the long dreaded attack took place; another and another shriek proclaimed a loss of limbs; some were torn from the boat to which they vainly endeavored to cling; some, it was supposed, sank from fear alone; all were in dreadful peril. Mr. Smith, even now, when of all horrible deaths the most horrible seemed to await him, gave his orders with clearness and coolness; and to the everlasting honor of the poor departed crew be it known, they were obeyed; again the boat was righted, and again two men were in her. Incredible as it may appear, still, however, it is true, that the voice of the officer was heard amidst the danger; and the survivors, actually as before, clung to the gun-wale, and kept the boat upright. Mr. Smith himself held to the stern, and cheered and applauded his men. The sharks had tasted the blood, and were not to be driven from their feast; in one short moment, when Mr. Smith ceased splashing, as he looked into the boat to watch the progress, a shark seized both legs, and bit them off just above the knees. Human nature was not strong enough to bear the immense pain without a groan; but Mr. Smith endeavored to conceal the misfortune; nature, true to herself, resisted the endeavor, and the groan was deep and audible. The crew had long respected their gallant commander; they knew his worth and his courage:—on hearing him express his pain, and seeing him relinquish his hold to sink, two of the men grasped their dying officer, and placed him in the stern sheets. Even now, in almost insupportable agony, that gallant fellow forgot his own sufferings, and thought only of rescuing the remaining few from the untimely grave which awaited them; he told them again of their only hope, deplored their perilous state, and concluded with these words: "if any of you survive this fatal night, and return to Jamaica, tell the admiral (Sir Lawrence Halstead) that I was, in search of the pirate when this lamentable occurrence took place, tell him I hope I have always done my duty, and that I—" Here the endeavor of some of the men to get into the boat gave her a heel on one side; the men who were supporting poor Smith relinquished him for a moment, and he rolled overboard and was drowned. His last bubbling cry was soon lost amidst the shrieks of his former companions; he sank to rise no more.

At eight o'clock in the evening, the Magpie was upset; it was calculated by the two survivors, that their companions had all died by nine. The sharks seemed satisfied for the moment, and they, with gallant hearts, resolved to profit by the precious time in order to save themselves; they righted the boat, and one getting over the bows, and the other over the stern, they found themselves, although nearly exhausted, yet alive, and in comparative security; they began the work of baling, and soon lightened the boat sufficiently not to be easily upset, when both set down to rest. The return of the sharks was a signal for their return to labor. The voracious monsters endeavored to upset the boat; they swam by its side in seeming anxiety for their prey, but after waiting sometime, they separated: the two rescued seamen found themselves free from their insatiable enemies, and, by the blessing of God, saved. Tired as they were, they continued their labor until the boat was nearly dry, when both lay down to rest, the one forward, and the other aft; so completely had fear operated on their minds, that they did not dare even to move, dreading that an incautious step might have capsized the boat. They soon, in spite of the horrors they had witnessed, fell into a sound sleep, and day had dawned before they awoke to horrible reflections, and apparently worse dangers. The sun rose clear and unclouded; the cool calm of the night was followed by the sultry calm of the morning, and heat, hunger, thirst, and fatigue, seemed to settle on the unfortunate men, rescued by Providence and their own exertions from the jaws of a horrible death. They awoke and looked at each other; the very gaze of despair was appalling; far as the eye could reach, no object could be discerned; the bright haze of the morning added to the strong refraction of light; one smooth, interminable plain, one endless ocean, one cloudless sky and one burning sun, were all they had to gaze upon. The boat lay like the ark, in a world alone! They had no oar, no mast, no sail, nothing but the bare planks and themselves, without provisions or water, food or raiment. They lay upon the calm ocean, hopeless, friendless, and miserable. It was a time of intense anxiety, their eyes rested upon each other in silent pity, not unmixed with fear. Each knew the dreadful alternative to which nature would urge them. The cannibal was, already, in their looks, and fearful would have been the first attack, on either side, for they were both brave and stout men, and equal in strength and courage.

It now being about half past six in the morning, the sun was beginning to prove its burning power, the sea was as smooth as a looking glass, and saving now and then, the slight cat's paw of air, which ruffled the face of the water for a few yards, all was calm and hushed. In vain they strained their eyes, in vain they turned from side to side to escape the burning rays of the sun; they could not sleep, for now anxiety and fear kept both vigilant and on their guard; they dared not to court sleep, for that might have been the last of mortal repose. Once they nearly quarrelled, but, fortunately, the better feelings of humanity overcame the bitterness of despair. The foremost man had long complained of thirst, and had frequently dipped his hand into the water, and sucked the fluid; this was hastily done, for all the horrors of the night were still before them, and not unfrequently the sharp fin of a shark was seen not very far from the boat. In the midst of the excruciating torments of thirst, heightened by the salt water, and the irritable temper of the bowman, as he stamped his impatient feet against the bottom boards, and tore his hair with unfeeling indifference, he suddenly stopped the expression of rage and called out—"A sail!"

Whilst they stood watching in silence the approach of the brig, which slowly made her way through the water, and at the very instant that they were assuring each other that they were seen, and that the vessel was purposely steered on the course she was keeping, to reach them, the whole fabric of hope was destroyed in a second; the brig kept away about three points, and began to make more sail. Then was it an awful moment; their countenances saddened as they looked at each other; for in vain they hailed, in vain they threw their jackets in the air; it was evident they had never been seen, and that the brig was steering her proper course.

The time was slipping away, and if once they got abaft the beam of the brig, every second would lessen the chance of being seen, besides the sea breeze might come down, and then she would be far away, and beyond all hope in a quarter of an hour. Now was it, that the man who had been so loudly lamenting his fate, seemed suddenly inspired with fresh hope and courage; he looked attentively at the brig, then at his companion, and said, "By heaven, I'll do it, or we are lost!" "Do what?" said the shipmate. "Though," said the first man, "it is no trifle to do, after what we have seen and known; yet I will try, for if she passes us, what can we do? I tell you, Jack, I'll swim to her; if I get safe to her, you are saved; if not, why I shall die without adding, perhaps murder, to my crimes." "What! jump overboard, and leave me all alone!" replied his companion; "look, look at that shark, which has followed us all night; why, it is only waiting for you to get into the water to swallow you, as it did perhaps half of our messmates; no, no, wait, do wait; perhaps another vessel may come; besides, I cannot swim half the distance, and I should be afraid to remain behind; think, Tom, only think of the sharks and of last night."

He jumped overboard with as much calmness as if he was bathing in security. No sooner had he begun to strike out in the direction he intended, than his companion turned towards the sharks. The first had disappeared, and it was evident they had heard the splash, and would soon follow their prey. It is hard to say, who suffered the most anxiety. The one left in the boat cheered his companion, looked at the brig, and kept waving his jacket, then turned to watch the sharks; his horror may be imagined when he saw three of these terrific monsters swim past the boat, exactly in the direction of his companion; he splashed his jacket in the water to scare them away, but they seemed quite aware of the impotency of the attack, and lazily pursued their course. The man swam well and strongly. There was no doubt he would pass within hail of the brig, provided the sharks did not interfere, and he, knowing that they would not be long in following him, kept kicking in the water and splashing, as he swam. There is no fish more cowardly, and yet more desperately savage than a shark. I have seen one harpooned twice, with a hook in his jaws, and come again to a fresh bait; yet will they suffer themselves to be scared by the smallest noise, and hardly ever take their prey without it is quite still. Generally speaking, any place surrounded by rocks where the surf breaks, although there may be no passage for a ship, will be secure from sharks. It was not until a great distance had been accomplished, that the swimmer became apprized of his danger, and saw by his side one of the terrific creatures; still, however, he bravely swam and kicked; his mind was made up for the worst, and he had little hope of success. In the mean time the breeze had gradually freshened, and the brig passed with greater velocity through the water; every stitch of canvas was spread. To the poor swimmer, the sails seemed bursting with the breeze, and as he used his utmost endeavor to propel himself so as to cut off the vessel, the spray appeared to dash from the bow and the brig to fly through the sea. He was now close enough to hope his voice might be heard; but he hailed and hailed in vain not a soul was to be seen on deck; the man who steered was too intent upon his avocation to listen to the call of mercy. The brig passed, and the swimmer was every second getting further in the distance, every hope was gone, not a ray of that bright divinity remained, the fatigue had nearly exhausted him, and the sharks only waited for the first quiet moment to swallow their victim. It was in vain, he thought of returning towards the boat, for he never could have reached her, and his companion had no means of assisting him. In the act of offering up his last prayer, ere he made up his mind to float and be eaten, he saw a man looking over the quarter of the brig; he raised both his hands, he jumped himself up in the water, and by the singularity of his motions, fortunately attracted notice. A telescope soon made clear the object; the brig was hove to, a boat sent, and the man saved. The attention of the crew was then awakened to the Magpie's boat; she was soon alongside, and thus, through the bold exertions of as gallant a fellow as ever breathed, both were rescued from their perilous situation.

THE LOSS OF THE PEGGY.

On the 28th of September, 1785, the Peggy, commanded by captain Knight, sailed from the harbor of Waterford, Ireland, for the port of New York, in America.

Here it is necessary to observe, that the Peggy was a large unwieldy Dutch-built ship, about eight hundred tons burden, and had formerly been in the Norway and timber trade, for which, indeed, she seemed, from her immense bulk, well calculated. There being no freight in readiness for America, we were under the necessity of taking in ballast: which consisted of coarse gravel and sand, with about fifty casks of stores, fresh stock, and vegetables, sufficient to last during the voyage; having plenty of room, and having been most abundantly supplied by the hospitable neighborhood, of which we were about to take our leave.

We weighed anchor, and with the assistance of a rapid tide and pleasant breeze, soon gained a tolerable offing: we continued under easy sail the remaining part of the day, and towards sunset, lost sight of land.

September 29th, made the old head of Kingsale; the weather continued favorable, we shortly came within sight of cape Clear, from whence we took our departure from the coast of Ireland.

Nothing material occurred for several days, during which time we traversed a vast space of the Western ocean.

October 12th, the weather now became hazy and squally; all hands turned up to reef top-sails, and strike top-gallant-yards. Towards night, the squalls were more frequent, indicating an approaching gale;—we accordingly clued, reefed top-sails, and struck top-gallant-masts; and having made all snug aloft, the ship weathered the night very steadily.

On the 13th, the crew were employed in setting up the

rigging, and occasionally pumping, the ship having made much water, during the night. The gale increasing as the day advanced, occasioned the vessel to make heavy rolls, by which an accident happened, which was near doing much injury to the captain's cabin. A puncheon of rum, which was lashed on the larboard side of the cabin, broke loose, a sudden jerk having drawn asunder the cleets to which it was fastened. By its velocity, it stove in the state-rooms, and broke several utensils of the cabin furniture. The writer of this, with much difficulty, escaped with whole limbs: but not altogether unhurt, receiving a painful bruise on the right foot: having, however, escaped from the cabin, the people on deck were given to understand that the rum was broken loose. The word rum soon attracted the sailors' attention, and this cask being the ship's only stock, they were not tardy (as may be supposed) in rendering their assistance to double lash, what they anticipated—the delight of frequently splicing the mainbrace therewith, during their voyage.

On the 14th, the weather became moderate, and the crew were employed in making good the stowage of the stores in the hold, which had given way during the night; shaking reefs out of the top-sails, getting up the top-gallant masts and yards, and rigging out studding-sails. All hands being now called to dinner, a bustle and confused noise took place on deck. The captain (who was below) sent the writer of this, to discover the cause thereof, but before he could explain, a voice was crying out in a most piteous and vociferous tone. The captain and chief mate jumped on deck, and found the crew had got the cook laid on the windlass, and were giving him a most severe cobbing with a flat piece of his own firewood. As soon as the captain had reached forward, he was much exasperated with them for their precipitate conduct, in punishing without his knowledge and permission; and having prohibited such proceedings in future cases, he inquired the cause of their grievance. The cook, it seems, having been serving out fresh water to dress vegetables for all hands, had inadvertently used it for some other purpose, and boiled the greens in a copper of salt water, which rendered them so intolerably tough, that they were not fit for use; consequently the sailors had not their expected garnish, and a general murmur taking place, the above punishment was inflicted.

A steady breeze ensued, all sails filled and the ship made way, with a lofty and majestic air: and at every plunge of her bows, which were truly Dutch-built, rose a foam of no small appearance.

During four days, the weather continued favorable, which flattered the seamen with a speedy sight of land.

On the 19th, we encountered a very violent gale, with an unusual heavy sea;—the ship worked greatly, and took in much water through her seams; the pumps were kept frequently going. At mid-day, while the crew were at dinner, a tremendous sea struck the ship right aft, which stove in the cabin windows, upset the whole of the dinner, and nearly drowned the captain, mate, and myself, who was at that time holding a dish on the table, while the captain was busily employed in carving a fine goose, which, much to our discomfiture, was entirely drenched by the salt-water. Some of the coops were washed from the quarter-deck, and several of the poultry destroyed.

In consequence of the vessel's shipping so great a quantity of water, the pumps were doubly manned, and soon gained on her. The gale had not in the least abated during the night. The well was plumbed, and there was found to be a sudden and alarming increase of water. The carpenter was immediately ordered to examine the ship below, in order to find the cause of the vessel's making so much water. His report was, she being a very old vessel, her seams had considerably opened by her laboring so much; therefore, could devise no means, at present, to prevent the evil. He also reported the mizzen-mast to be in great danger.

The heel of the mizzen-mast being stepped between decks, (a very unusual case, but probably it was placed there in order to make more room for stowage in the after-hold,) was likely to work from its step, and thereby might do considerable damage to the ship.

The captain now held a consultation with the officers, when it was deemed expedient to cut the mast away, without delay: this was accordingly put into execution the following morning, as soon as the day made its appearance. The necessary preparations having been made, the carpenter began hewing at the mast, and quickly made a deep wound. Some of the crew were stationed ready to cut away the stays and lanyards, whilst the remaining part were anxiously watching the momentary crash which was to ensue; the word being given to cut away the weather-lanyards, as the ship gave a lee-lurch, the whole of the wreck of the mast plunged, without further injury, into the ocean.

The weather still threatening a continuance, our principal employ was at the pumps, which were kept continually going. The sea had now risen to an alarming height, and frequently struck the vessel with great violence. Towards the afternoon, part of the starboard bulwark was carried away by the shock of a heavy sea, which made the ship broachto, and before she could answer her helm again, a sea broke through the fore-chains, and swept away the caboose and all its utensils from the deck: fortunately for the cook, he was assisting at the pumps at the time, or he inevitably must have shared the same fate as his galley.

Notwithstanding the exertions of the crew, the water gained fast, and made its way into the hold, which washed a great quantity of the ballast through the timber-holes into the hull, by which the suckers of the pumps were much damaged, and they thereby frequently choked. By such delays the leaks increased rapidly. We were under the necessity of repeatedly hoisting the pumps on deck, to apply different means which were devised to keep the sand from entering, but all our efforts proved ineffectual, and the pumps were deemed of no further utility. There was now no time to be lost; accordingly it was agreed that the allowance of fresh water should be lessened to a pint a man; the casks were immediately hoisted from the hold, and lashed between decks. As the water was started from two of them, they were sawed in two, and formed into buckets, there being no other casks on board fit for that purpose; the whips were soon applied, and the hands began baling at the fore and after hatchways, which continued without intermission the whole of the night, each man being suffered to take one hour's rest, in rotation.

The morning of the 22d, presented to our view a most dreary aspect,—a dismal horizon encircling—not the least appearance of the gale abating—on the contrary, it seemed to come with redoubled vigor—the ballast washing from side to side of the ship at each roll, and scarce a prospect of freeing her. Notwithstanding these calamities, the crew did not relax their efforts. The main-hatchway was opened, and fresh buckets went to work; the captain and mate alternately relieving each other at the helm. The writer's station was to supply the crew with grog, which was plentifully served to them every two hours. By the motion of the ship, the buckets struck against the combings of the hatchways with great violence, and in casting them into the hold to fill, they frequently struck on the floating pieces of timber which were generally used as chocks in stowing the hold. By such accidents, the buckets were repeatedly stove, and we were under the necessity of cutting more of the water casks to supply their place. Starting the fresh water overboard was reluctantly done, particularly as we now felt the loss of the caboose, and were under the necessity of eating the meat raw, which occasioned us to be very thirsty. Night coming on, the crew were not allowed to go below to sleep; each man, when it came to his turn, stretched himself on the deck.

October 23. Notwithstanding the great quantity of water baled from the vessel, she gained so considerably, that she had visibly settled much deeper in the water. All hands were now called aft, in order to consult on the best measures. It was now unanimously resolved to make for the island of Bermuda, it being the nearest land. Accordingly we bore away for it, but had not sailed many leagues before we found that the great quantity of water in the vessel had impeded her steerage so much that she could scarcely answer her helm; and making a very heavy lurch, the ballast shifted, which gave her a great lift to the starboard, and rendered it very difficult to keep a firm footing on deck. The anchors which were stowed on the larboard bow were ordered to be cut away, and the cables, which were on the orlop deck, to be hove overboard in order to right her; but all this had a very trifling effect, for the ship was now become quite a log.

The crew were still employed in bailing; one of whom, in preventing a bucket from being stove against the combings, let go his hold, and fell down the hatchway; with great difficulty he escaped being drowned or dashed against the ship's sides. Having got into a bucket which was instantly lowered, he was providentially hoisted on deck without any injury.

During the night, the weather became more moderate, and on the following morning, (October 25,) the gale had entirely subsided, but left a very heavy swell. Two large whales approached close to the ship. They sported around the vessel the whole of the day, and after dusk, disappeared.

Having now no further use of the helm, it was lashed down, and the captain and mate took their spell at the buckets. My assistance having been also required, a boy of less strength, whose previous business was to attend the cook, now took my former station of serving the crew with refreshments. This lad had not long filled his new situation of drawing out rum from the cask, before he was tempted to taste it, which having repeatedly done, he soon became intoxicated, and was missed on deck for some time. I was sent to look for him. The spigot I perceived out of the cask, and the liquor running about, but the boy I could not see for some time; however looking down the lazeretto, (the trap-door of which was lying open,) I found him fast asleep. He had luckily fallen on some sails which were stowed there, or he must have perished.

On the 26th and 27th of October, the weather continued quite clear, with light baffling winds. A man was constantly kept aloft to look out for a sail. The rest of the crew were employed at the whips.

On the 28th, the weather began to lower, and appeared inclined for rain. This gave some uneasiness, being apprehensive of a gale. The captain therefore directed the carpenter to overhaul the long-boat, caulk her, and raise a streak, which orders were immediately complied with; but when he went to his locker for oakum, he found it plundered of nearly the whole of his stock—all hands were therefore set to picking, by which means he was soon supplied.

It was totally clear on the 29th, with a fresh breeze, but the ship heeled so much that her gunwale at times was under water, and the crew could scarcely stand on deck. All hands were now ordered to assemble aft, when the captain in a short address, pointed out the most probable manner by which they could be saved. All agreed in opinion with him, and it was resolved that the long-boat should be hoisted out as speedily as possible, and such necessaries as could be conveniently stowed, to be placed in her. Determined no longer to labor at the buckets, the vessel, which could not remain above water many hours after we had ceased bailing, was now abandoned to her fate.

I now began to reflect on the small chance we had of being saved—twenty-two people in an open boat—upwards of three hundred miles from the land, in a boisterous climate, and the whole crew worn out with fatigue! The palms of the crew's hands were already so flayed it could not be expected that they could do much execution with the oars; while thus reflecting on our perilous situation, one of our oldest seamen, who at this moment was standing near me, turned his head aside to wipe away a tear; I could not refrain from sympathizing with him, my heart was already full; the captain perceiving my despondency bade me be of good cheer, and called me a young lubber.

The boat having been hoisted out, and such necessaries placed in her as were deemed requisite, one of the hands was sent aloft to lash the colors downwards to the main-top-mast shrouds; which having done, he placed himself on the crosstrees, to look around him, and almost instantly hallooed out,—"A sail." It would be impossible to describe the ecstatic emotions of the crew: every man was aloft, in order to be satisfied; though a minute before, not one of the crew was able to stand upright.

The sail was on our weather-bow, bearing right down on us with a smart breeze. She soon perceived us, but hauled her wind several times, in order to examine our ship. As she approached nearer she clearly perceived our calamitous situation, and hastened to our relief.

She proved to be a Philadelphia schooner, bound to cape Francois, in St. Domingo. The captain took us all on board in the most humane and friendly manner, and after casting our boat adrift, proceeded on his voyage. When we perceived our ship from the vessel on which we were now happily on board, her appearance was truly deplorable.

The captain of the schooner congratulated us on our fortunate escape, and expressed his surprise that the ship should remain so long on her beam ends, in such a heavy sea, without capsizing. We soon began to distance the wreck, by this time very low in the water, and shortly after lost sight of her.

The evening began to approach fast, when a man loosing the main-top-sail, descried a sail directly in the same course on our quarter. We made sail for her, and soon came within hail of her. She proved to be a brig from Glasgow, bound to Antigua. It was now determined, between the captains, that half of our people should remain in the schooner, and the captain, mate, eight of the crew, and myself, should get on board the brig. On our arrival at Antigua we met with much kindness and humanity.

Loss of the Halsewell. *Page* 205.

LOSS OF THE HALSEWELL EAST INDIAMAN.

The Halsewell East Indiaman, of seven hundred and fifty-eight tons burthen, Richard Pierce, Esq. commander, having been taken up by the Directors to make her third voyage to coast and bay, fell down to Gravesend the 16th of November, 1785, and there completed her lading. Having taken the ladies and other passengers on board at the Hope, she sailed through the Downs on Sunday, January the 1st, 1786, and the next morning, being abreast of Dunnose, it fell calm.

The ship was one of the finest in the service, and supposed to be in the most perfect condition for her voyage; and the commander a man of distinguished ability and exemplary character. His officers possessed unquestionable knowledge in their profession; the crew, composed of the best seamen that could be collected, was as numerous as the establishment admits. The vessel likewise contained a considerable body of soldiers, destined to recruit the forces of the company in Asia.

The passengers were Miss Eliza Pierce, and Miss Mary Anne Pierce, daughters of the commander; Miss Amy Paul, and Miss Mary Paul, daughters of Mr. Paul, of Somersetshire, and relations of captain Pierce; Miss Elizabeth Blackburne, daughter of captain B. likewise in the service of the East India company: Miss Mary Haggard, sister to an officer on the Madras establishment; Miss Ann Mansell, a native of Madras, but of European parents, who had received her education in England; and John George Schutz, Esq. returning to Asia, where he had long resided, to collect a part of his fortune which he had left behind.

On Monday, the 2d of January, at three P. M. a breeze springing up from the south, they ran in shore to land the pilot. The weather coming on very thick in the evening, and the wind baffling, at nine they were obliged to anchor in eighteen fathoms water. They furled their top-sails, but were unable to furl their courses. the snow falling thick and freezing as it fell.

Tuesday, the 3d, at four o'clock A. M. a violent gale came on from E. N. E. and the ship driving, they were obliged to cut their cables and run out to sea. At noon, they spoke with a brig to Dublin, and having put their pilot on board of her, bore down channel immediately. At eight in the evening, the wind freshening, and coming to the southward, they reefed such sails as were judged necessary. At ten, it blew a violent gale at south, and they were obliged to carry a press of sail to keep the ship off the shore. In this situation, the hause-plugs, which, according to a recent improvement, were put inside, were washed in, and the hause-bags washed away, in consequence of which they shipped a great quantity of water on the gun-deck.

Upon sounding the well, they found that the vessel had sprung a leak, and had five feet of water in her hold; they clued up the main top-sail, hauled up the main-sail, and immediately attempted to furl both, but failed in the attempt. All the pumps were set to work, on the discovery of the leak.

Wednesday the 4th, at two A. M. they endeavored to wear the ship, but without success. The mizzen-mast was instantly cut away, and a second attempt made to wear, which succeeded no better than the former. The ship having now seven feet of water in her hold, and the leak gaining fast on the pumps, it was thought expedient for the preservation of the ship, which appeared to be in immediate danger of foundering, to cut away the main-mast. In its fall, Jonathan Moreton, coxswain, and four men, were carried overboard by the wreck and drowned. By eight o'clock, the wreck was cleared, and the ship got before the wind. In this position she was kept about two hours, during which the pumps reduced the water in the hold two feet.

At ten in the morning the wind abated considerably, and the ship labored extremely, rolled the fore top-mast over on the larboard side, which, in the fall, tore the fore-sail to pieces. At eleven, the wind came to the westward, and the weather clearing up, the Berry-Head was distinguished, at the distance of four or five leagues. Having erected a jury main-mast, and set a top-gallant-sail for a main-sail, they bore up for Portsmouth, and employed the remainder of the day in getting up a jury mizzen-mast.

On Thursday the 5th, at two in the morning, the wind came to the southward, blew fresh, and the weather was very thick. At noon, Portland was seen, bearing north by east, distant about two or three leagues. At eight at night, it blew a strong gale at south; the Portland lights were seen bearing north-west, distant four or five leauges, when they wore ship and got her head to the westward. Finding they lost ground on that tack, they wore her again, and kept stretching to the eastward, in the hope of weathering Peverel Point, in which case they intended to have anchored in Studland bay. At eleven, they saw St. Alban's Head, a mile and a half to the leeward, upon which they took in sail immediately, and let go the small bower anchor, which brought up the ship at a whole cable, and she rode for about an hour, and then drove. They now let go the sheet anchor, and wore away a whole cable; the ship rode about two hours longer when she drove again.

In this situation the captain sent for Mr. Henry Meriton, the chief officer, and asked his opinion concerning the probability of saving their lives. He replied with equal candor and calmness, that he apprehended there was very little hope, as they were then driving fast on shore, and might expect every moment to strike. It was agreed that the boats could not then be of any use, but it was proposed that the officers should be confidentially requested, in case an opportunity presented itself, of making it serviceable, to reserve the long boat for the ladies and themselves, and this precaution was accordingly taken.

About two, in the morning of Friday the 6th, the ship still driving, and approaching the shore very fast, the same officer again went into the cuddy where the captain then was. Captain Pierce expressed extreme anxiety for the preservation of his beloved daughters, and earnestly asked Mr. Meriton, if he could devise any means of saving them. The latter expressed his fears that it would be impossible, adding, that their only chance would be to wait for the morning, upon which the captain lifted up his hands in silent distress.

At this moment the ship struck with such violence, as to dash the heads of those who were standing in the cuddy against the deck above them, and the fatal blow was accompanied by a shriek of horror, which burst at the same instant from every quarter of the ship.

The seamen, many of whom had been remarkably inattentive and remiss in their duty during a great part of the storm, and had actually skulked into their hammocks, leaving the working of the pump, and the other labors required by their situation, to the officers, roused to a sense of their danger, now poured upon the deck, to which the utmost endeavors of their officers could not keep them while their assistance might have been useful. But it was now too late; the ship continued to beat upon the rocks, and soon bilged, falling with her broadside towards the shore. When the ship struck, several of the men caught hold of the ensign staff, under the apprehension of her going to pieces immediately.

At this critical juncture, Mr. Meriton offered his unhappy companions the best advice that possibly could be given. He recommended that they should all repair to that side of the ship which lay lowest on the rocks, and take the opportunities that might then present themselves of escaping singly to the shore. He then returned to the round-house, where all the passengers and most of the officers were assembled. The latter were employed in affording consolation to the unfortunate ladies, and with unparalleled magnanimity, suffering their compassion for the amiable companions of their own danger, and the dread of almost inevitable destruction. At this moment what must have been the feelings of a father—of such a father as captain Pierce?

The ship had struck on the rocks near Seacombe, on the island of Purbeck, between Peverel-point and St.

Alban's Head. On this part of the shore the cliff is of immense height, and rises almost perpendicularly. In this particular spot the cliff is excavated at the base, presenting a cavern ten or twelve yards in depth, and equal in breadth to the length of a large ship. The sides of the cavern are so nearly upright as to be extremely difficult of access, and the bottom of it is strewed with sharp and uneven rocks which appear to have been rent from above by some convulsion of nature. It was at the mouth of this cavern that the unfortunate vessel lay stretched almost from side to side, and presented her broadside to the horrid chasm. But, at the time the ship struck it was too dark to discover the extent of their danger, and the extreme horror of their situation.

The number in the round-house was now increased to nearly fifty, by the admission of three black women and two soldier's wives, with the husband of one of the latter, though the sailors, who had demanded entrance to get a light, had been opposed and kept out by the officers. Captain Pierce was seated on a chair, or some other movable, between his two daughters, whom he pressed alternately to his affectionate bosom. The rest of the melancholy assembly were seated on the deck, which was strewed with musical instruments, and the wreck of furniture, boxes, and packages.

Here Mr. Meriton, after having lighted several wax candles, and all the glass lanthorns he could find, likewise took his seat, intending to wait till daylight, in the hope that it would afford him an opportunity of effecting his own escape, and also rendering assistance to the partners of his danger. But, observing that the ladies appeared parched and exhausted, he fetched a basket of oranges from some part of the round-house, with which he prevailed on some of them to refresh themselves.

On his return he perceived a considerable alteration in the appearance of the ship. The sides were visibly giving way, the deck seemed to heave, and he discovered other evident symptoms that she could not hold together much longer. Attempting to go forward to look out, he instantly perceived that the ship had separated in the middle and that the fore-part had changed its position, and lay rather farther out towards the sea. In this emergency he determined to seize the present moment, as the next might have been charged with his fate, and to follow the example of the crew and the soldiers, who were leaving the ship in numbers, and making their way to a shore, with the horrors of which they were yet unacquainted.

To favor their escape an attempt had been made to lay the ensign-staff from the ship's side to the rocks, but without success, for it snapped to pieces before it reached them. By the light of a lanthorn, however, Mr. Meriton discovered a spar, which appeared to be laid from the ship's side to the rocks, and upon which he determined to attempt his escape. He accordingly lay down upon it, and thrust himself forward, but soon found that the spar had no communication with the rock. He reached the end and then slipped off, receiving a violent contusion in his fall. Before he could recover his legs, he was washed off by the surge, in which he supported himself by swimming till the returning wave dashed him against the back of the cavern. Here he lay hold of a small projection of the rock, but was so benumbed that he was on the point of quitting it, when a seaman, who had already gained a footing, extended his hand and assisted him till he could secure himself on a little shelf of the rock, from which he clambered still higher till he was out of the reach of the surf.

Mr. Rogers, the third mate, remained with the captain and the ladies nearly twenty minutes after Mr. Meriton had left the ship. The latter had not long quitted the round house, before the captain inquired what was become of him, and Mr. Rogers replied, that he had gone upon deck to see what could be done. A heavy sea soon afterwards broke over the ship, upon which the ladies expressed great concern at the apprehension of his loss. Mr. Rogers proposed to go and call him, but this they opposed, fearful lest he might share the same fate.

The sea now broke in at the fore part of the ship, and reached as far as the main-mast. Captain Pierce and

Mr. Rogers then went together, with a lamp, to the stern gallery, where, after viewing the rocks, the captain asked Mr. Rogers if he thought there was any possibility of saving the girls. He replied, he feared not; for they could discover nothing but the black surface of the perpendicular rock, and not the cavern which afforded shelter to those who had escaped. They then returned to the round house, where captain Pierce again seated himself between his two daughters, struggling to suppress the parental tear which then started into his eye.

The sea continuing to break in very fast, Mr. Rogers, Mr. Schutz, and Mr. M'Manus, a midshipman, with a view to attempt their escape, made their way to the poop. They had scarcely reached it, when a heavy sea breaking over the wreck, the round house gave way, and they heard the ladies shriek at intervals, as if the water had reached them; the noise of the sea at other times drowned their voices.

Mr. Brimer had followed Mr. Rogers to the poop, where, on the coming of the fatal sea, they jointly seized a hen-coop, and the same wave which whelmed those who remained below in destruction, carried him and his companion to the rock, on which they were dashed with great violence, and miserably bruised.

On this rock were twenty-seven men; but it was low water, and being convinced that, upon the flowing of the tide, they must all be washed off, many endeavored to get to the back or sides of the cavern beyond the reach of the returning sea. Excepting Mr. Rogers and Mr. Brimer, scarcely more than six succeeded in this attempt. Of the remainder, some experienced the fate they sought to avoid, others perished in endeavoring to get into the cavern.

Mr. Rogers and Mr. Brimer, however, having reached the cavern, climbed up the rock, on the narrow shelves of which they fixed themselves. The former got so near to his friend, Mr. Meriton, as to exchange congratulations with him; but between these gentlemen, there were about twenty men, none of whom could stir but at the most imminent hazard of his life. When

Mr. Rogers reached this station, his strength was so nearly exhausted, that had the struggle continued a few minutes longer he must inevitably have perished.

They soon found that though many who had reached the rocks below, had perished in attempting to ascend, yet that a considerable number of the crew, seamen, soldiers, and some of the inferior officers, were in the same situation with themselves. What that situation was, they had still to learn. They had escaped immediate death; but they were yet to encounter a thousand hardships for the precarious chance of escape. Some part of the ship was still discernible, and they cheered themselves in this dreary situation, with the hope that it would hold together till day break. Amidst their own misfortunes, the sufferings of the females filled their minds with the acutest anguish; every returning sea increased their apprehensions for the safety of their amiable and helpless companions.

But, alas! too soon were these apprehensions realized. A few minutes after Mr. Rogers had gained the rock, a general shriek, in which the voice of female distress was lamentably distinguishable, announced the dreadful catastrophe! In a few moments, all was hushed, excepting the warring winds and the dashing waves. The wreck was whelmed in the bosom of the deep, and not an atom of it was ever discovered. Thus perished the Halsewell, and with her, worth, honor, skill, beauty, and accomplishments!

This stroke was a dreadful aggravation of wo to the trembling and scarcely half-saved wretches, who were clinging about the sides of the horrid cavern. They felt for themselves, but they wept for wives, parents, fathers, brothers, sisters,—perhaps lovers!—all cut off from their dearest, fondest hopes!

Their feelings were not less agonized by the subsequent events of that ill-fated night. Many who had gained the precarious stations on the rocks, exhausted with fatigue, weakened by bruises, and benumbed with cold, quitted their hold, and falling headlong, either upon the rocks below, or into the surf, perished beneath the feet of their wretched associates, and by their dying groans and loud acclamations, awakened terrific apprehensions of a similar fate in the survivors.

At length, after three hours of the keenest misery, the day broke on them, but, far from bringing with it the expected relief, it served only to discover to them all the horrors of their situation. They were convinced, that had the country been alarmed by the guns of distress, which they continued to fire several hours before the ship struck, but, which, from the violence of the storm, were unheard, they could neither be observed by the people above, as they were completely ingulphed in the cavern, and overhung by the cliff; nor was any part of the wreck remaining to indicate their probable place of refuge. Below, no boat could live to search them out, and had it been possible to acquaint those who were willing to assist them, with their exact situation, they were at a loss to conceive how any ropes could be conveyed into the cavern to facilitate their escape.

The only method, that afforded any prospect of success, was to creep along the side to its outer extremity, to turn the corner on a ledge scarcely as broad as a man's hand, and to climb up the almost perpendicular precipices, nearly two hundred feet in height. In this desperate attempt, some succeeded, while others, trembling with terror, and exhausted with bodily and mental fatigue, lost their precarious footing, and perished.

The first men who gained the summit of the cliff were the cook, and James Thompson, a quarter-master. By their individual exertions they reached the top, and instantly hastened to the nearest house, to make known the situation of their fellow-sufferers. Eastington, the habitation of Mr. Garland, steward, or agent, to the proprietors of the Purbeck quarries, was the house at which they first arrived. That gentleman immediately assembled the workmen under his direction, and with the most zealous humanity exerted every effort for the preservation of the surviving part of the crew of the unfortunate ship.

Mr. Meriton had, by this time, almost reached the

edge of the precipice. A soldier, who preceded him, stood upon a small projecting rock, or stone, and upon the same stone Mr. Meriton had fastened his hands to assist his progress. Just at this moment the quarrymen arrived, and seeing a man so nearly within their reach they dropped a rope, of which he immediately laid hold. By a vigorous effort to avail himself of the advantage, he loosened the stone, which giving way, Mr. Meriton must have been precipitated to the bottom, had not a rope been lowered to him at the instant, which he seized, while in the act of falling, and was safely drawn to the summit.

The fate of Mr. Brimer was peculiarly severe. He had been married only nine days before the ship sailed, to the daughter of Captain Norman, of the Royal Navy, came on shore, as it has been observed, with Mr. Rogers, and, like him, got up the side of the cavern. Here he remained till the morning, when he crawled out; a rope was thrown him, but he was either so benumbed with the cold as to fasten it about him improperly, or so agitated as to neglect to fasten it at all. Whatever was the cause, the effect proved fatal; at the moment of his supposed preservation he fell from his stand, and was unfortunately dashed to pieces, in sight of those who could only lament the deplorable fate of an amiable man and skilful officer.

The method of affording help was remarkable, and does honor to the humanity and intrepidity of the quarrymen. The distance from the top of the rock to the cavern, over which it projected, was at least one hundred feet: ten of these formed a declivity to the edge, and the remainder was perpendicular. On the very brink of this precipice stood two daring fellows, with a rope tied round them, and fastened above to a strong iron bar fixed into the ground. Behind these, in like manner, stood others, two and two. A strong rope, likewise properly secured, passed between them, by which they might hold, and support themselves from falling. Another rope, with a noose ready fixed, was then let down below the cavern, and the wind blowing hard, it was sometimes forced under the projecting rock, so that the sufferers could reach it without crawling to the edge. Whoever laid hold of it, put the noose round his waist, and was drawn up with the utmost care and caution by their intrepid deliverers.

In this attempt, however, many shared the fate of the unfortunate Mr. Brimer. Unable, through cold, perturbation of mind, weakness, or the inconvenience of the stations they occupied, to avail themselves of the succor that was offered them, they were precipitated from the stupendous cliff, and either dashed to pieces on the rocks, or falling into the surge, perished in the waves.

Among these unhappy sufferers, the death of a drummer was attended with circumstances of peculiar distress. Being either washed off the rocks by the sea, or falling into the surf, he was carried by the returning waves beyond the breakers. His utmost efforts to regain them were ineffectual, he was drawn further out to sea, and being a remarkably good swimmer, continued to struggle with the waves, in the view of his commiserating companions, till his strength was exhausted, and he sank,—to rise no more!

It was late in the day when all the survivors were carried to a place of safety, excepting William Trenton, a soldier, who remained on his perilous stand till the morning of Saturday, the 7th, exposed to the united horrors of extreme personal danger, and the most acute disquietude of mind.

The surviving officers, seamen, and soldiers, being assembled at the house of their benevolent deliverer, Mr. Garland, they were mustered, and found to amount to 74, out of more than 240, which was nearly the number of the crew and passengers when she sailed through the Downs. Of the rest, it is supposed that fifty or more sank with the Captain and the ladies in the round house, and that upwards of seventy reached the rocks, but were washed off, or perished in falling from the cliffs. All those who reached the summit survived, excepting two or three, who expired while being drawn up, and a black who died a few hours after he was brought to the house. Many, however, were so miserably bruised, that their lives were doubtful, and it was a considerable time before they perfectly recovered their strength.

The benevolence and generosity of the master of the Crown Inn, at Blanford, deserves the highest praise. When the distressed seamen arrived at that town he sent for them all to his house, and having given them the refreshment of a comfortable dinner, he presented each man with half a crown to help him on his journey

---

LOSS OF THE NOTTINGHAM GALLEY, OF LONDON.

The Nottingham Galley, of and from London, of 120 tons, ten guns, fourteen men, John Dean, commander, having taken in cordage in England, and butter, cheese, &c. in Ireland, sailed for Boston in New-England, the 25th of September, 1710. Meeting with contrary winds and bad weather, it was the beginning of December, when we first made land to the eastward of Piscataqua, and proceeding southward for the bay of Massachusetts, under a hard gale of wind at northeast, accompanied with rain, hail and snow; having no observation for ten or twelve days, we, on the 11th, handed all our sails, excepting our fore-sail and maintop sail double reefed, ordering one hand forward to look out. Between eight and nine o'clock, going forward myself, I saw the breakers ahead, whereupon I called out to put the helm hard to starboard, but before the ship could wear, we struck upon the east end of the rock, called Boon Island, four leagues to the Eastward of Piscataqua.

The second or third sea heaved the ship alongside of it; running likewise so very high, and the ship laboring so excessively, that we were not able to stand upon deck; and though it was not distant above thirty or forty yards, yet the weather was so thick and dark, that we could not see the rock, so that we were justly thrown into con-

Loss of the Nottingham Galley. *Page* 206.

sternation at the melancholy prospect of immeidately perishing in the sea. I presently called all hands down to the cabin, where we continued a few minutes, earnestly supplicating the mercy of heaven; but knowing that prayers, alone, are vain, I ordered all up again to cut the masts by the board, but several were so oppressed by the terrors of conscience that they were incapable of any exertion. We, however went upon deck, cut the weathermost shrouds, and the ship heeling toward the rocks, the force of the sea soon broke the masts, so that they fell towards the shore.

One of the men went out on the bowsprit, and returning, told me he saw something black ahead, and would venture to go on shore, accompanied with any other person: upon which I desired some of the best swimmers (my mate and one more) to go with him, and if they gained the rock, to give notice by their calls, and direct us to the most secure place. Recollecting some money and papers that might be of use, also ammunition, brandy, &c., I then went down and opened the place in which they were; but the ship bilging, her decks opened, her back broke, and her beams gave way, so that the stern sank under water. I therefore hastened forward to escape instant death, and having heard nothing of the men who had gone before, concluded that they were lost. Notwithstanding, I was under the necessity of making the same adventure upon the foremast, moving gradually forward betwixt every sea, till at last quitting it, I threw myself with all the strength I had, toward the rock; but it being low water, and the rock extremely slippery, I could get no hold, and tore my fingers, hands, and arms, in the most deplorable manner, every sea fetching me off again, so that it was with the utmost peril and difficulty that I got safe on shore at last. The rest of the men ran the same hazards, but through the mercy of Providence we all escaped with our lives.

After endeavoring to discharge the salt water and creeping a little way up the rock, I heard the voices of the three men above mentioned, and by ten o'clock we all met together, when, with grateful hearts, we returned thanks to Providence for our deliverance from such imminent danger. We then endeavored to gain shelter to the leeward of the rock, but found it so small and inconsiderable, that it would afford none, (being about one hundred yards long and fifty broad,) and so very craggy that we could not walk to keep ourselves warm, the weather still continuing extremely cold, with snow and rain.

As soon as day light appeared I went toward the place where we came on shore, not doubting but that we should meet with provisions enough from the wreck for our support, but found only some pieces of the masts and yards among some old junk and cables heaped together, which the anchors had prevented from being carried away, and kept moving about the rock at some distance. Part of the ship's stores with some pieces of plank and timber, old sails, canvas, &c. drove on shore, but nothing eatable, excepting three small cheeses which we picked up among the rock-weed.

We used our utmost endeavors to get fire, having a steel and flint with us, and also by a drill, with a very swift motion; but having nothing which had not been water-soaked, all our attempts proved ineffectual.

At night we stowed ourselves under our canvas, in the best manner possible, to keep each other warm. The next day the weather clearing a little, and inclining to a frost, I went out, and perceiving the main land, I knew where we were, and encouraged my men with the hope of being discovered by fishing shallops, desiring them to search for and bring up any planks, carpenter's tools, and stores they could find, in order to build a tent and a boat. The cook then complained that he was almost starved, and his countenance discovering his illness, I ordered him to remain behind with two or three more the frost had seized. About noon the men acquainted me that he was dead; we therefore laid him in a convenient place for the sea to carry him away. None mentioned eating him, though several, with myself, after wards acknowledged that they thought of it.

After we had been in this situation two or three days, the frost being very severe, and the weather extremely cold, it affected most of our hands and feet to such a degree as to take away the sense of feeling, and render them almost useless; so benumbing and discoloring them as gave us just reason to apprehend mortification. We pulled off our shoes, and cut off our boots; but in getting off our stockings, many, whose legs were blistered, pulled off skin and all, and some, the nails of their toes. We then wrapped up our legs and feet as warmly as we could in oakum and canvas.

Now we began to build our tent in a triangular form, each side being about eight feet, covered it with the old sails and canvas that came on shore, having just room for each to lie down on one side, so that none could turn, unless all turned, which was about every two hours, when notice was given. We also fixed a staff to the top of our tent, upon which, as often as the weather would permit, we hoisted a piece of cloth in the form of a flag, in order to discover ourselves to any vessel that might approach.

We then commenced the building of our boat with planks and timber belonging to the wreck. Our only tools were the blade of a cutlass, made into a saw with our knives, a hammer, and a caulking mallet. We found some nails in the clefts of the rock, and obtained others from the sheathing. We laid three planks flat for the bottom, and two up each side, fixed to stanchions and let into the bottom timbers, with two short pieces at each end, and one breadth of new Holland duck round the sides to keep out the spray of the sea. We caulked all we could with oakum drawn from the old junk, and in other places filled up the spaces with long pieces of canvas, all of which we secured in the best manner possible. We found also some sheet lead and pump-leather, which proved of use. We fixed a short mast and square sail, with seven paddles to row, and a longer one to steer with. But our carpenter, whose services were now most wanted, was, on account of illness, scarcely capable of affording us either assistance or advice; and all

18*

the rest, excepting myself and two others, were so benumbed and feeble as to be unable to move. The weather, too, was so extremely cold, that we could seldom stay out of the tent more than four hours in the day and some days we could do nothing at all.

When we had been upon the rock about a week, without any kind of provisions, excepting the cheese abovementioned, and some beef bones, which we eat, after beating them to pieces, we saw three boats, about five leagues from us, which, as may easily be imagined, rejoiced us not a little, believing that the period of our deliverance had arrived. I directed all the men to creep out of the tent and halloo together, as loud as their strength would permit. We likewise made all the signals we could, but in vain, for they neither heard nor saw us. We, however, received no small encouragement from the sight of them, as they came from the southwest; and the wind being at north-east when we were cast away, we had reason to suppose that our distress might have been made known by the wreck driving on shore, and to presume that they had come out in search of us, and would daily do so when the weather should permit. Thus we flattered ourselves with the pleasing but delusive hope of deliverance.

Just before we had finished our boat, the carpenter's axe was cast upon the rock, by which we were enabled to complete our work, but then we had scarcely strength sufficient to get her into the water.

About the 21st of December, the boat being finished, the day fine, and the water smoother than I had yet seen it since we came there, we consulted who should attempt to launch her; I offered myself as one to venture in her; this was agreed to, as I was the strongest, and therefore the fittest to undergo the extremities to which we might possibly be reduced. My mate also offered himself, and desiring to accompany me, I was permitted to take him, together with my brother and four more. Thus commending our enterprize to Providence, all that were able came out, and with much difficulty, got our poor patched-up boat to the water-side. The surf run ning very high, we were obliged to wade very deep to launch her, upon which I and another got into her. The swell of the sea heaved her along the shore and overset upon us, whereby we again narrowly escaped drowning. Our poor boat was staved to pieces, our enterprize totally disappointed, and our hopes utterly destroyed.

What heightened our afflictions, and served to aggravate our miserable prospects, and render our deliverance less practicable, we lost, with our boat, both our axe and hammer, which would have been of great use to us if we should afterwards have attempted to construct a raft. Yet we had reason to admire the goodness of God in producing our disappointment for our safety; for, that afternoon, the wind springing up, it blew so hard, insomuch that, had we been at sea in that imitation of a boat, we must, in all probability, have perished, and those left behind, being unable to help themselves, must doubtless soon have shared a similar fate.

We were now reduced to the most melancholy and deplorable situation imaginable; almost every man but myself was weak to an extremity, nearly starved with hunger and perishing with cold; their hands and feet frozen and mortified; large and deep ulcers in their legs; the smell of which was highly offensive to those who could not creep into the air, and nothing to dress them with but a piece of linen that was cast on shore. We had no fire: our small stock of cheese was exhausted, and we had nothing to support our feeble bodies but rock-weed and a few muscles, scarce and difficult to be procured, at most not above two or three for each man a day; so that our miserable bodies were perishing, and our disconsolate spirits overpowered by the deplorable prospect of starving, without any appearance of relief. To aggravate our situation, if possible, we had reason to apprehend, lest the approaching springtide if accompanied with high winds, should entirely overflow us. The horrors of such a situation it is impossible to describe; the pinching cold and hunger; extremity of weakness and pain; racking and horrors of conscience in many; and the prospect of a certain, painful, and lingering death, without even the most remote views of deliverance! This is, indeed, the height of misery; yet such alas! was our deplorable case: insomuch that the greater part of our company were ready to die of horror and despair.

For my part, I did my utmost to encourage myself, exhort the rest to trust in God, and patiently await their deliverance. As a slight alleviation of our fate, Providence directed towards our quarters a sea-gull, which my mate struck down and joyfully brought to me. I divided it into equal portions, and though raw, and scarcely affording a mouthful for each, yet we received and eat it thankfully.

The last method of rescuing ourselves we could possibly devise, was to construct a raft capable of carrying two men. This proposal was strongly supported by a Swede, one of our men, a stout, brave fellow, who, since our disaster, had lost the use of both his feet by the frost. He frequently importuned me to attempt our deliverance in that way, offering himself to accompany me, or, if I refused, to go alone. After deliberate consideration we resolved upon a raft, but found great difficulty in clearing the fore-yard, of which it was chiefly to be made, from the junk, as our working hands were so few and weak.

This done, we split the yard, and with the two parts made side-pieces, fixing others, and adding some of the lightest planks we could find, first spiking, and afterwards making them firm. The raft was four feet in breadth. We fixed up a mast, and out of two hammocks that were driven on shore we made a sail, with a paddle for each man, and a spare one in case of necessity. This difficulty being thus surmounted, the Swede frequently asked me whether I designed to accompany him, giving me to understand, that if I declined, there was another ready to offer himself for the enterprise.

About this time we saw a sail come out of Piscataqua river, about seven leagues to the westward. We again made all the signals we could, but the wind being northwest, and the ship standing to the eastward, she was presently out of sight, without ever coming near us which proved an extreme mortification to our hopes. The next day, being moderate, with a small breeze toward the shore in the afternoon, and the raft being wholly finished, the two men were very anxious to have it launched; but this was as strenuously opposed by the mate, because it was so late, being two in the afternoon. They, however, urged the lightness of the nights, begged me to suffer them to proceed, and I at length consented. They both got upon the raft, when the swell, rolling very high, soon overset them, as it did our boat. The Swede not daunted by this accident, swam on shore, but the other being no swimmer, continued some time under water; as soon as he appeared, I caught hold of and saved him, but he was so discouraged that he was afraid to make a second attempt. I desired the Swede to wait for a more favorable opportunity, but he continued resolute, begged me to go with him, or help him to turn the raft, and he would go alone.

By this time another man came down and offered to adventure; when they were upon the raft, I launched them off, they desiring us to go to prayers, and also to watch what became of them. I did so, and by sunset judged them half-way to the mainland and supposed that they might reach the shore by two in the morning. They, however, probably fell in with some breakers, or were overset by the violence of the sea and perished; for, two days afterwards, the raft was found on shore, and one man dead about a mile from it, with a paddle fastened to his wrist; but the Swede, who was so very forward to adventure, was never heard of more.

We, who were left on the desolate island, ignorant of what had befallen them, waited daily for deliverance. Our expectations were the more raised by a smoke we observed, two days afterwards in the woods, which was the signal appointed to be made if they arrived safely. This continued every day, and we were willing to believe that it was made on our account, though we saw no appearance of any thing toward our relief. We supposed that the delay was occasioned because they were not able to procure a vessel so soon as we desired, and this idea served to bear up our spirits and to support us greatly.

Still our principal want was that of provision, having nothing to eat but rock weed, and a very few muscles; indeed, when the spring-tide was over, we could scarcely get any at all. I went myself as no other person was able, several days at low water, and could find no more than two or three apiece. I was frequently in danger of losing my hands and arms, by putting them so often into the water after the muscles, and when obtained, my stomach refused them, and preferred rockweed.

Upon our first arrival we saw several seals upon the rocks, and supposing they might harbor there in the night, I walked round at midnight, but could never meet with any thing. We saw likewise, a great number of birds, which perceiving us daily there, would never lodge upon the rock, so that we caught none.

This disappointment was severe, and tended to aggravate our miseries still more; but it was particularly afflicting to a brother I had with me, and another young gentleman, neither of whom had before been at sea, or endured any kind of hardship. They were now reduced to the last extremity, having no assistance but what they received from me.

Part of a green hide, fastened to a piece of the main-yard, being thrown up by the sea, the men importuned me to bring it to the tent, which being done, we minced it small and swallowed it

About this time I set the men to open junk, and when the weather would permit I thatched the tent with the rope yarn in the best manner I was able, that it might shelter us the better from the extremities of the weather. This proved of so much service as to turn two or three hours rain, and preserve us from the cold, pinching winds which were always very severe upon us.

Toward the latter part of December, our carpenter, a fat man, and naturally of a dull, heavy, phlegmatic disposition, aged about forty-seven, who, from our first coming on shore, had been constantly very ill, and lost the use of his feet, complained of excessive pain in his back, and stiffness in his neck. He was likewise almost choked with phlegm, for want of strength to discharge it, and appeared to draw near his end. We prayed over him, and used our utmost endeavors to be serviceable to him in his last moments; he showed himself sensible, though speechless, and died that night. We suffered the body to remain till morning, when I desired those who were most able, to remove it; creeping out myself to see whether Providence had sent us any thing to satisfy the excessive cravings of our appetites. Returning before noon, and not seeing the dead body without the tent, I inquired why they had not removed it, and received for answer, they were not all of them able; upon which, fastening a rope to the body, I gave the utmost of my assistance, and with some difficulty we dragged it out of the tent. But fatigue, and the consideration of our misery, so overcame my spirits, that being ready to faint, I crept into the tent, and was no sooner there, than, to add to my trouble, the men began to request my permission to eat the dead body, the better to support their lives.

This circumstance was, of all the trials I had encountered, the most grievous and shocking:—to see myself and company, who came hither laden with provisions but three weeks before, now reduced to such a deplorable situation; two of us having been absolutely starved to death, while, ignorant of the fate of two others, the rest, though still living, were reduced to the last extremity, and requiring to eat the dead for their support.

After mature consideration of the lawfulness or sinfulness, on the one hand, and absolute necessity on the other, judgment and conscience were obliged to submit to the more prevailing arguments of our craving appetites. We, at length, determined to satisfy our hunger, and support our feeble bodies with the carcass of our deceased companion. I first ordered his skin, head, hands, feet, and bowels, to be buried in the sea, and the body to be quartered, for the convenience of drying and carriage, but again received for answer, that none of them being able, they intreated I would perform that labor for them. This was a hard task; but their incessant prayers and entreaties at last prevailed over my reluctance, and by night I had completed the operation.

I cut part of the flesh into thin slices, and washing it in salt water, brought it to the tent and obliged the men to eat rock-weed with it instead of bread. My mate and two others refused to eat any that night, but the next morning they complied, and earnestly desired to partake with the rest.

I found that they all eat with the utmost avidity, so that I was obliged to carry the quarters farther from the tent, out of their reach, lest they should injure themselves by eating too much, and likewise expend our small stock too soon.

I also limited each man to an equal portion, that they might not quarrel or have cause to reflect on me or one another. This method I was the more obliged to adopt, because, in a few days, I found their dispositions entirely changed, and that affectionate, peaceable temper they had hitherto manifested, totally lost. Their eyes looked wild and staring, their countenances fierce and barbarous. Instead of obeying my commands, as they had universally and cheerfully done before, I now found even prayers and entreaties vain and fruitless; nothing was now to be heard but brutal quarrels, with horrid oaths and imprecations, instead of that quiet submissive spirit of prayer and supplication they had before manifested.

This, together with the dismal prospect of future want, obliged me to keep a strict watch over the rest of the body, lest any of them, if able, should get to it, and if that were spent we should be compelled to feed upon the living, which we certainly must have done, had we remained in that situation a few days longer.

The goodness of God now began to appear, and to make provision for our deliverance, by putting it into the hearts of the good people on the shore to which our raft was driven, to come out in search of us, which they did on the 2d of January, in the morning.

Just as I was creeping out of the tent I saw a shallop half way from the shore, standing directly toward us. Our joy and satisfaction, at the prospect of such speedy and unexpected deliverance, no tongue is able to express, nor thought to conceive.

Our good and welcome friends came to an anchor to the south-west, at the distance of about one hundred yards, the swell preventing them from approaching nearer; but their anchor coming home obliged them to stand off till about noon, waiting for smoother water upon the flood. Meanwhile our passions were differently agitated; our expectations of deliverance, and fears of miscarriage, harried our weak and disordered spirits strangely.

I gave them an account of all our miseries, excepting the want of provisions, which I did not mention, lest the fear of being constrained by the weather to remain with us, might have prevented them from coming on shore. I earnestly entreated them to attempt our immediate deliverance, or at least to furnish us if possible, with fire, which, with the utmost hazard and difficulty they at last accomplished, by sending a small canoe, with one man, who, after great exertion, got on shore.

After helping him up with his canoe, and seeing nothing to eat, I asked him if he could give us fire:—he answered in the affirmative, but was so affrighted by my thin and meagre appearance that, at first, he could scarcely return me an answer. However, recollecting himself, after several questions asked on both sides, he went with me to the tent, where he was surprised to see so many of us in such a deplorable condition. Our flesh was so wasted, and our looks were so ghastly and frightful, that it was really a very dismal spectacle.

With some difficulty we made a fire, after which, determining to go on board myself with the man, and to send for the rest, one or two at a time, we both got into the canoe; but the sea immediately drove us against the rock with such violence that we were overset, and being very weak, it was a considerable time before I could recover myself, so that I had again a very narrow escape from drowning. The good man with great difficulty got on board without me, designing to return the next day with better conveniences, if the weather should permit.

It was an afflicting sight to observe our friends in the shallop, standing away for the shore without us. But God, who orders every thing for the best, doubtless had designs of preservation in denying us the appearance of present deliverance: for the wind coming about to south-east, it blew so hard that the shallop was lost, and the crew with extreme difficulty, saved their lives. Had we been with them it is more than probable that we should all have perished, not having strength sufficient to help ourselves.

When they had reached the shore they immediately sent an express to Portsmouth, in Piscataqua, where the good people made no delay in hastening to our deliverance as soon as the weather would allow. To our great sorrow, and as a farther trial of our patience, the next day continued very stormy, and though we doubted not but the people on shore knew our condition, and would assist us as soon as possible, yet our flesh being nearly consumed, being without fresh water, and uncertain how long the unfavorable weather might continue, our situation was extremely miserable. We, however, received great benefit from our fire, as we could both warm ourselves and broil our meat.

The next day, the men being very importunate for flesh, I gave them rather more than usual, but not to their satisfaction. They would certainly have eaten up the whole at once, had I not carefully watched them, with the intention of sharing the rest next morning, if the weather continued bad. The wind, however, abated that night, and early next morning a shallop came for us, with my much esteemed friends captain Long and captain Purver, and three other men, who brought a large canoe, and in two hours got us all on board, being obliged to carry almost all of us upon their backs from the tent to the canoe, and fetch us off by two or three at a time.

When we first came on board the shallop, each of us eat a piece of bread, and drank a dram of rum, and most of us were extremely sea-sick: but after we had cleansed our stomachs and tasted warm nourishing food, we became so exceeding hungry and ravenous, that had not our friends dieted us, and limited the quantity for two or three days, we should certainly have destroyed ourselves with eating.

Two days after our coming on shore, my apprentice lost the greater part of one foot; all the rest recovered their limbs, but not their perfect use; very few, excepting myself, escaping without losing the benefit of fingers or toes, though otherwise all were in perfect health.

LOSS OF THE FRENCH SHIP DROITS DE L'HOMME.

On the 5th of January, 1797, returning home on leave of absence from the West Indies, in the Cumberland letter of marque, for the recovery of my health, saw a large man-of-war off the coast of Ireland, being then within four leagues of the mouth of the river Shannon. She hoisted English colors, and decoyed us within gun-shot, when she substituted the tri-colored flag, and took us. She proved to be les Droits de L'Homme, of 74-guns, commanded by the *ci devant* baron, now citizen La Crosse, and had separated from a fleet of men-of-war, on board of which were twenty thousand troops, intended to invade Ireland. On board of this ship was General Humbert, who afterwards effected a descent in Ireland (in 1799) with nine hundred troops and six hundred seamen.*

On the 7th of January, went into Bantry Bay to see if any of the squadron were still there, and on finding none, the ship proceeded to the southward. Nothing

* Sir Edward Pellew has since told me that the official account from France, on which he has received head money, amounted to one thousand seven hundred and fifty souls at the time of the shipwreck.

extraordinary occurred until the evening of the 13th, when two men-of-war hove in sight, which afterwards proved to be the Indefatigable and Amazon frigates. It is rather remarkable that the captain of the ship should inform me, that the squadron which was going to engage him was Sir Edward Pellew's, and declared, as was afterwards proved by the issue, that "he would not yield to any two English frigates, but would sooner sink his ship with every soul on board." The ship was then cleared for action, and we English prisoners, consisting of three infantry officers, two captains of merchantmen, two women, and forty-eight seamen and soldiers, were conducted down to the cable tier at the foot of the foremast.

The action began with opening the lower deck ports, which, however, were soon shut again, on account of the great sea, which occasioned the water to rush in to such a degree that we felt it running on the cables. I must here observe, that the ship was built on a new construction, considerably longer than men-of-war of her rate, and her lower deck, on which she mounted thirty-two pounders French, equal to forty pounders English, was two feet and a half lower than usual. The situation of the ship, before she struck on the rocks, has been fully represented by Sir Edward Pellew, in his letter of the 17th of January, to Mr. Nepean: the awful task is left for me to relate what ensued.

At about four in the morning, a dreadful convulsion, at the foot of the foremast, roused us from a state of anxiety for our fate to the idea that the ship was sinking!—It was the fore-mast that fell over the side; in about a quarter of an hour an awful mandate from above was re-echoed from all parts of the ship: *Pauvres Anglais! pauvres Anglais! Montez bien vite; nous sommes tous perdus!*—"Poor Englishmen! poor Englishmen! come on deck as fast as you can, we are all lost!" Every one rather flew than climbed. Though scarcely able to move before, from sickness, yet I now felt an energetic strength in all my frame, and soon gained the upper deck, but what a sight! dead, and wounded, and living, intermingled in a state terrible beyond description: not a mast standing, a dreadful loom of the land, and breakers all around us. The Indefatigable, on the starboard quarter, appeared standing off, in a most tremendous sea, from the Penmark Rocks, which threatened her with instant destruction. To the great humanity of her commander, those few persons who survived the shipwreck, are indebted for their lives, for had another broadside been fired, the commanding situation of the Indefatigable must have swept off, at least, a thousand men.—On the starboard side was seen the Amazon, within two miles, just struck on shore. Our own fate drew near. The ship struck and immediately sunk! Shrieks of horror and dismay were heard from all quarters, while the merciless waves tore from the wreck many early victims. Day-light appeared, and we beheld the shore lined with people, who could render us no assistance. At low water, rafts were constructed, and the boats were got in readiness to be hoisted out. The dusk arrived, and an awful night ensued. The dawn of the day brought with it still severer miseries than the first, for the wants of nature could scarcely be endured any longer, having been already near thirty hours without any means of subsistence, and no possibility of procuring them. At low water a small boat was hoisted out, and an English captain and eight sailors succeeded in getting to the shore. Elated at the success of these men, all thought their deliverance at hand, and many launched out on their rafts, but, alas! death soon ended their hopes.

Another night renewed our afflictions. The morning of the third, fraught with still greater evils, appeared; our continual sufferings made us exert the last effort, and we, English prisoners, tried every means to save as many of our fellow-creatures as lay in our power.—Larger rafts were constructed, and the largest boat was got over the side. The first consideration was to lay the surviving wounded, the women, and helpless men, in the boat, but the idea of equality so fatally promulgated among the French, destroyed all subordination, and nearly one hundred and twenty having jumped into the boat, in defiance of their officers, they sank her.—The most dreadful sea that I ever saw, seemed at that fatal moment to aggravate the calamity; nothing of the boat was seen for a quarter of an hour, when the bodies floated in all directions; then appeared, in all their horrors, the wreck, the shores, the dying and the drowned! Indefatigable in acts of humanity, an adjutant-general, Renier, launched himself into the sea, to obtain succor from the shore, and perished in the attempt.

Nearly one half of the people had already perished, when the horrors of the fourth night renewed all our miseries. Weak, distracted, and destitute of every thing, we envied the fate of those whose lifeless corpses no longer wanted sustenance. The sense of hunger was already lost, but a parching thirst consumed our vitals. Recourse was had to urine and salt water, which only increased our want; half a hogshead of vinegar indeed floated up, of which each had half a wine glass: it afforded a momentary relief, yet soon left us again in the same state of dreadful thirst. Almost at the last gasp, every one was dying with misery, and the ship, now one third shattered away from the stern, scarcely afforded a grasp to hold by, to the exhausted and helpless survivors.

The fourth day brought with it a more serene sky, and the sea seemed to subside, but to behold, from fore to aft, the dying in all directions, was a sight too shocking for the feeling mind to endure. Almost lost to a sense of humanity, we no longer looked with pity on those whom we considered only as the forerunners of our own speedy fate, and a consultation took place, to sacrifice some one to be food for the remainder. The die was going to be cast, when the welcome sight of a man-of-war brig renewed our hopes. A cutter speedily followed, and both anchored at a short distance from the wreck. They then sent their boats to us, and by means of large rafts, about one hundred, out of four hundred, who attempted it, were saved by the brig that evening. Three hundred and eighty were left to endure another night's misery, when, dreadful to relate, above one half were found dead the next morning!

I was saved about ten o'clock, on the morning of the 18th, with my two brother officers, the Captain of the ship, and General Humbert. They treated us with great humanity on board the cutter, giving us a little weak brandy and water every five or six minutes, and after that, a basin of good soup. I fell on the locker in a kind of trance for nearly thirty hours, and swelled to such a degree as to require medical aid to restore my decayed faculties. Having lost all our baggage, we were taken to Brest almost naked, where they gave us a rough shift of clothes, and in consequence of our sufferings, and the help we afforded in saving many lives, a cartel was fitted out by order of the French government to send us home, without ransom or exchange. We arrived at Plymouth on the 7th of March following.

To that Providence, whose great workings I have experienced in this most awful trial of human afflictions, be ever offered the tribute of my praise and thanksgiving.

LOSS OF THE EARL OF ABERGAVENNY EAST INDIAMAN.

THE universal concern occasioned by the loss of the Earl of Abergavenny, has induced us to lay before our readers an accurate statement of this melancholy disaster, chiefly collected from the accounts which were given at the India-House, by Cornet Burgoyne, of his majesty's eighth regiment of light dragoons, who had the command of the troops on board the above vessel, and by the fourth officer of the ship, (who were among the few who fortunately escaped from the wreck,) and from the best information afterwards received.

On Friday, February the 1st, the Earl of Abergavenny, East-Indiaman, captain Wadsworth, sailed from Portsmouth, in company with the royal George, Henry Addington, Wexford, and Bombay Castle, under convoy of his majesty's ship Weymouth, captain Draper.

The Earl of Abergavenny was engaged in the company's service for six voyages, and this was the fourth on which she was proceeding.

Her company consisted of

Seamen, &c.	160
Troops, King's and Company's	159
Passengers at the Captain's table . . .	40
Ditto, at the Third Mate's	11
Chinese	32
Total	402

In going through the Needles, they unfortunately separated from the convoy. The fleet, in consequence, lay to nearly the whole of the next day; but seeing nothing of the Weymouth, proceeded under moderate sail towards the next port, in hopes of being joined by the convoy. On the 5th, the convoy not appearing, it was deemed expedient to wait her arrival in Portland Roads, particularly as the wind had become rather unfavorable, having shifted several points from the N. E. Captain Clarke of the Wexford, being senior-commander, and consequently commodore, made the signal for those ships that had taken Pilots on board, to run into the Roads.

The Earl of Abergavenny having at about half past three, P. M. got a pilot on board, bore up for Portland Roads with a steady wind, when on a sudden the wind slackened, and the tide setting in fast, drove her rapidly on the Shambles. The nearer she approached, the less she was under management; and being at last totally ungovernable, was driven furiously on the rocks, off the Bill of Portland, about two miles from the shore. She remained on the rocks nearly an hour, beating incessantly with great violence, the shocks being so great, that the officers and men could scarcely keep their footing on the deck. At four P. M. the shocks became less violent, and in about a quarter of an hour she cleared the rocks. The sails were immediately set, with an intention to run for the first port, as the ship made much water; but the leak increased so fast that the ship would not obey the helm. In this situation, it was considered necessary to fire signal guns of distress. Twenty were fired: the danger did not, however, appear to those on board sufficient to render it necessary for the ship's boats to be hoisted out at this moment, as the weather was moderate, and the ship in sight of the fleet and shore.

The leak increased fast upon the pumps at five, P. M. Soon after striking, the hand pumps started above six inches, and shortly after the water increased from six to eight feet in spite of every exertion at the pumps. All endeavors to keep the water under were found in vain, and night setting in rendered the situation of all on board melancholy in the extreme; the more so, as it was then ascertained that the ship had received considerable damage in her bottom, immediately under the pumps. All hands took their turn at the pumps, alternately bailing at the fore-hatchway. At eight o'clock their situation became still more dreadful, when it was found impossible to save the ship, which was eventually sinking fast, and settling into the water. Signal guns were again discharged incessantly. The purser, with the third officer, Mr. Wadsworth, and six seamen, were sent on shore, in one of the ship's boats, to give notice to the inhabitants of the distressed state of the ship and crew. At this time a pilot boat came off, and Mr. Evan's with his daughter, Mr. Routledge, Mr. Taylor, a cadet, and Miss Jackson, passengers, embarked for the shore, notwithstanding a dreadful sea, which threatened them with almost instant destruction.

For a few moments the general attention of the crew was diverted in observing the boats leave the ship; but these unfortunate people were soon reminded of their own approaching fate, by a heavy swell, which baffled almost every attempt to keep the ship above water. Every one seemed assured of his fate, and notwithstanding the unremitting attention of the officers, confusion commenced on board, as soon as it was given out that the ship was sinking. At ten, P. M. several sailors intreated to be allowed more liquor, which being refused, they attacked the spirit-room, but were repulsed by the officers, who never once lost sight of their character, or that dignity so necessary to be preserved on such an occasion, but continued to conduct themselves with the utmost fortitude to the last. One of the officers, who was stationed at the door of the spirit-room, with a brace of pistols to guard against surprise in so critical a moment, at which post he remained even while the ship was sinking, was much importuned by a sailor, while the water poured in on all sides, to grant him some liquor. The man said he was convinced "it would be all one with them in an hour hence." The officer, however, true to his trust in this perilous moment, had courage enough to repulse the man, and bid him go to his duty with his fellow-comrades, observing, "that if it was God's will they should perish, they should die like men."

At half past ten the water had got above the orlop-deck, in spite of the endeavors of the officers and crew who behaved in the most cool and exemplary manner. All on board were now anxiously looking out for boats from the shore, many wishing they had taken refuge in those that had already left the ship, as their destruction on board appeared inevitable. The utmost exertions became necessary to keep the ship above water till the boats came off from the shore. Unfortunately in the general distress and agony of the moment, the ship's boats were not hoisted out, when every soul on board might possibly have been saved. At eleven o'clock, a fatal swell gave the ship a sudden shock: she gave a surge, and sank almost instantaneously, two miles from Weymouth beach; with scarcely five minutes warning, she went down by the head in twelve fathom water, after a heavy heel, when she righted and sank with her masts and rigging standing. Many clung to loose spars, and floated about the wreck, but the majority took refuge in the shrouds. The severe shock of the ship going down, made several let go their hold, whilst others, by the velocity of the ship's descent, had not power to climb sufficiently fast to keep above the water. The Halsewell East Indiaman was wrecked within a few miles from this spot.

When the hull of the ship touched the ground, about one hundred and eighty persons were supposed to be in the tops and rigging: their situation was terrible beyond description: the yards only were above water, and the sea was breaking over them, in the dead of a cold and frosty night. In about half an hour their spirits were revived, by the sound of several boats beating against the waves at a short distance: but, alas! how vain their hopes, when on hailing the boats, not one of them came to their assistance. The sound of them died away, and they were again left to the mercy of the rude waves. By twelve o'clock their numbers had much decreased: the swell had swept off some, whilst others were, from the piercing cold, unable longer to retain their hold. Every moment they perceived some friend floating around them, for awhile, then sinking into the abyss to rise no more.

About this time a sloop was discovered; she had fortunately heard the signal guns, and came to an anchor close by the ship. The weather was moderate, and those who had survived were now promised a speedy delivery. The sloop's boat was immediately manned, and proceeded to the rigging that remained above water, when every person was taken off. The boat returned three times, taking twenty each return. Nothing could be more correct than the conduct of the crew on this occasion: they coolly got into the boat, one by one and those only as they were named by their officers. When it was supposed that every one was brought off, and the boat was about to depart for the last time, a person was observed in one of the tops: he was hailed but did not answer. Mr. Gilpin, the fourth officer, (whose extraordinary exertions on this occasion, as well as throughout the whole of this unfortunate affair, entitled him to the highest commendation,) returned to the wreck, and there found a man in an inanimate state, exhausted from the severe cold. He most humanely brought him down on his back, and took him to the boat; the man proved to be sergeant Heart of the 22d regiment. Every possible care was taken of him, but to no effect: he died about twelve hours after he had landed. The sloop having now, as was supposed, taken on board all the survivors of the ship, returned to Weymouth. She had not however, proceeded far, before it was perceived that Mr. Baggot, the chief officer, was close astern. The sloop immediately lay to for him; but this noble spirited young man, although certain of securing his own life, disregarded his own safety, on perceiving Mrs. Blair, an unfortunate fellow passenger, floating at some distance from him. He succeeded in coming up with her, and sustained her above water, while he swam towards the sloop; but just as he was on the point of reaching it, a swell came on, and his strength being totally exhausted, he sank and never rose again. The unfortunate Mrs. Blair sank after him, and this generous youth thus perished in vain. It was nearly two o'clock. before the sloop weighed anchor from the wreck, but the wind being favorable she soon reached the port. On mustering those who had landed, it appeared that only one hundred and fifty-five persons had reached the shore out of four hundred and two who had embarked!

The greatest attention was paid to the unfortunate sufferers by the mayor and aldermen as well as the principal inhabitants of Weymouth; and the purser was immediately dispatched to the India House with the melancholy intelligence.

At daylight, February the 6th, the top-masts of the ship were seen from Weymouth. During the time the passengers and crew remained in the tops she appeared to have sunk eight feet, and was considerably lower in the morning; it was therefore conjectured, that she had sunk on a mud-bank. The Greyhound cutter was immediately stationed to guard the wreck, and the boats from the Rover succeeded in stripping the masts of the rigging. On the 7th her decks had not been blown up, and she appeared to remain in exactly the same state in which she had sunk. Her sinking so steadily is attributed to the great weight of her cargo, her floorings consisting chiefly of earthern ware. The cargo of the ship was estimated at two hundred thousand pounds, besides which she had on board dollars to the amount of two hundred and seventy-five thousand ounces, and is supposed to have been one of the richest ships that ever sailed for India. She was of the largest tonnage, and inferior only to the Ganges in the service, being at least fifteen hundred tons burthen, and built for the China trade.

About eighty officers and seamen were saved, eleven passengers, fifteen Chinese, five out of thirty-two cadets and forty-five recruits. The captain was drowned. He was nephew to captain Wadsworth, who formerly commanded the Earl of Abergavenny, and was considered one of the first navigators in the service. He was on his third voyage as captain, and, painful to relate, perished with his ship, disdaining to survive the loss of so valuable a charge: his conduct throughout the distressing scene, has been spoken of in terms of the highest praise. It is an extraordinary fact that he felt such an unaccountable depression of spirits, that he could not be persuaded to go through the usual ceremony of taking leave of the court of directors on the day appointed; and it was not till the Wednesday following, which was specially fixed for that purpose, that he yielded to the wishes of his friends, and reluctantly attended the court! He was a man of remarkably mild manners; his conduct was, in every instance, so well tempered, that he was known among his shipmates, by the title of "the Philosopher." As soon as the ship was going down, Mr. Baggot, the chief officer, went on the quarter deck, and told him, "that all exertions were now in vain; the ship was rapidly sinking." Captain Wadsworth, who, no doubt, expected it, steadfastly looked him in the face, and, at last, with every appearance of a heart-broken man, faintly answered: "Let her go! God's will be done." These were the last words he uttered; from that instant he was motionless. In a few moments the ship sank, and many who were climbing the shrouds endeavored to save him, but without success. In this endeavor Mr. Gilpin was foremost, and made several unsuccessful attempts, at the evident risk of his own life.

LOSS OF THE CATHARINE, VENUS AND PIEDMONT TRANSPORTS; AND THREE MERCHANT SHIPS.

The miseries of war are in themselves great and terrible, but the consequences which arise indirectly from it, though seldom known and little adverted to, are no less deplorable. The destruction of the sword sometimes bears only an inconsiderable proportion to the havoc of disease, and, in the pestilential climates of the western colonies, entire regiments, reared in succession, have as often fallen victims to their baneful influence.

To prosecute the war with alacrity, it had been judged expedient to transport a strong body of troops on foreign service, but their departure was delayed by repeated adversities, and at length the catastrophe which is about to be related ensued.

On the 15th of November, 1795, the fleet, under convoy of Admiral Christian's squadron, sailed from St. Helen's. A more beautiful sight than it exhibited cannot be conceived; and those who had nothing to lament in leaving their native country, enjoyed the spectacle as the most magnificent produced by the art of man, and as that which the natives of this island contemplate with mingled pride and pleasure.

Next day, the wind continued favorable, carried the fleet down the channel; and as the Catharine transport came within sight of the isle of Perbeck, Lieutenant Jenner, an officer on board, pointed out to another person, the rocks where the Halsewell and so many unfortunate individuals had perished. He and Cornet Burns, had been unable to reach Southampton until the Catharine had sailed therefore they hired a boy to overtake her; and on embarking at St. Helen's, the former expressed his satisfaction, in a letter to his mother, that he had been so fortunate as to do so.

On Tuesday, the 17th, the fleet was off Portland, standing to the westward; but the wind shifting and blowing a strong gale at south-south-west, the admiral, dubious whether they could clear the channel, made a signal for putting into Torbay, which some of the transports were then in sight of. However, they could not make the bay; the gale increased, and a thick fog came on; therefore the admiral thought it expedient to alter his design, and about five in the afternoon made a signal for standing out to sea. Of the circumstances relative to the Catharine, a more detailed account has been preserved than respecting the other vessels of the fleet; and they are preserved by a female, with whose name we are unacquainted, in these words.

"The evening of the 17th was boisterous and threatening; the master said he was apprehensive that we should have bad weather; and when I was desired to go on deck and look at the appearance of the sky, I observed that it was troubled and red, with great heavy clouds flying in all directions, and with a sort of dull mist surrounding the moon. On repeating this to the other passengers, two of whom had been at sea before, they said we should certainly have a stormy night, and indeed it proved so very tempestuous, that no rest was to be obtained. Nobody, however, seemed to think that there was any danger, though the fog was so thick that the master could see nothing by which to direct his course; but he thought that he had sufficient sea-room.

'The fatigue I had suffered from the tossing of the ship, and the violence with which she continued to roll, had kept me in bed. It was about ten o'clock in the morning of the 18th, when the mate looked down into the cabin and cried, 'save yourselves if you can.'

'The consternation and terror of that moment cannot be described; I had on a loose dressing gown, and wrapping it round me I went up, not quite on deck, but to the top of the stairs, from whence I saw the sea break mountain high against the shore. The passengers and soldiers seemed thunder-struck by the sense of immediate and inevitable danger, and the seamen, too conscious of the hopelessness of any exertion, stood in speechless agony, certain of meeting in a few moments that destruction which now menaced them.

'While I thus surveyed the scene around me in a kind of dread which no words can figure, Mr. Burns, an officer of dragoons, who had come up in his shirt, called to Mr. Jenner and Mr. Stains for his cloak; nobody, however, could attend to any thing in such a moment but self preservation.

'Mr. Jenner, Mr. Stains and Mr. Dodd the surgeon, now passed me, their countenances sufficiently expressing their sense of the situation in which we all were. Mr. Burns spoke cheerfully to me; he bade me take good courage, and Mr. Jenner observed, there was a good shore near, and all would do well.

'These gentlemen then went to the side of the ship, with the intention, I believe, of seeing whether it was possible to get on shore. The master of the vessel alone remained near the companion; when suddenly a tremendous wave broke over the ship, and struck me with such violence, that I was stunned for a moment, and, before being able to recover myself, the ship struck with a force so great as to throw me from the stairs into the cabin, the master being thrown down near me. At the same instant, the cabin, with a dreadful crash, broke in upon us, and planks and beams threatened to bury us in ruins. The master, however, soon recovered himself, he left me to go again upon deck, and I saw him no more.

A sense of my condition lent me strength to disengage myself from the boards and fragments by which I was surrounded, and I once more got upon the stairs, I hardly know how. But what a scene did I behold! The masts were all lying across the shattered remains of the deck, and no living creature appeared on it; all was gone, though I knew not then that they were gone forever. I looked forward to the shore, but there I could see nothing except the dreadful surf that broke against it, while behind the ship, immense black waves rose like tremendous ruins. I knew that they must overwhelm her, and thought that there could be no escape for me.

Believing, then, that death was immediate and unavoidable, my idea was to regain my bed in the cabin, and there, resigning myself to the will of God, await the approaching moment. However, I could not reach it, and for awhile was insensible; then the violent striking and breaking up of the wreck again roused me to recollection; I found myself near the cabin windows, and the water was rising around me. It rapidly increased, and the horrors of drowning were present to my view; yet do I remember seeing the furniture of the cabin float about. I sat almost enclosed by pieces of the wreck, and the water now reached my breast.

The bruises I had received made every exertion extremely difficult, and my loose gown was so entangled among the beams and fragments of the ship, that I could not disengage it. Still the desire of life, the hope of being welcomed on shore, whither I thought my friends had escaped, and the remembrance of my child, all united in inspiring me with courage to attempt saving myself. I again tried to loosen my gown, but found it impossible, and the wreck continued to strike so violently, and the ruins to close so much more around me, that I now expected to be crushed to death. As the ship drifted higher on the stones, the water rather lessened as the waves went back, but on their return, continued to cover me, and I once or twice lost my breath, and for a moment, my recollection. When I had power to think, the principle of self preservation still urged me to exertion.

The cabin now broke more and more, and through a large breach I saw the shore very near. Amidst the tumult of the raging waves I had a glimpse of the people, who were gathering up what the sea drove towards them; but I thought they could not see me, and from them I despaired of assistance.—Therefore I determined to make one effort to preserve my life. I disengaged my arms from the dressing gown, and, finding myself able to move, I quitted the wreck, and felt myself on the ground. I attempted to run, but was too feeble to save myself from a raging wave, which overtook and overwhelmed me. Then I believed myself gone; yet, half suffocated as I was, I struggled very much, and I remember that I thought I was very long dying. The waves left me; I breathed again, and made another attempt to get higher upon the bank, but, quite exhausted, I fell down and my senses forsook me.

By this time I was observed by some of the people on the bank, and two men came to my assistance. They lifted me up; I once more recovered some faint recollection; and, as they bore me along, I was sensible that one of them said the sea would overtake us; that he must let me go and take care of his own life. I only remember clinging to the other and imploring him not to abandon me to the merciless waves. But I have a very confused idea of what passed, till I saw the boat, into which I was to be put to cross the Fleet water; I had then just strength to say, for God's sake do not take me to sea again.

I believe the apprehension of it, added to my other sufferings, tended to deprive me of all further sensibility, for I have not the least recollection of any thing afterwards until roused by the remedies applied to restore me in a farmhouse whither I was carried. There I heard a number of women around me, who asked a great number of questions which I was unable to answer. I remember hearing one say I was a French woman; another say that I was a negro, and indeed I was so bruised, and in such a disfigured condition, that the conjectures of these people are not surprising.

'When recovering some degree of confused recollection, and able to speak, I begged that they would allow me to go to bed. This, however. I did not ask with any expectation of life, for I was now in such a state of suffering, that my only wish was to be allowed to lie down and die in peace.

'Nothing could exceed the humanity of Mr. Abbot, the inhabitant of Fleet-farm-house, nor the compassionate attention of his sister, Miss Abbot, who not only afforded me immediate assistance, but continued for some days to attend me with such kindness and humanity, that I shall always remember it with the sincerest gratitude."

The unfortunate sufferer who gives the preceding account, was tended with great humanity by Mr. Bryer, while a wound in her foot, and the dangerous bruises she had received, prevented her from quitting the shelter she first found under the roof of Mr. Abbot, at Fleet. As soon as she was in a condition to be removed to Weymouth, Mr. Bryer, a surgeon there, received her into his own house, where Mrs. Bryer assisted in administering to her recovery such benevolent offices of consolation as her deplorable situation admitted. Meantime the gentlemen of the south battalion of the Gloucester Militia, who had done every thing possible towards the preservation of those who were the victims of the tempest, now liberally contributed to alleviate the pecuniary distresses of the survivors. None seemed to have so forcible a claim on their pity as this forlorn and helpless stranger; and she alone, of forty souls, except a single ship-boy, survived the wreck of the Catharine. There perished, twelve seamen, two soldiers' wives, twenty-two dragoons and four officers, Lieutenant Stains, Mr. Dodd of the hospital-staff, Lieutenant Jenner, the representative of an ancient and respectable family in Gloucestershire, aged thirty-one, and Cornet Burns, the son of an American loyalist of considerable property who was deprived of every thing for his adherence to the British government. —Having no dependence but on the promises of government to indemnify those who had suffered on that account he, after years of distress and difficulty, obtained a cornetcy in the 26th regiment of dragoons, then going to the West Indies, and was thus lost in his twenty-fourth year. This officer had intended embarking in another transport, and actually sent his horse on board, when finding the Catharine more commodious, he gave her the preference, while the other put back to Spithead in safety. The mangled remains of Lieutenant Jenner were two days afterwards found on the beach and interred with military honors.

But the Catharine was not the only vessel which suffered in the tempest. Those, who on shore had listened to it raging on the preceding evening, could not avoid feeling the most lively alarm for the consequences; and early in the morning on the 18th of November, several pilots and other persons assembled on the promontory called the Look-out at Weymouth. Thence they too evidently discovered the distress and danger of many of the transports.

Soon after, a lieutenant of the navy, residing at Weymouth, applied to the major of a militia regiment, for a guard to be sent to the Chisell Bank, as a large ship, supposed to be a frigate, was on shore. This was immediately granted, and the major himself marched along with a captain's guard.

The violence of the wind was so great, that the party could with difficulty reach the place of their destination. There they found a large merchantman, the Æolus, laden with timber for government, on shore. Lieutenant Mason of the navy, and his brother, a midshipman, perished in her, and a number of men who would probably have been saved had they understood the signals from shore. The men of Portland, who crowded down to the scene of desolation, meant to express, by throwing small pebbles at them, that they should remain on board, (to make them hear was impossible,) because they foresaw the ship would drive high on the bank. Should that be the case, they might soon leave her without hazard; and accordingly those who continued on board were saved, though many of them were dreadfully bruised.

Not far from the same place, the Golden Grove, another merchantman, was stranded, and in her Dr. Stevens and Mr. Burrows of St. Kits, were lost.

Lieutenant colonel Ross, who was also there, escaped on shore. These two vessels had struck against a part of the Passage-house, almost on the same spot where a French frigate, the Zenobia, had gone to pieces in 1763.

But the scene of distress was infinitely greater about four miles to the westward, where, as already related, the Catharine was wrecked. Along with her, nearly opposite to the villages of Fleet and Chickerell, the Piedmont and Venus, two transports, and soon after, the Thomas, a merchantman, shared the same fate.

One hundred and thirty-eight soldiers of the 63d regiment, under the command of captain Barcroft, were on board the Piedmont; also lieutenant Ash, and Mr. Kelly, surgeon of the same regiment. Of all these, only sergeant Richardson, eleven privates, and four seamen, survived the catastrophe; all the rest perished.

Captain Barcroft's life had been passed in the service. While yet a very young man, he served in America during the war between England and her colonies; and being then taken prisoner, was severely treated. On commencement of the war which has so many years desolated Europe, he raised a company in his native country, and served with it on the Continent during the campaign of 1794. Under a heavy fire of the enemy, he was one of the last men who retreated with it along a single plank, knee-deep in water, from the seige of Nimeguen. In a few months after the disastrous retreat on the Continent, in the winter 1794, he was ordered to the West Indies, and, in the outset of his voyage, perished in the tempest.

Of the few who reached the shore from the Piedmont, there was scarce one who was not dreadfully bruised, and some had their limbs broken. An unfortunate veteran of the 63d, though his leg was shockingly fractured, had sufficient resolution to creep for shelter under a fishing boat which lay inverted on the further side of the bank. There his groans were unheard until a young gentleman, Mr. Smith, a passenger in the Thomas, who had himself been wrecked, and was now wandering along the shore, discovered him. In this ship, the Thomas, bound to Oporto, the master, Mr. Brown, his son, and all the crew, except the mate, three seamen, and Mr. Smith, were lost. The last was on his way to Lisbon; but his preservation was chiefly in consequence of his remaining on board after all the rest had left the ship, or were washed away by the waves. She had then drifted high on the bank, when he leaped out of her and reached the ground.

Though weak and encumbered by his wet clothes, he gained the opposite side of the bank, but on gazing on the dreary beach around him, he considered himself cast away on an uninhabited coast. At length he observed a fishing boat, and approaching it, heard the groans of the unfortunate old soldier, whom he attempted to relieve. But alone he found himself unable to fulfil his intention, and it was a considerable time before he observed any means of assistance near. At last, perceiving a man at some distance, he hastened to him, eagerly inquiring whether a surgeon could be procured for a poor creature with a broken limb, who lay under the boat. Probably the man showed little alacrity, for Mr. Smith found it necessary to purchase his good offices by a gift of half a guinea, which he imagined would induce him to seek what was so much required. But the man pocketing the half-guinea with the greatest composure, said he was a king's officer, and must see what bales of goods were driven on shore; then telling Mr. Smith there was a ferry about four miles off, by which he might get to Weymouth. The youth was thus disappointed of his humane design, and the soldier died in that deplorable condition before any other aid attained him.

In the Thomas, the vessel to which Mr. Smith belonged, he witnessed scenes not less distressing. Mr. Brown the master of the vessel, was carried away by an immense wave just as he was stripping off his clothes to endeavor to save himself. His son exclaiming, "Oh my father! my poor father!" instantly followed. The bodies of both were afterwards found and interred at Wyke.

Of ninety-six persons on board the Venus, only Mr. John Darley of the hospital staff, sergeant-major Hearne, twelve soldiers, four seamen and a boy were saved. Mr. Darley escaped by throwing himself from the wreck at a moment when it drifted high on the stones; he reached them without broken limbs, but, overtaken by the furious sea, he was carried back, not so far, however, that he was incapable of regaining the ground. Notwithstanding the weight of his clothes and his exhausted state, he got to the top of the bank, but there the power of farther exertion failed, and he fell. While lying in this situation, trying to recover breath and strength, a great many people from the neighboring villages passed him; they had crossed the Fleet-water in the hopes of sharing the plunder of the vessels which the lower inhabitants of the coast are too much accustomed to consider their right.

Mr. Darley seems to have been so far from meeting with assistance from those who were plundering the dead, without thinking of the living, that although he saw many boats passing and repassing the Fleet-water, he found great difficulty in procuring a passage for himself and two or three fellow-sufferers who had now joined him. But having passed it he soon met with Mr. Bryer, to whose active humanity all the sufferers were eminently indebted.

Before the full extent of this dreadful calamity was known at Weymouth, the officers of the South Gloucester Militia, with equal humanity, were devising how they might best succor the survivors, and perform the last duties to the remains of those who had perished. On the morning of the 19th of November, one of them, accompanied by Mr. Bryer of Weymouth, rode to the villages where those who had escaped from the various wrecks had found a temporary shelter. In a house at Chickerell, they found sergeant Richardson and eleven privates of the 63d regiment; two of the latter had fractured limbs, and almost all the rest either wounds or bruises. In other houses the sufferers had been received, and were as comfortably accommodated as circumstances would admit.

The gentlemen then crossed the Fleet-water to the beach, and there, whatever idea was previously formed of it, the horror of the scene infinitely surpassed expectation; no celebrated field of carnage ever presented, in proportion to its size, a more awful sight than the Chisell Bank now exhibited. For about two miles it was strewed with the dead bodies of men and animals, with pieces of wreck and piles of plundered goods, which groups of people were carrying away, regardless of the sight of drowned bodies that filled the new spectators with sorrow and amazement.

On the mangled remains of the unfortunate victims, death appeared in all its hideous forms. Either the sea or the people who had first gone down to the shore, had stripped the bodies of the clothes which the sufferers had wore at the fatal moment. The remnants of the military stock, the wristbands, or collar of a shirt, or a piece of blue pantaloons, were all the fragments left behind.

The only means of distinguishing the officers was the different appearance of their hands from those of men accustomed to hard labor; but some were known by the description given of them by their friends or by persons who were in the vessels along with them. The remains of captain Barcroft were recognised by the honorable scars he had received in the service of his country; and his friends and relatives, as well as those of several others had the satisfaction of learning that their bodies were rescued from the sea, and interred with military honors.

Early in the morning of the 20th of November, a lieutenant of the militia regiment who had been appointed to superintend the melancholy office of interment, repaired to the scene of destruction. But from the necessary preliminaries of obtaining the authority of a magistrate to remove the bodies, not more than twenty-five were buried that day. The bodies of captain Barcroft, lieutenant Sutherland, Cornet Graydon, lieutenant Ker and two women, were then selected to be put into coffins. Next day, those of lieutenant Jenner and Cornet Burns, being found, were distinguished in the like manner.

The whole number of dead found on the beach, amounted to two hundred and thirty-four; so that the duty of interment was so heavy and fatiguing, that it was not until the twenty-third that all the soldiers and sailors were deposited. Of these there were two hundred and eight, and they were committed to the earth as decently as circumstances would admit, in graves dug on the Fleet side of the beach, beyond the reach of the sea, where a pile of stones was raised on each, to mark where they lay. Twelve coffins were sent to receive the bodies of the women, but nine only being found, the supernumerary ones were appointed to receive the remains of the officers.

Two wagons were next sent to the Fleet-water to receive the coffins, in which the shrouded bodies of seventeen officers and nine women had been placed, and on the 24th were carried to the church-yard at Wyke, preceded by a captain, subaltern and fifty men of the Gloucester Militia, and attended by the young gentleman before mentioned, Mr. Smith, as chief mourner. The officers were interred in a large grave, north of the church-tower, with military honors, and lieutenant Ker in a grave on the other side of the tower. The remains of the nine women, which had been deposited in the church during the ceremony, were next committed to the earth.

Two monuments have been erected in commemoration of the unfortunate sufferers, the first bearing the following inscription :—

"To the memory of Captain Ambrose William Barcroft, Lieutenant Harry Ash, and Mr. Kelly, surgeon of the 63d regiment of Light Infantry; of Lieutenant Stephen Jenner, of the 6th West-India regiment; Lieutenant Stains of the 2d West India regiment; and two hundred and fifteen soldiers and seamen and nine women, who perished by shipwreck on Portland Beach, opposite the villages of Langton, Fleet, and Chickerell, on Wednesday the 18th day of November, 1795."

On the second monument is inscribed,

"Sacred to the memory of Major John Charles Ker, Military Commandant of Hospitals in the Leeward Islands, and to that of his son, Lieutenant James Ker, of the 40th regiment of foot, who both departed this life on the 18th of November, 1795, the first aged forty and the latter fourteen years."

The fate of both was truly deplorable, and is a melancholy example of the uncertainty of human affairs.

They were embarked in the Venus transport, and left Portsmouth the 16th of November, with a fleet full of troops, destined to the West Indies, under the command of General Sir Ralph Abercrombie.

A storm having arisen on the 17th which lasted till the next day, many of the ships were lost, and the Venus wrecked on Portland Beach.

The major's body could not be found, although it is possible it may have been among the many others which were driven ashore and buried in this church-yard.

His son's corpse was recognised and lies interred under this stone, which was raised by his brother, John William Ker, Esq.

WRECK OF THE BRITISH SHIP SIDNEY.

On a reef of rocks in the South Sea.

The Sidney left Port Jackson, on the coast of New Holland, on the 12th of April, 1806, bound to Bengal. Intending to proceed through Dampier's Straits, her course was directed as nearly as possible in the track of Captain Hogan, of the Cornwallis, which, as laid down in the charts, appeared a safe and easy passage. But, on the 20th of May, at one, A. M., we ran upon a most dangerous rock, or shoal, in 3 20 south latitude, and 146 50 east longitude, and as this reef is not noticed in any map or chart, it appears that we were its unfortunate discoverers.

On Sunday, 25 fathoms of water were found over the taffrail, and six fathoms over the larboard gangway; only nine feet on the starboard side, and 12 feet over the bows. One of the boats was immediately got out with a bower-anchor; but on sounding, at the distance of ten fathoms from the ship, no ground could be found with sixty fathoms of line.

When she struck it must have been high water, for at that time there was no appearance of any reef or breaker; but as the water subsided, the shoal began to show itself, with a number of small black rocks. The ship had been striking very hard, and began to yield forward.—At three, A. M. there were six feet water in the hold.

and increasing rapidly; at five, the vessel was settling aft, and her top-sides parting from the floor-heads.

Upon consultation with my officers, it was our unanimous opinion that the ship was gone beyond recovery, and that no exertions could avail for her safety. We therefore employed all hands in getting the boats ready to receive the crew, who were 108 in number. Eight bags of rice, six casks of water, and a small quantity of salted beef and pork, were put into the long-boat as provisions for the whole; the number of the people prevented us from taking a larger stock, as the three boats were barely sufficient to receive us all with safety.

We remained with the Sidney until five, P. M. on the twenty-first of May, when there were three feet of water on the orlop-deck; therefore we now thought it full time to leave the ship to her fate, and seek our safety in the boats. Accordingly, I embarked in the long-boat with Mr. Trounce, second officer, and seventy-four Lascars; Mr. Robson and Mr. Halkart, with sixteen Lascars, were in the cutter, and the jolly-boat was allotted to fifteen Dutch Malays, and one Sepoy.

Being desirous to ascertain the position of the reef, which could be done by making the Admiralty Islands, our course was shaped thither, steering north by east and half east. During the night, it blew fresh, and the long-boat having made much water, we were obliged to lighten her, by throwing a great deal of lumber, and two casks of water, overboard. The three boats kept close in company, the long-boat having the jolly-boat in tow.

Finding, at day-light, that the cutter sailed considerably better, I directed Mr. Robson that the jolly-boat might be taken in tow by her. But the wind increasing as the morning advanced, and a heavy swell rising, the jolly-boat, while in tow by the cutter, sank at ten o'clock, and all on board, to the number of sixteen, perished. It was lamentable to witness the fate of these unhappy men, and the more so, as it was not in our power to render them the smallest assistance.

The Admiralty Islands were seen at noon of the 22d, bearing N. N. E. three or four leagues distant, and as we had run about fifty-eight miles in the boats, upon a N. by E. half E. course, the situation of the shoal where the Sidney struck was accurately ascertained, and will be found as above laid down.

From the Admiralty Islands, we continued standing to the westward, and on the 25th, made a small island, on which, from its appearance, I was induced to land in quest of a supply of water. Therefore Mr. Robson, myself, and twenty of our best hands, armed with heavy clubs, brought from New Caledonia, (our fire-arms being rendered useless from exposure to the rain) landed through a high surf, to the utmost astonishment of the inhabitants.

As far as might be judged, they had never before seen people of our complexion. The men were tall and well made, wearing their hair plaited and raised above the head; they had no resemblance to Malays or Caffres;—and excepting their color, which was of a light copper, they had the form and features of Europeans. They were entirely naked. We also saw a number of women, who were well formed, and had mild and pleasing features.

We were received on the beach by about twenty natives, who immediately supplied each of us with a cocoa-nut. We succeeded in making them understand that we wanted water, on which they made signs for us to accompany them to the interior of the island; on compliance, after walking about a mile, they conducted us into a thick jungle, and, as their number was quickly increasing, I judged it imprudent to proceed further.—Thus returning to the beach, I was alarmed to find that one hundred and fifty, or more, of the natives had assembled, armed with spears eight or ten feet long. One of them, an old man of venerable appearance, and who seemed to be their chief, approached and threw his spear at my feet, expressive, as I understood, of his wish that we should part with our clubs in like manner. Perceiving, at this time, that a crowd of women had got hold of the stern-fast of the cutter, and were endeavoring to haul her on shore from the grapnel, we hastily tried to gain the boat. The natives followed us closely; some of them pointed their spears at us as we retreated, and some were thrown, though happily without effect; and to us they seemed to be very inexpert in the management of their weapons. On my getting into the water, three or four of the natives followed me, threatening to throw their spears, and when I was within reach of the boat, one of them made a thrust, which was prevented from taking effect by Mr. Robson, who warded off the weapon. When we had got into the boat, and were putting off, they threw, at least, two hundred spears, none of which struck, excepting one, which gave a severe wound to my cook, entering immediately above the jaw, and passing through his mouth.

Having escaped this perilous adventure we pursued our course, and got as far as Dampier's Straits, in as favorable circumstances as our situation could well admit. But the Lascars, now being within reach of land, became impatient to be put on shore. It was in vain that I exhorted them to persevere; they would not listen to argument, and expressed their wish rather to meet with immediate death on shore, than to be starved to death in the boats. Yielding to their importunity, I at length determined to land them on the northwest extremity of the island of Ceram, from whence they might travel to Amboyna in two or three days. Being off that part of the island on the ninth of June, Mr. Robson volunteered to land a portion of the people in the cutter, to return to the long-boat, and the cutter to be then given up to such further portion of the crew as chose to join the party first landed. Accordingly he went ashore with the cutter, but to my great mortification, after waiting two days, there was no appearance of his return or of the cutter.

We concluded that the people had been detained either by the Dutch or the natives. Yet as the remaining part of the Lascars were desirous to be landed, we stood-in with the long-boat, and put them on shore near the point where we supposed the cutter to have landed her people.

Our number in the long-boat were now reduced to seventeen, consisting of Mr. Trounce, Mr. Halkart, myself and fourteen Lascars and others. Our stock of provision was two bags of rice and one gang cask of water. with which we conceived we might hold out until reaching Bencoolen, whither we determined to make the best of our way. The allowance to each man we fixed as one tea-cupful of rice and a pint of water daily, but we soon found it necessary to make a considerable reduction.

Proceeding through the straits of Bantam, we met in our course several Malay prows, none of which took notice of us excepting one, which gave chase for a day, and would have come up with us had we not got off under cover of a very dark night. Continuing onwards, we passed through the strait of Saypay, where we caught a large shark. Our spirits were much elated by this valuable prize, which we lost no time in getting on board; and having kindled a fire in the bottom of the boat, it was roasted with all expedition. Such was the keenness of our appetite, that although the shark must have weighed one hundred and fifty or one hundred and sixty pounds, not a vestige of it remained at the close of the day. But we were afflicted on the following day with the most violent complaint of the stomach and bowels, which reduced us exceedingly, and left us languid and spiritless, insomuch that we now despaired of safety.

On the second of July, I lost an old and faithful servant, who died from want of sustenance; and on the fourth, we made Java head; at the same time catching two large boobies, which afforded all hands a most precious and refreshing meal. At midnight of the ninth, we came to off Pulo Penang, on the west coast of Sumatra; but at daylight, when endeavoring to weigh our anchor and run close in shore, we were so much exhausted that our united strength proved insufficient to get it up.

On a signal of distress being made, a sanpan with two Malays came off, and as I was the only person in the long-boat who had sufficient strength to move, I accompanied them on shore. However, I found myself so weak on landing that I fell to the ground, and it was necessary to carry me to an adjacent house. Such refreshments as could be procured were immediately sent off to the long-boat, and we recruited so rapidly, that in two days we found ourselves in a condition to proceed on our voyage. Having weighed anchor on the 12th of July, we set sail, and on the 19th, arrived off the island of Bencoolen.

Here I met with an old friend, captain Chauvet of the Perseverance, whose kindness and humanity I shall ever remember and gratefully acknowledge. On the day subsequent to my arrival, I waited on Mr. Parr the resident, from whom I received every attention.

Leaving Bencoolen on the 17th of August, in the Perseverance, I arrived at Penang on the 27th, where I was agreeably surprised to meet my late chief-mate, Mr. Robson, who, along with the Lascars, had landed at Ceram. They reached Amboyna in safety, where they were received by the Dutch governor, Mr. Cranstoun, with a humanity and benevolence that reflect honor on his character. He supplied them with whatever their wants required. Mr. Robson was accommodated at his own table, and, on leaving Amboyna, he furnished him money for himself and his people, for the amount of which he refused to take any receipt or acknowledgment. He also gave Mr. Robson letters to the governor-general of Batavia, recommending him to his kind offices. Such honorable conduct from the governor of a foreign country, and with which we were at war, cannot be too widely promulgated. From Amboyna, Mr. Robson embarked in the Pallas, a Dutch frigate, for Batavia, which on the passage thither was captured by his majesty's ships Greyhound and Harriet, and brought to Prince of Wales' island.

From Penang I sailed to Bengal with the Paruna, captain Denison, and arrived safely in Calcutta in the beginning of May, 1806.

LOSS OF THE RAMILLIES IN THE ATLANTIC OCEAN.

ADMIRAL (afterwards Lord) Graves having requested leave to return to England in 1782, was appointed by lord Rodney to command the convoy sent home with the numerous fleet of merchantmen from the West Indies in the month of July. He accordingly hoisted his flag on board the Ramillies, of seventy-four guns, and sailed on the 25th from Blue Fields, having under his orders the Canada and Centaur of seventy-four guns each, the Pallas frigate of thirty-six guns, and the following French ships, taken by lord Rodney and Sir Samuel Hood, out of the armament commanded by the count de Grasse, viz. the Ville de Paris, of one hundred and ten guns; the Glorieux and Hector, of seventy-four guns each; the Ardent, Caton, and Jason, of six guns each. Those which were originally British ships had been in so many actions, and so long absent from England, as to have become extremely out of condition, while that of the prizes was still more deplorable, and the following authentic account of the various disasters which attended this distressed convoy will be found equally melancholy and interesting.

Soon after the fleet had sailed, the officers of the Ardent united in signing such a representation of her miserable plight as induced admiral Graves to order her back to Port Royal; and the Jason, by not putting to sea with the convoy, from want of water, never joined him at all. The rest proceeded, and after those vessels that were bound for New York had separated, the whole convoy was reduced to ninety-two or three sail.

On the 8th of September the Caton springing a leak, made such alarming complaints, that the admiral directed her and the Pallas, also became leaky, to bear away immediately, and keep company together, making for

Halifax, which then bore N. N. W. and was but eighty-seven leagues distant.

The afternoon of the 16th of September showing indications of a gale and foul weather from the south-east quarter, every preparation was made on board the flag-ship for such an event, not only on account of her own safety, but also as an example to the rest of the fleet. The admiral collected the ships about six o'clock, and brought to under his mainsail on the larboard tack, having all his other sails furled, and his top-gallant yards and masts lowered down.

The wind soon increasing, blew strong from the E. S. E. with a very heavy sea, and about three o'clock in the morning of the 17th flew suddenly round to the contrary point, blowing most tremendously, and accompanied with rain, thunder, and lightning; the Ramillies was taken by the lee, her main-sail thrown back, her main-mast went by the board, and mizzen-mast half way up; the fore-top mast fell over the starboard bow, the fore-yard broke in the slings, the tiller snapped in two, and the rudder was nearly torn off. Thus was this capital ship, from being in perfect order, reduced, within a few minutes, to a mere wreck, by the fury of the blast and the violence of the sea, which acted in opposition to each other. The ship was pooped, the cabin, where the admiral lay, was flooded, his cot-bed jerked down by the violence of the shock and the ship's instantaneous revulsion, so that he was obliged to pull on his boots half leg deep in water, without any stockings, to huddle on his wet clothes, and repair upon deck. On his first coming thither, he ordered two of the lieutenants to examine into the state of the affairs below, and to keep a sufficient number of people at the pumps, while he himself and the captain kept the deck, to encourage the men to clear away the wreck, which, by its constant swinging backwards and forwards by every wave against the body of the ship, had beaten off much of the copper from the starboard side, and exposed the seams so much to the sea that the decayed oakum washed out, and the whole frame became at once exceedingly porous and leaky.

At dawn of day they perceived a large ship lying under their lee, upon her side, water-logged, her hands attempting to wear her by first cutting away the mizzen-mast, and then her main-mast; hoisting her ensign, with the union downwards in order to draw the attention of the fleet; but to no purpose, for no succor could be given, and she very soon went down head foremost, the fly of her ensign being the last thing visible. This was the Dutton, formerly an East Indiaman, and then a store-ship, commanded by a lieutenant of the navy, who in his agitation, leaped from her deck into the sea; but, as might be expected, was very soon overwhelmed by its billows. Twelve or thirteen of the crew contrived, however, to slide off one of the boats, and running with the wind, first endeavored to reach a large ship before them, which, not being able to fetch, and afraid of filling if they attempted to haul up for the purpose, they made up for another ship more to the leeward, who fortunately descrying them, threw a number of ropes, by the help of which these desperate fellows scrambled up her sides, and fortunately saved their lives. Out of ninety four or five sail, seen the day before, scarcely twenty could now be counted; of the ships of war, there were discerned the Canada, half hull down upon the lee-quarter, having her main-top-mast and mizzen-mast gone, the main-top damaged, the main-yard aloft, and the main-sail furled; the Centaur was far to windward, without masts, bowsprit, or rudder; and the Glorieux without foremast, bowsprit, or main-top-mast. Of these the two latter perished with all their crews, excepting the captain of the Centaur, and a few of his people, who contrived to slip off her stern into one of the boats unnoticed, and thus escaped the fate of the rest of the crew.

The Ville de Paris appeared to have received no injury, and was commanded by a most experienced seaman, who had made twenty-four voyages to and from the West Indies, and had, therefore, been pitched upon to lead the ship through the gulf; nevertheless she was afterwards buried in the ocean with all on board her consisting of above eight hundred people. Of the convoy, besides the Dutton, before mentioned, and the British Queen, seven others were discovered without masts or bowsprits; eighteen lost masts, and several others had foundered.

In the course of this day the Canada crossed upon and passed the Ramillies; some of the trade attempted to follow the Canada, but she ran at such a rate that they soon found it to be in vain, and then returned towards the flag-ship; the Ramillies had at this time six feet water in her hold, and the pumps would not free her, the water having worked out the oakum, and her beams amid-ship being almost drawn from their clamps.

The admiral, therefore, gave orders for all the buckets to be manned, and every officer to help towards freeing the ship; the mizzen-top-sail was set upon the fore-mast, the main-top-gallant-sail on the stump of the mizzen-mast, and the tiller shipped. In this condition, by bearing away, she scudded on at so good a rate that she held pace with some of the merchantmen.

The day having been spent in bailing and pumping, without materially gaining on the water, the captain, in the name of the officers, represented to the admiral the necessity of parting with the guns for the relief of the ship, but he objected, that there would then be left no protection for the convoy. At length, however, after great difficulty, he consented to their disposing of the fore-castle and after-most quarter-deck guns, together with some of the shot, and other articles of very great weight. The ensuing night was employed in bailing and endeavoring to make the pumps useful, for the ballast, by getting into the well, had choked and rendered them useless, and the chains had broken every time they were repaired. The water had risen to seven feet in the hold. The wind from the westward drove a vast sea before it, and the ship being old, strained most violently.

On the morning of the 18th, nothing could be seen of the Canada, she having pushed on at her greatest speed for England. The frame of the Ramillies having opened during the night, the admiral was prevailed upon, by the renewed and pressing remonstrances of the officers, although with great reluctance, to let six of the forwardmost and four of the aftermost guns of the main-deck to be thrown overboard, together with the remainder of those on the quarter-deck; and the ship still continuing to open very much, he ordered tarred canvas and hides to be nailed fore and aft from under the sills of the ports on the main-deck under the fifth plank above, or within the water-ways, and the crew, without orders, did the same on the lower deck. Her increasing complaints requiring still more to be done, the admiral directed all the guns on the upper deck, the shot, both on that and the lower deck, and various heavy stores to be thrown overboard; a leakage in the light room of the grand magazine having almost filled the ship forward, and there being eight feet water in the magazine, every gentleman was compelled to take his turn at the whips, or in handing the buckets. The ship was besides frapped from the fore-mast to the mainmast.

Notwithstanding their utmost efforts the water still gained on them; the succeeding night, the wind blowing very hard, with extremely heavy squalls, a part of the orlop-deck fell into the hold; the ship herself seemed to work excessively, and to settle forward.

On the morning of the 19th, under these very alarming circumstances, the admiral commanded both the bower-anchors to be cut away, all the junk to be flung overboard, one sheet and one bower cable to be reduced to junk and served the same way, together with every remaining ponderous store that could be got at, and all the powder in the grand magazine (it being damaged;) the cutter and pinnace to be broken up and tossed overboard, the skidds having already worked off the side; every soul on board was now employed in bailing. One of the pumps was got up, but to no purpose, for the shot-lockers being broken down, some of the shot, as well as the ballast, had fallen into the well; and as the weather moderated a little, every thing was made ready to heave the lower deck guns into the sea, the admiral being anxious to leave nothing undone for the relief of the ship.

When evening approached, there being twenty merchant ships in sight, the officers united in beseeching him to go into one of them, but this he positively refused to do, deeming it, as he declared, unpardonable in a commander-in-chief to desert his garrison in distress; that his living a few years longer was of very little consequence, but that, by leaving his ship at such a time, he should discourage and slacken the exertions of the people, by setting a very bad example. The wind lulling somewhat during the night; all hands bailed the water, which, at this time, was six feet fore and aft.

On the morning of the 20th, the admiral ordered the the spare and stream anchors to be cut away, and within the course of the day all the lower deck guns to be thrown overboard. When evening came, the spirits of the people in general, and even of the most courageous, began to fail, and they openly expressed the utmost despair, together with the most earnest desire of quitting the ship, lest they should founder in her. The admiral hereupon advanced and told them, that he and their officers had an equal regard for their own lives, and that the officers had no intention of deserting either them or the ship; that, for his part, he was determined to try one night more in her; he, therefore, hoped and entreated they would do so too, for there was still room to imagine, that one fair day, with a moderate sea, might enable them, by united exertions, to clear and secure the well against the encroaching ballast which washed into it; that if this could be done, they might be able to restore the chains to the pumps, and use them; and that then hands enough might be spared to raise jury-masts, with which they might carry the ship to Ireland; that her appearance alone, while she could swim, would be sufficient to protect the remaining part of her convoy; above all, that as every thing that could be thought of had now been done for her relief, it would be but reasonable to wait the effect. He concluded with assuring them, that he would make the signal directly for the trade to lie by them during the night, which he doubted not they would comply with.

This temperate speech had the desired effect; the firmness and confidence with which he spoke, and their reliance on his seamanship and judgment, as well as his constant presence and attention to every accident, had a wonderful effect upon them; they became pacified, and returned to their duty and their labors. Since the first disaster, the admiral had, in fact, scarcely ever quitted the deck; this they had all observed, together with his diligence in personally inspecting every circumstance of distress. Knowing his skill and experience, they placed great confidence in them; and he instantly made, according to his promise, a signal for all the merchantmen.

At this period, it must be confessed, there was great reason for alarm, and but little for hope; for all the anchors and guns, excepting one, together with every other matter of weight, had been thrown overboard, and yet the ship did not seem at all relieved. The strength of the people was, likewise, so nearly exhausted, having had no sleep since the first fatal stroke, that one half of the crew were ordered to bail and the other to repose; so that, although the wind was much abated, the water still gained upon them, in spite of all their efforts, and the ship rolled and worked most prodigiously in a most unquiet sea.

At three in the morning of the 21st, being the fourth night, the well being quite broken in, the casks, ballast and remaining shot rushed together and destroyed the cylinders of the pumps; the frame and carcass of the ship began to give way in every part, and the whole crew exclaimed that it was impossible to keep her any longer above water.

In this extremity, the admiral resolved within himself not to lose a moment in removing the people whenever daylight should arrive, but told the captain not to communicate any more of his design than that he intended to remove the sick and lame at day-break; and for this purpose he should call on board all the boats of the merchantmen. He, nevertheless, gave private orders to the captain, while this was doing, to have all the bread brought upon the quarter-deck, with a quantity of beef, pork, and flour, to settle the best distribution of the people according to the number of the trade-ships that should obey their signal, and to allow an officer to each division of them ; to have the remaining boats launched, and as soon as the sick were disposed of, to begin to remove the whole of the crew, with the utmost despatch, but without risking too many in a boat.

Accordingly at dawn, the signal was made for the boats of the merchantmen, but nobody suspected what was to follow, until the bread was entirely removed and the sick gone. About six o'clock, the rest of the crew were permitted to go off, and between nine and ten, there being nothing further to direct and regulate, the admiral himself, after shaking hands with every officer, and leaving his barge for their better accommodation and transport, quitted forever the Ramillies, which had then nine feet of water in her hold. He went into a small leaky boat, loaded with bread, out of which both him and the surgeon who accompanied him were obliged to bail water all the way. He was in his boots, with his surtout over his uniform, and his countenance as calm and as composed as ever. He had, at going off, desired a cloak, a cask of flour and a cask of water, but could get only the flour, and he left behind all his stock, wines, furniture, books and charts, which had cost him upwards of one thousand pounds, being unwilling to employ even a single servant in saving or packing up what belonged to himself alone, in a time of such general calamity, as to appear better in that respect than any of the crew.

The admiral rowed for the Belle, Captain Forster, being the first of the trade that had borne up to the Ramillies the preceding night in her imminent distress, and by his anxious humanity set such an example to his brother traders as had a powerful influence upon them—an influence which was generally followed by sixteen others.

By three o'clock, most of the crew were taken out, at which time the Ramillies had thirteen feet of water in her hold, and was evidently foundering in every part; at half past four the captain, and first and third lieutenants, left her, with every soul excepting the fourth lieutenant, who staid behind only to execute the admiral's orders for setting fire to her wreck when finally deserted. The carcass burned rapidly, and the flames quickly reaching the powder which was filled in the after-magazine, and had been lodged very high; in thirty-five minutes the decks and upper works blew up with a horrid explosion and cloud of smoke, while the lower part of the hull was precipitated to the bottom of the ocean.

All this time the admiral, in the Belle, stood for the wreck to see his last orders executed, as well as to succor any boats that might be too full of men, the swell of the sea being prodigious, although the weather had been moderate ever since noon of the foregoing day. There were, however, at intervals, some squalls, with threats of the weather soon becoming violent. It was not long before they were realized, for within two hours after the last of the crew were put on board their respective ships, the wind rose to a great height, and so continued, with intermission, for six or seven successive days, so that no boat could, during that time, have lived in the water. On such a small interval depended the salvation of more than six hundred lives! Indeed, during the four days immediately preceding this catastrophe, it blew such a strong gale, and such a heavy sea followed the Ramillies, that it was always necessary to keep her with the wind upon her quarter, with seldom more than the sprit-sail hoisted upon her foremast, and at times with no sail at all, in which state she would run at the rate of six miles an hour. Whenever the main-top-gallant-sail was set on the stump of the mizzen-mast she commonly griped so much, as to render the steerage very difficult, and yet this had been carried, whenever it could be, in order to keep pace with the merchantmen, the slowest of which went nearly as fast under their bare poles.

Even in running thus, the Ramillies rolled prodigiously, and as she grew lighter every day her motion became the more uneasy, so that the men could scarcely stand to their work or keep their legs without something to lay hold by. There was no such thing as real repose for them when sitting or lying down upon deck, nor steadiness enough to eat or drink with any security; no meat could be dressed, nor did any man or officer go into bed. Until the afternoon of the 20th, there was no venturing to bring her to, even for a boat to come on board; but notwithstanding this desperate condition, when some were hourly dropping through fatigue and want of sleep, and the decks were covered with water, the whole of the crew behaved with the utmost obedience, attention and sobriety, and omitted no possible exertion for the preservation of the ship.

Upon their separation taking place, the officers, who were distributed with portions of the crew among the Jamaica-men, had orders respectively to deliver them to the first man-of-war or tender they should meet with, and to acquaint the Secretary of the Admiralty, by the earliest opportunity, of their proceedings. A pendant was hoisted on board the Belle, by way of distinction, that she might, if possible, lead the rest. Some of the trade kept with her, and others made the best of their way, apprehensive lest they should soon fall short of provisions, as they had so many more to feed.

The Silver-Eel transport, which had sailed from Bluefields with the invalids of Sir George Rodney's fleet, and was under the command of a lieutenant of the navy, had been ordered to keep near the Ramillies. That ship was accordingly at hand on the 21st of September, the day of her destruction, and in consequence of several deaths on the passage had room enough for the reception of all who were now ailing or maimed, and was therefore charged with them, being properly fitted for their accommodation.

The Silver-Eel parted from the admiral in latitude 42 48 N. and longitude 45 19 W. after seeing the Ramillies demolished, and being ordered to make for the first port, ran into Falmouth the 6th of October, on the afternoon of which day, one of the trade-ships, with a midshipman and sixteen of the crew of the Ramillies, reached Plymouth sound. Another of the same convoy, having on board another part of the crew, with the captain and first lieutenant, anchored in the same place before daylight the next morning. The Canada, however, having exerted her utmost speed, had, prior to all these, on the 4th of the same month, got to Portsmouth, where she spread the news of the dispersion of this miserable fleet, which being conveyed to France, her privateers immediately put to sea in hopes of making prizes of them. Some of the Jamaica-men, with part of the crew of the Ramillies, fell into their hands; two of the West Indiamen were captured in sight of the Belle, but she herself with the admiral and thirty-three of his crew, arrived safe, though singly, on the 10th of October, in Cork harbor, where was the Myrmidon frigate. The Admiral immediately hoisted his flag on board the latter, and sailing with the first fair wind, arrived, on the 17th, in Plymouth Sound, apparently in good health, but with a settled oppression upon his breast, from having been so long and so dreadfully exposed upon the deck of the Ramillies in the horrid night when she was first overtaken by the storm; nor could he remove that complaint for upwards of six months. He brought away with him nothing but a few of his private papers, the rest of his effects having shared the same fate as the ship.

It was calculated that by the destruction of the fleet, upwards of twenty one thousand and five hundred persons perished. The loss of property has been estimated by the British Government to be upwards of £20,000,000. The gale, which continued for six days, was the most tremendous one on record

---

PRESERVATION OF NINE MEN,

IN A SMALL BOAT, SURROUNDED BY ISLANDS OF ICE.

We sailed from Plymouth under convoy of H. B. Majesty's ship St. Alban's, and two other ships of war, together with a fleet of merchantmen bound to the Mediterranean, having a fresh gale at north-east.

The wind still continuing, we kept company with the fleet until reaching 120 leagues to the westward; then judging ourselves clear of privateers, we proceeded on our voyage. But before gaining 300 leagues, on the 17th of March, we came up with an English-built ship of about 200 tons, carrying twelve guns, and sailing under a jury main-mast. On our approach she hoisted English colors; and, on being hailed, told us she belonged to London, and was now bound from Virginia homewards, which seemed probable, as many tame fowl were on board; and a red bird flew from her to us.

Our captain seeing the vessel disabled, desired her to bring to; saying, if any thing was wanted on board, we should hoist out our boat and carry it thither; but this was obstinately refused; the captain declared, that our boat should not approach, and unless we kept further off, he would fire into us. This induced suspicion on our part, wherefore we ran up with the vessel, and commanded her to bring to. On this she fired, and engaged us from eleven in the morning until six in the evening; then, being much damaged, she struck, and called to us to save the lives of the crew. But this request came too late, for the wind increasing, raised a great sea, which forced our ship under a reefed main-sail, whence we could not hoist out our boat, without endangering our own lives. However, by means of a light which she carried, we kept close to her, intending to hoist the boat out when it became practicable. But towards midnight her light became very low; and by a loud cry, which was heard about one o'clock, we judged that she foundered.

When the vessel struck she told us that she had fourteen Frenchmen on board, whence we conjectured her to be an English Virginia-man taken by the French; and that she had lost her main-mast in the engagement. We followed her chasing and fighting, about thirty leagues; and when she struck we were in 45 50 north latitude.

Our booty being thus lost, we made the best of our way to Newfoundland, being bound thither on a fishing voyage. One trouble, however, seldom comes alone, and so it happened to us; for on the 26th of March, we saw some shattered ice, at four in the afternoon, which was supposed to be the harbor ice now broken up. We were now in 46 50 north latitude, and conceived ourselves fifty leagues, though it afterwards proved seventy, from the land. The wind being at east, the top-sails were handed; and we stood northward, under our courses, hoping to get clear of the ice before night. But finding rather more than less, we tacked to the Southward, which was found unproductive of any change. Therefore, for further security, the fore-sail was furled, and the ship brought to under the mainsail, as night approached, and as there was a dead wind, so that we could lie off on either tack; we trusted if we should fall in with the greater ice, to meet with the less shocks.

About eight or nine o'clock, we discovered a field of ice, of which we ran foul, notwithstanding our exertions to keep clear of it; and although we hung cables, coils of rope, hoops and such things, over the ship to defend her, she struck so hard, that at eleven she bilged, whence we had much difficulty to keep her afloat till day-light, by two pumps going, and bailing at three hatch-ways.

At the approach of day, our men were much fatigued, the water increased, and against noon the hold was half full. No one knew what to advise another, and all began to despair of their lives: we continued pumping, though to little purpose, and concluded, that if now were our appointed time, we must submit patiently to it.

But amidst this disaster, it pleased God to put it into the thoughts of some us, that several might be preserved in the boat, upon which the captain was entreated to hoist her out, and commit a few of us there.

The captain answered, that, although God could work wonders, it was improbable that so small a boat should preserve us; that it was but living a few days longer in misery; and, seeing God had cast this calamity to his lot, he was resolved to take his chance, and die with his men.

Nevertheless, being much importuned, he ordered the boat out, and William Saunders and five others in her;

and, that the men might not suspect their design it was given out that the boat should go ahead to tow the ship clear of the ice. How likely that was the reader may judge, there being but one oar, all the rest were broken by defending the ship from the ice. However, the purpose advanced.

The boat being out, and finding no effect produced in towing the ship, fell a-stern, intending to take in the captain and as many as it could safely carry, while some were preparing necessaries for a miserable voyage. A compass, and other things ready, were conveyed into it.

The captain, doctor and several others, having got out at the cabin windows and galleries, I, amongst the rest, endeavored to escape at the gallery, intending likewise, if possible, to get into the boat; but being discovered by the men, they took small arms, and kept off the boat, resolving, as they could not preserve all, that the whole should perish together.

This design being frustrated, every one, except myself and William Langmead, got into the ship again; but we were so low that we could not recover ourselves. No person coming to relieve us, we were at length forced to let go our hold, and trust to the mercy of those in the boat, who seeing us swimming towards them, hove out a rope and took us in.

We were now eight in number in the boat; and, willing to save our captain, lay hovering about the ship till night; but the men persisting in their resolution, fired at the boat and kept her off. We began to seek shelter as night approached; and, having gone among the shattered ice, made our boat fast to a small lump, and drove with it; and as we came foul of great ice, we removed and made fast to another piece, and so continued during the remainder of the night. Looking around in the morning, the ship was seen about three leagues to the eastward in the same position as we had left her, whereon a consultation was held, whether or not we should return and make another attempt to save the captain, and as many more as possible. This proposal, however, was negatived, every one alleging that the men would either fire on us, or inconsiderately crowd into the boat and sink her; therefore it was resolved to make the best of our way to the shore. But I, considering how little it would tend to my honor to save my life, and see my captain perish, endeavored to persude them that the ship still swam buoyant, that I hoped the leak was stopped, and that we might proceed on our voyage; but this was unavailing. When I saw myself unable to prevail thus, I desired them to row up and set me on that part of the ice next the ship, whence I should walk to her, and die with my commander.

This being unanimously agreed to, we rowed up to the ice; but when we reached it, I was loth to get out. However, on calling the captain to us, Mr. John Maddick came first, and after him the doctor and some others, which the captain perceiving, came also.

The captain having left the ship, the multitude crowded so eagerly after him that we had like to have spoiled all; but by chance the boat was got off, and twenty-one people in her and hanging to her sides. Some were forced to slip; others perished on the ice, not being able to return to the ship, where the rest were lost.

On the 25th of March, we took a miserable farewell of our distressed brethren, the heart of every one being so overloaded with his own misery as to have little room to pity another. Next, on considering what course to follow, we resolved to make for the shore.

Our only provision was a small barrel of flour, and a five gallon rundlet of brandy, which had been thrown overboard, and was taken up by us. We also took up an old chest, which stood us in good stead, for having but one oar, and our ship's handspikes, and a hatchet being by chance in the boat, we could split the chest, and nail it to the handspikes, which were our oars. Nails we had only by drawing them from different parts of the boat; and the rest of the chest was used to kindle a fire. It also happened that our main tarpauling, which had been newly tarred, was put into the boat. Of it we made a main-sail; and of an old piece of canvas, that had been a sail to a yawl, we made a fore-sail. In this condition we turned towards the shore, and observing the surrounding ice lie north and south, we steered north, and in the morning were clear of it.

Having now got into the ocean, and the wind being still easterly, we hoisted our sail, and steered W. N. W. about fourteen leagues, when we fell in with another field of ice. Attempting to sail through it, we were enclosed by many great islands, which drove so fast together, that we were forced to haul up our boat on the ice, otherwise we should have perished.

Here we lay eleven days without once seeing the sea. As the ice was thick, we caught as many seals as we chose, for they were in great abundance. Our fire-hearth was made of the skin, and the fat melted so easily, that we could boil the lean with it.

But by lying so long in this cold region, the men began to complain of their feet; and our boat being too small to afford room for all, there was always a hideous cry among us of hurting each other, though for this there was no remedy. We kept watch six and six, both for the convenience of room, and to guard against the ice breaking under our boat, which often happened, and then it was necessary to launch, or carry her to a place which we thought strong enough to bear her weight.

In eleven days we saw the sea, and, with great difficulty, got out the boat. We sailed about ten or twelve leagues N. N. W. as before, when we were again enclosed; and this was repeated five several times. The last ice, however, was worse than any before, and although it was so thick that we could not force the boat through it, yet it was not so solid as to bear the weight of a man; therefore, notwithstanding we daily saw enough seals, we could take none of them.

It fortunately happened, that when we parted from the hard ice, we had seven seals in store, and one that we took dead, which was consumed without consulting how it had died.

We were next reduced to short allowance, having only one among us to serve two days, which, with about three ounces of flour, mixed with water, and boiled in the fat of the seal, was all our provision. At length we were obliged to share both feet and skin, each of us allowing a little fat to make a fire. But being constrained to eat the whole, skin and bone also, scarcely boiled, injured our stomachs so much, that some of our number died, and I myself suffered severely.

On getting clear of the loose ice, if the wind was so adverse as to prevent our rowing, we made fast the boat to an island of ice until better weather. Although this sheltered us, we were often in great danger, from the islands driving foul of us, so that it was wonderful we escaped.

We drank the ice mixed with brandy; and our provisions, with good management, lasted until our coming ashore, for it pleased God to save some of us by taking others to himself. Our companions began to die two or three in a day, until we were at last reduced to nine.

The feet of several who died were bit in such a manner by the frost, that, on stripping them, which was done to give the clothes to the survivors, their toes came away with the stockings. The last who died was the boatswain, who lived until the day before we saw land.

Our compass was broken by the last field of ice through which we passed, and soon after we lost our water-bucket, which was used for bailing. Our course was directed by the sun in the day-time, and the stars by night.

Though many other accidents befel us, it pleased the Lord to bring us safe to land, after passing twenty-eight days in the boat.

On the 24th of April, we arrived at Baccalew, and thence repaired to the bay of Verds, in Newfoundland, where we found three men providing for a fishing voyage, who carried us to their house, and gave us such things as they had. But they being indifferently stored, and unable to maintain us, we determined to go to St. John's, notwithstanding some of us were so much frost-bit, as to be obliged to be carried to the boat. Before getting to cape St. Francis, however, the wind veered to the southwest, which compelled us to row all night. In

Loss of the Æneas Transport. *Page* 265.

the morning we reached Portugal Cove, where to our unspeakable joy, some men were found preparing for the summer's fishing. They showed us so much compassion as to launch a boat, and tow us over to Belleisle, and there we were courteously received. All were so weak that we were carried ashore on men's shoulders and we were besides so disfigured with hunger, cold, and the oil of seals, that people could hardly recognise us as men, except for the shape. At Belleisle we remained ten days, when, being somewhat recruited, we went to St. John's. Thus, in all this extremity, God miraculously preserved nine out of ninety-six that were in the ship.

LOSS OF THE ÆNEAS TRANSPORT.

The Æneas transport sailed with three hundred and forty-seven souls on board, including a party of men belonging to the 100th regiment of foot, as also some officers, together with several women and children. About four in the morning of the 23d of October, 1805, the vessel struck violently on a rock, and received such damage that her total wreck soon became evident to all on board. For the first few minutes after this alarming occurrence, the women and children clung to their husbands and fathers; but in a short time, a prodigious wave swept not less than two hundred and fifty of those miserable people into the ocean. The rock whereon the vessel had struck, speedily forced its way through the decks, and then it appears, from her parting, thirty-five of the survivors were driven on a small island before eight in the morning, about a quarter of a mile distant, but when she had entirely gone to pieces.

The narrative of these events was collected from one of the survivors, a soldier of the 100th regiment, who could give no correct account of how he and the others got ashore, but he supposed they were floated in by part of the wreck. He remembered to have observed one of the boys endeavoring to save major Bertram, whose arm was broken by some timber, and he was on the point of sinking; he held him up as long as his strength permitted; but to save his own life, was forced to let go his hold, and the major perished.

The thirty-five men who gained the shore, consisted of part of the regiment, two of whom were officers, lieutenant Dawson and ensign Faulkner, and seven sailors. Immediately on landing, the wind unfortunately changed, so that not an article of any kind was saved from the wreck. Mr. Faulkner was aware of the real situation they had reached, judging the main-land, which they saw about a mile distant, to be Newfoundland, and that they were about three hundred miles distant from the town of St. John's.

After passing one night on the little island, they constructed a raft, by means of which, thirty of them arrived on the main-land. Previous to this, however, four survivors of the shipwreck had died, among whom was the poor fellow who had endeavored to save major Bertram. Another, who had both his legs broken, was missing, as he had crawled away from his comrades, that he might die in quiet. But, eight days afterwards, he was found alive, though in a shocking state, as his feet were frozen off. Yet he survived all this, and reached Quebec at a future period. Most of the party set out, leaving three behind them, who were unable to walk from bruises, and directed their course towards the rising sun; but when the first day had elapsed, lieutenant Dawson became incapable of keeping up with the remainder; and two soldiers staid to attend him. These three toiled onwards without any food, except the berries which they found; and lieutenant Dawson was then unable to stand, unless supported. On reaching the banks of a river, one of the soldiers attempted to carry him across on his back; but having waded up to the neck, he was obliged to return, and lay him down on the bank. There Mr. Dawson entreated his faithful attendants to make the best of their way, and leave him to his fate; and at the same time, affectionately squeezing their hands, he entreated them to inform his father of his melancholy end. Here the soldier, who was one of them, and who related these affecting incidents, burst into a flood of tears before he could proceed. "We staid with him," said he, "until we did not know whether he was alive or dead."

The two survivors continued wandering in a weak and feeble state for twelve days longer, making twenty-six in all from the period of their shipwreck, and subsisting on what they could find on a barren and inhospitable land. But after the first four or five days, they suffered no hunger, for, as they themselves said, their misfortunes were so great as to banish its influence, and to deprive them of the sense of feeling. The snow besides was so deep during the last two days, as to prevent them from getting the berries as usual.

At last they were found by a man belonging to a hunting party, who, little suspecting to see human beings in that desolate region, took them, at a distance, for deer, and had concealed himself behind a fallen tree, with his gun pointed towards one of them, when his dog, leaping towards them, began to bark, and showed his error. When they related their shipwreck, and the sufferings they had endured, tears stole down the cheeks of the huntsman, and, taking the moccasins from his feet, gave them to the poor miserable creatures. He invited them to his hunting-cabin, saying it was only a mile off, though the real distance was at least twelve miles; but, by degrees, he enticed them to proceed, and at length they gained it. On approaching the hut, four or five men came out with long, bloody knives in their hands, when the narrator, turning to his comrade, exclaimed, "After all we have escaped, are we brought here to be butchered and ate up?" But they soon discovered their mistake, for the men had been cutting up some deer, the fruit of their chase, and the appearance of the unfortunate soldiers quickly excited sentiments of pity in their breast, they produced a bottle of rum wherewith they were refreshed.

Every possible comfort was ministered by the hunters

to the unfortunate wanderers, and, from the accounts and description given to them, they set out in quest of the others. They luckily succeeded in finding the man who remained the first day on the island, and also the other two who were unable to leave the shore.

Those two men who had accompanied lieutenant Dawson, appeared to have made but little progress during twenty-six days of travelling, for they were discovered in a place not very remote from whence they set out. Thus, involved among the woods, they must have returned over the same ground that they had passed.

Those whom the huntsman first met endeavored to make them understand where they might find the remains of lieutenant Dawson, and ensign Faulkner, and his party, but they could speak too vaguely of where they had themselves been, to give any pointed directions on the subject. But two of the latter were found by a man on another hunting excursion, about ninety miles distant, apparently lifeless; though on being carried to an adjacent settlement they recovered. Of the whole thirty-five who survived the wreck of the transport, accounts could be heard only of these five.

Ensign Faulkner was a strong, active, enterprising man, and fully capable of adopting whatever means could be devised for preservation. Both he and lieutenant Dawson, who was scarce more than seventeen years of age, were of the greatest promise. While the transport lay about three miles from Portsmouth, they are said to have swum to the ship, when the former climbed up her side, but the latter was nearly exhausted.

A brig from Port, which touched at Newfoundland, carried five of the survivors from thence to Quebec; and when they arrived there in the barrack-square, a most affecting scene ensued. Men and women eagerly flocked around them, with anxious inquiries for some friend or brother who was on board the ill-fated vessel. But all they could answer was, "If you do not see him here, be assured he has perished; for, of three hundred and forty-seven souls, we five Irish lads and two sailors are all that remain alive." The tears and exclamations following these words can scarce be described.

LOSS OF THE NAUTILUS SLOOP OF WAR,

On a rock in the Archipelago.

A MISUNDERSTANDING having originated between the court of Great Britain and the Ottoman Porte, a powerful squadron was ordered to proceed to Constantinople, for the purpose of enforcing compliance with rational propositions. The object, however, proved abortive; and the expedition terminated in a way which did not enhance the reputation of these islands in the eyes of the Turks.

Sir Thomas Louis, commander of the squadron sent to Dardanelles, having charged captain Palmer with despatches of the utmost importance for England, the Nautilus got under weigh at daylight on the third of January, 1807. A fresh breeze from north-east carried her rapidly out of the Hellespont, passing the celebrated castles in the Dardanelles, which severely galled the British. Soon afterwards she passed the island of Tenedos, off the north end of which, two vessels of war were seen at anchor; they hoisted Turkish colors, and in return the Nautilus showed those of Britain. In the course of this day, many of the other islands abounding in the Greek Archipelago came in sight, and in the evening, the ship approached the island of Negropont, lying in 38 30 north latitude, and 24 8 east longitude; but now the navigation became more intricate, from the increasing number of islands, and from the narrow entrance between Negropont and the island of Andros.

The wind still continued to blow fresh, and as night was approaching, with the appearance of being dark and squally, the pilot, who was a Greek, wished to lie to until morning, which was done accordingly; and at daylight the vessel again proceeded. His course was shaped for the island Falconera, in a track which has been so elegantly described by Falconer, in a poem as far surpassing the uncouth productions of modern times, as the Ionian temples surpassed those flimsy structures contributed to render the fame of the originals eternal. This island, and that of Anti Milo, were made in the evening, the latter distant fourteen or sixteen miles from the more extensive island of Milo, which could not then be seen, from the thickness and haziness of the weather.

The pilot never having been beyond the present position of the Nautilus, and declaring his ignorance of the further bearings, now relinquished his charge, which was resumed by the captain. All possible attention was paid to the navigation; and captain Palmer, after seeing Falconera so plainly, and anxious to fulfil his mission with the greatest expedition, resolved to stand on during the night. He was confident of clearing the Archipelago by morning, and himself pricked the course from the chart which was to be steered by the vessel. This he pointed out to his coxswain, George Smith, of whose ability he entertained a high opinion. Then he ordered his bed to be prepared, not having had his clothes off for the three preceding nights, and having scarce had any sleep from the time of leaving the Dardanelles.

A night of extreme darkness followed, with vivid lightning constantly flashing in the horizon; but this circumstance served to inspire the captain with a greater degree of confidence; for being enabled by it to see so much further at intervals, he thought, that should the ship approach any land, the danger would be discovered in sufficient time to be avoided.

The wind continued still increasing; and though the ship carried but little sail, she went at the rate of nine miles an hour, being assisted by a lofty following sea, which with the brightness of the lightning, made the night particularly awful. At half past two in the morning, high land was distinguished, which those who saw it supposed to be the island of Cerigotto, and thence thought all safe, and that every danger had been left behind. The ship's course was altered to pass the island, and she continued on her course until half past four, at the changing of the watch, when the man on the lookout exclaimed, "breakers ahead!" and immediately the vessel struck with a most tremendous crash. Such was the violence of the shock, that people were thrown from their beds, and, on coming upon deck, were obliged to cling to the cordage. All was now confusion and alarm; the crew hurried on deck, which they had scarce time to do when the ladders below gave way, and indeed left many persons struggling in the water, which already rushed into the under part of the ship. The captain it appeared had not gone to bed, and immediately came on deck when the Nautilus struck; there having examined her situation, he immediately went round, accompanied by his second lieutenant, Mr. Nesbit, and endeavored to quiet the apprehensions of the people. He then returned to his cabin, and burnt his papers and private signals. Meantime every sea lifted up the ship, and then dashed her with irresistible force on the rocks; and in a short time, the crew were obliged to resort to the rigging, where they remained an hour, exposed to the surges incessantly breaking over them. There they broke out into the most lamentable exclamations, for their parents, children, and kindred, and the distresses they themselves endured. The weather was so dark and hazy, that the rocks could be seen only at a very small distance, and in two minutes afterwards the ship had struck.

At this time the lightning had ceased, but the darkness of the night was such, that the people could not see the length of the ship from them; their only hope rested in the falling of the main-mast, which they trusted would reach a small rock, which was discovered very near them. Accordingly, about half an hour before daybreak, the main-mast gave way, providentially falling towards the rock, and by means of it they were enabled to gain the land.

The struggles and confusion to which this incident gave birth, can better be conceived than described; some of the crew were drowned, one man had his arm broke, and many were cruelly lacerated; but captain Palmer refused to quit his station, while any individual remained on board; and not until the whole of his people had gained the rock, did he endeavor to save himself. At that time, in consequence of remaining by the wreck, he had received considerable personal injury, and must infallibly have perished, had not some of the seamen ventured through a tremendous sea to his assistance. The boats were staved in pieces; several of the people endeavored to haul in the jolly-boat, which they were incapable of accomplishing.

The hull of the vessel being interposed, sheltered the shipwrecked crew a long time from the beating of the surf; but as she broke up, their situation became more perilous every moment, and they soon found that they should be obliged to abandon the small portion of the rock, which they had reached, and wade to another, apparently somewhat larger. The first lieutenant, by watching the breaking of the seas, had got safely thither, and it was resolved by the rest to follow his example. Scarce was this resolution formed, and attempted to be put into execution, when the people encountered an immense quantity of loose spars, which were immediately washed into the channel which they had to pass; but necessity would admit of no alternative. Many in crossing between the two rocks were severely wounded; and they suffered more in this undertaking than in gaining the first rock from the ship. The loss of their shoes was now felt in particular, for the sharp rocks tore their feet in a dreadful manner, and the legs of some were covered with blood.

Daylight beginning to appear, disclosed the horrors by which those unfortunate men were surrounded. The sea was covered with the wreck of their ill fated ship; many of their unhappy comrades were seen floating away on spars and timbers; and the dead and dying were mingled together without a possibility of the survivors affording assistance to any that might still be rescued. Two short hours had been productive of all this misery, the ship destroyed and her crew reduced to a situation of despair. Their wild and affrighted

Loss of the Nautilus. Page 272.

looks indicated the sensations by which they were agitated; but on being recalled to a sense of their real condition, they saw that they had nothing left but resignation to the will of Heaven.

The shipwrecked mariners now discovered that they were cast away on a coral-rock almost level with the water, about three or four hundred yards long, and two hundred broad. They were at least twelve miles from the nearest islands, which were afterwards found to be those of Cerigotto and Pera, on the north end of Candia, about thirty miles distant. At this time it was reported that a small boat, with several men, had escaped; and although the fact was true, the uncertainty of her fate induced those on the rock to confide in being relieved by any vessel accidentally passing in sight of a signal of distress they had hoisted on a long pole; the neighboring islands being too distant.

The weather had been extremely cold, and the day preceding the shipwreck, ice had lain on the deck; now, to resist its inclemency, a fire was made, by means of a knife and a flint preserved in the pocket of one of the sailors; and with much difficulty, some damp powder, from a small barrel washed on shore, was kindled. A kind of tent was next made, with pieces of old canvass, boards, and such things as could be got about the wreck, and the people were thus enabled to dry the few clothes they had saved. But they passed a long and comfortless night, though partly consoled with the hope of their fire being descried in the dark, and taken for a signal of distress. Nor was this hope altogether disappointed.

When the ship first struck, a small whale-boat was hanging over the quarter, into which, an officer, George Smith, the coxswain, and nine men, immediately got, and lowering themselves into the water, happily escaped. After rowing three or four leagues against a very high sea, and the wind blowing hard, they reached the small island of Pera. This proved to be scarce a mile in circuit, and containing nothing but a few sheep and goats, belonging to the inhabitants of Cerigo, who come in the summer months to carry away their young.

They could find no fresh water, except a small residue from rain in the hole of a rock, and that was barely sufficient though most sparingly used. During the night, having observed the fire above-mentioned, the party began to conjecture that some of their shipmates might have been saved, for until then, they had deemed their destruction inevitable. The coxswain, impressed with this opinion, proposed again hazarding themselves in the boat for their relief, and, although some feeble objections were offered against it, he continued resolute to his purpose, and persuaded four others to accompany him.

About nine in the morning of Tuesday, the second day of the shipwreck, the approach in the little whale-boat was descried by those on the rock; all uttered an exclamation of joy, and in return, the surprise of the coxswain and his crew to find so many of their shipmates still surviving is not to be described. But the surf ran so high as to endanger the safety of the boat, and several of the people imprudently endeavored to get into it. The coxswain tried to persuade captain Palmer to come to him, but he steadily refused, saying, "No, Smith, save your unfortunate shipmates, never mind me." After some little consultation, he desired him to take the Greek pilot on board, and make the best of his way to Cerigotto, where the pilot said there were some families of fishermen, who doubtless would relieve their necessities.

But it appeared as if Heaven had ordained the destruction of this unfortunate crew, for, soon after the boat departed, the wind began to increase, and dark clouds gathering around, excited among those remaining behind, all their apprehensions for a frightful storm. In about two hours it commenced with the greatest fury; the waves rose considerably, and soon destroyed the fire. They nearly covered the rock, and compelled the men to fly to the highest part for refuge, which was the only one that could afford any shelter. There, nearly ninety people passed a night of the greatest horror; and the only means of preventing themselves from being swept away by the surf, which every moment broke over them, was by a small rope fastened round the summit of the rock, and with difficulty holding on by each other.

The fatigues which the people had previously undergone, added to what they now endured, proved too overpowering to many of their number; several became delirious; their strength was exhausted, and they could hold on no longer. Their afflictions were still further aggravated by an apprehension that the wind, veering more to the north, would raise the sea to their present situation, in which case a single wave would have swept them all into oblivion.

The hardships which the crew had already suffered were sufficient to terminate existence, and many had met with deplorable accidents. One in particular, while crossing the channel between the rocks at an unsuitable time, was dashed against them so as to be nearly scalped, and exhibited a dreadful spectacle to his companions. He lingered out the night, and next morning, expired. The more fortunate survivors were but ill prepared to meet the terrible effects of famine; their strength enfeebled, their bodies unsheltered, and abandoned by hope. Nor were they less alarmed for the fate of their boat. The storm came on before she could have reached the intended island, and on her safety, their own depended. But the scene which daylight presented was still more deplorable. The survivors beheld the corpses of their departed shipmates, and some still in the agonies of death. They were themselves altogether exhausted, from the sea's all night breaking over them, and the inclemency of the weather, which was such, that many, among whom was the carpenter, perished from excessive cold.

But this unfortunate crew had now to suffer a mortification, and to witness an instance of inhumanity, which leaves an eternal stain of infamy on those who merit the reproach. Soon after day broke, they observed a vessel with all sail set, coming down before the wind, steering directly for the rock. They made every possible signal of distress which their feeble condition admitted, nor without effect, for they were at last seen by the vessel, which bore to and hoisted out her boat. The joy which this occasioned may be easily conceived, for nothing short of immediate relief was anticipated; and they hastily made preparations for rafts to carry them through the surf, confident that the boat was provided with whatever might administer to their necessities. Approaching still nearer, she came within pistol-shot, full of men dressed in the European fashion, who after having gazed at them a few minutes, the person who steered, waved his hat to them and then rowed off to his ship. The pain of the shipwrecked people at this barbarous proceeding was acute, and heightened even more, by beholding the stranger vessel employed the whole day in taking up the floating remains of that less fortunate one which had so lately borne them.

Perhaps the abandoned wretches guilty of so unfeeling an act may one day be disclosed, and it would surely excite little compassion to learn that they suffered that retribution which such inhuman conduct merits. That people dressed in the habit of Englishmen, though belonging to a different nation, could take advantage of misery instead of relieving it, will scarce seem creditable at the present day, were not some instances of a similar nature related elsewhere than in these volumes.

After this cruel disappointment, and bestowing an anathema which the barbarity of the strangers deserved, the thoughts of the people were, during the remainder of the day, directed towards the return of the boat; and being disappointed there also, their dread that she had been lost was only further confirmed. They began to yield to despondency, and had the gloomy prospect of certain death before them. Thirst then became intolerable; and in spite of being warned against it by instances of the terrific effects ensuing, some in desperation resorted to salt water. Their companions had soon the grief of learning what they would experience by following their example; in a few hours, raging madness followed, and nature could struggle no longer.

Another awful night was to be passed, yet the weather being considerably more moderate, the sufferers entertained hopes that it would be less disastrous than the one preceding; and to preserve themselves from the cold, they crowded close together and covered themselves with their few remaining rags. But the ravings of their comrades who had drank salt water, were truly horrible; all endeavors to quiet them, were ineffectual, and the power of sleep lost its influence. In the middle of the night they were unexpectedly hailed by the crew of the whale-boat; but the only object of the people on the rock was water; they cried out to their shipmates for it, though in vain. Earthern vessels only could have been procured, and these would not bear being conveyed through the surf. The coxswain then said they should be taken off the rock by a fishing-vessel in the morning, and with this assurance they were forced to be content. It was some consolation to know that the boat was safe, and that relief had so far been obtained.

All the people anxiously expected morning, and, for the first time since being on the rock, the sun cheered them with its rays. Still the fourth morning came and no tidings either of the boat or vessel. The anxiety of the people increased, for inevitable death from famine, was staring them in the face. What were they to do for self-preservation? The misery and hunger which they endured, were extreme; they were not ignorant of the means whereby other unfortunate mariners in the like situation had protracted life, yet they viewed them with disgust. Still when they had no alternative, they considered their urgent necessities and found them affording some excuse. Offering prayers to Heaven for forgiveness of the sinful act, they selected a young man who had died the preceding night, and ventured to appease their hunger with human flesh.

Whether the people were relieved is uncertain; for towards evening, death had made hasty strides among them, and many brave men drooped under their hardships. Among these were the captain and first lieutenant, two meritorious officers; and the sullen silence now preserved by the survivors, showed the state of their internal feelings. Captain Palmer was in the twenty-sixth year of his age; amidst his endeavors to comfort those under his command, his companions in misfortune, his personal injuries were borne with patience and resignation, and no murmurs escaped his lips; his virtuous life was prematurely closed by the overwhelming severities of the lamentable catastrophe he had shared.

During the course of another tedious night, many suggested the possibility of constructing a raft which might carry the survivors to Cerigotto; and the wind being favorable, might enable them to reach that island. At all events, attempting this seemed preferable to remaining on the rock to expire of hunger and thirst. Accordingly, at daylight they prepared to put their plan in execution. A number of the larger spars were lashed together, and sanguine hopes of success entertained. At length the moment of launching the raft arrived, but it was only to distress the people with new disappointments, for a few moments sufficed for the destruction of a work on which the strongest of the party had been occupied hours. Several from this unexpected failure became still more desperate, and five resolved to trust themselves on a few small spars slightly lashed together, and on which they had scarce room to stand. Bidding their companions adieu, they launched out into the sea, where they were speedily carried away by unknown currents, and vanished forever from sight.

Towards the same afternoon, the people were again rejoiced by the sight of the whale-boat, and the coxswain told them that he had experienced great difficulty in prevailing on the Greek fishermen of Cerigotto to venture in their boats, from dread of the weather. Neither would they permit him to take them unaccompanied by themselves; he regretted what his comrades had endured, and his grief at not being able yet to relieve them, but encouraged them with hopes, if the weather remained fine, that next day the boats might come. While the coxswain spoke this, twelve or fourteen men imprudently plunged from the rock into the sea, and very nearly reached the boat. Two, indeed, got so far as to be taken in; one was drowned, and the rest providentially recovered their former station. Those who thus escaped could not but be envied by their companions, while they reproached the indiscretion of the others, who, had they reached the boat, would without all doubt have sunk her, and thus unwittingly consigned the whole to irremediable destruction.

The people were wholly occupied in reflections on the passing incidents; but their weakness increased as the day elapsed; one of the survivors described himself as feeling the approach of annihilation, that his sight failed, and his senses became confused; that his strength was exhausted, and his eyes turned towards the setting sun, under the conviction that he should never see it rise again. Yet on the morning he survived, and he was surprised that Providence willed it should still be so, as several strong men had fallen in the course of the night. While the remainder were contemplating their forlorn condition, and judging this the last day of their lives, the approach of the boats was unexpectedly announced. From the lowest ebb of despair, they were now elated with the most extravagant joy; and copious draughts of water, quickly landed, refreshed their languid bodies. Never before did they know the blessings which the single possession of water could afford; it tasted more delicious than the finest wines.

Anxious preparations were made for immediate departure from a place, which had been fatal to so many unhappy sufferers. Of one hundred and twenty-two persons on board the Nautilus when she struck, fifty-eight had perished. Eighteen were drowned, it was supposed, at the moment of the catastrophe, and one in attempting to reach the boat; five were lost on the small raft, and thirty-four died of famine. About fifty now embarked in our fishing vessels, and landed the same evening at the island of Cerigotto, making altogether sixty-four individuals, including those who escaped in the whale-boat. Six days had been passed on the rock, nor had the people, during that time, received any assistance, excepting from the human flesh of which they had participated

The survivors landed at a small creek in the island of Cerigotto, after which they had to go to a considerable distance before reaching the dwellings of their friends. Their first care was to send for the master's mate, who had escaped to the island of Pori, and had been left behind when the whale-boat came down to the rock. He and his companions had exhausted all the fresh water, but lived on the sheep and goats, which they caught among the rocks, and had drank their blood. There they had remained in a state of great uncertainty concerning the fate of those who had left them in the boat.

Though the Greeks could not aid the seamen in the care of their wounds, they treated them with great care and hospitality; but medical assistance being important, from the pain the sufferers endured, and having nothing to bind up their wounds but shirts which they tore into bandages, they were eager to reach Cerigo. The island of Cerigotto, where they had landed, was a dependency on the other, about fifteen miles long, ten broad, and of a barren and unproductive soil, with little cultivation. Twelve or fourteen families of Greek fishermen dwelt upon it, as the pilot had said, who were in a state of extreme poverty. Their houses, or rather huts, consisting of one or two rooms on the same floor, were, in general, built against the side of a rock; the walls composed of clay and straw, and the roof supported by a tree in the centre of the dwelling. Their food was a coarse kind of bread, formed of boiled pease and flour, which was made into a kind of paste for the strangers, with once or twice a bit of kid; and that was all which they could expect from their deliverers. But they made a liquor from corn, which having an agreeable flavor, and being a strong spirit, was drank with avidity by the sailors.

Cerigo was about twenty-five miles distant, and there, it was also said, an English consul resided. Eleven days elapsed, however, before the crew could leave Cerigotto, from the difficulty of persuading the Greeks to adventure to sea, in their frail barks, during tempestuous weather. The wind at last proving fair, with a smooth sea, they bade a grateful adieu to the families of their deliverers, who were tenderly affected by their distresses, and shed tears of regret when they departed. In six or eight hours, they reached Cerigo, where they were received with open arms. Immediately on arrival, they were met by the English vice-consul, Signor Manuel Caluci, a native of the island, who devoted his house, bed, credit, and whole attention to their service; and the survivors unite in declaring their inability to express the obligations under which he laid them. The governor, commandant, bishop, and principal people, all showed equal hospitality, care, and friendship, and exerted themselves to render the time agreeable; insomuch that it was with no little regret that these shipwrecked mariners thought of forsaking the island.

After the people had remained three weeks at Cerigo, they learnt that a Russian ship of-war lay at anchor off the Morea, about twelve leagues distant, being driven in by bad weather, and immediately sent letters to her commanding officer, narrating their misfortunes, and soliciting a passage to Corfu. The master of the Nautilus determined to make the most of the opportunity, took a boat to reach the Russian vessel; but he was at first so unfortunate as to be blown on the rocks in a heavy gale of wind, where he nearly perished, and the boat was staved in pieces. However, he luckily got to the ship, and after some difficulty, succeeded in procuring the desired passage for himself and his companions to Corfu. Her commander, to accommodate them, came down to Cerigo, and anchored at a small port called St. Nicholas, at the eastern extremity of the island. The English embarked on the 5th, but, owing to contrary winds, did not sail until the 15th of February, when they bade farewell to their friends. They next touched at Zante, another small island, abounding in currants and olives; the oil from the latter of which constitutes the chief riches of the people. After remaining there four days, they sailed for Corfu, where they arrived on the 2d of March, 1807, nearly two months after the date of their shipwreck.

LOSS OF HIS B. MAJESTY'S SHIP AMPHION.

The Amphion frigate, Captain Israel Pellow, after having cruised some time in the North Seas, had at length received an order to join the squadron of frigates commanded by Sir Edward Pellow. She was on her passage, when a hard gale of wind occasioning some injury to the fore-mast, obliged her to put back into Plymouth, off which place she then was. She accordingly came into the Sound, anchored there on the 19th, and went up into harbor the next morning.

On the 22d, at about half past four P. M., a violent shock, as of an earthquake, was felt at Stone-house, and extended as far off as the Royal hospital and the town of Plymouth. The sky towards the Dock appeared red, like the effect of a fire; for near a quarter of an hour, the cause of this appearance could not be ascertained, though the streets were crowded with people running different ways in the utmost consternation.

When the alarm and confusion had somewhat subsided, it first began to be known that the shock had been occasioned by the explosion of the Amphion. Several bodies and mangled remains were picked up by the boats in Harmoaze; and their alacrity on this occasion was particularly remarked and highly commended. The few who remained alive of the crew were conveyed, in a mangled state, to the Royal Hospital. As the frigate was originally manned from Plymouth, the friends and relations of her unfortunate ship's company mostly lived in the neighborhood. It is dreadful to relate what a scene took place—arms, legs and lifeless trunks, mangled and disfigured by gunpowder, were collected and deposited at the hospital, having been brought in sacks to be owned. Bodies still living, some with the loss of limbs, others having expired as they were being conveyed thither; men, women and children, whose sons, husbands, and fathers were among the unhappy number, flocking round the gates, entreating admittance. During the first evening nothing was ascertained concerning the cause of this event, though numerous reports were instantly circulated. The few survivors, who, by the following day, had, in some degree, regained the use of their senses, could not give the least account. One man who was brought alive to the Royal Hospital, died before night, another before the following morning; the boatswain and one of the sailors appeared likely, with great care, to do well. Three or four men who were at work in the tops, were blown up with them, and falling into the water, were picked up with very little hurt. These, with the two before mentioned, and one of the sailors, wives, were supposed to be the only survivors, besides the captain and two of the lieutenants.

The following particulars were, however, collected from the examination of several persons before Sir Richard King, the port-admiral, and the information procured from those, who saw the explosion from the Dock.

The first person known to have observed any thing was a young midshipman in the Cambridge guard-ship, lying not far distant from the place where the Amphion blew up; who having a great desire to observe every thing relative to a profession into which he had just entered, was looking through a glass at the frigate, as she lay along side of the sheer-hulk, and was taking in her bowsprit. She was lashed to the hulk; and the Yarmouth, an old receiving ship, was lying on the opposite side, quite close to her, and both within a few yards of the Dock-yard jetty. The midshipman said, that the Amphion suddenly appeared to rise altogether upright from the surface of the water, until he nearly saw the keel; the explosion then succeeded; the masts seemed to be forced up into the air, and the hull instantly to sink. All this passed in the space of two minutes.

The man who stood at the Dock-yard stairs, said, that the first he heard of it was a kind of hissing noise, and then followed the explosion, when he beheld the masts blown up into the air. It was very strongly reported that several windows were broken in the Dock by the explosion, and that in the Dock-yard, much mischief was done by the Amphion's guns going off when she blew up; but though the shock was felt as far off as Plymouth, and at Stone-house, enough to shake the windows, yet it is a wonderful and miraculous fact, that surrounded as she was in the harbor, with ships close along-side of the jetty, and lashed to another vessel, no damage was done to any thing but herself. It is dreadful to reflect, that owing to their intention of putting to sea the next day, there were nearly one hundred men, women and children, more than her complement on board, taking leave of their friends, besides the company who were at two dinners given in the ship, one of which was by the captain.

Captain Israel Pellow, and captain William Swaffield, of his Majesty's ship Overyssel, who was at dinner with him and the first lieutenant, were drinking their wine; when the first explosion threw them off their seats, and struck them against the carlings of the upper deck, so as to stun them. Captain Pellow, however, had sufficient presence of mind to fly to the cabin-windows, and seeing the two hawsers, one slack in the bit and the other taut, threw himself with an amazing leap, which he afterwards said, nothing but his sense of danger could have enabled him to take, upon the latter, and by that means saved himself from the general destruction, though his face had been badly cut against the carlings, when he was thrown from his seat. The first lieutenant saved himself in the same manner, by jumping out of the window, and by being also a remarkably good swimmer; but captain Swaffield, being, as it was supposed, more stunned, did not escape. His body was found on the twenty-second of October, with his skull fractured, appearing to have been crushed between the sides of the vessels.

The sentinel at the cabin door happened to be looking at his watch; how he escaped no one can tell, not even himself. He was, however, brought on shore, and but little hurt; the first thing he felt was, that his watch was dashed out of his hands, after which he was no longer sensible of what happened to him. The boatswain was standing on the cat-head; the bowsprit had been stepped for three hours; the gammoning and every thing on; and he was directing the men in rigging out the jib-boom, when suddenly he felt himself driven upwards and fell into the sea. He then perceived that he was entangled in the rigging, and had some trouble to get clear; when being taken up by a boat belonging to one of the men of war, they found that his arm was broken. One of the surviving seamen declared to an officer of rank, that he was preserved in the following truly astonishing manner: —He was below at the time the Amphion blew up, and went to the bottom of the ship; he recollected that he had a knife in his pocket, and taking it out, cut his way through the companion of the gun-room, which was already shattered with the explosion; then letting himself up to the surface of the water, he swam unhurt to the shore. He showed his knife to the officer, and declared he had been under water full five minutes.

It was likewise said, that one of the sailor's wives had a young child in her arms; the fright of the shock made her take such fast hold of it, that though the upper part of her body alone remained, the child was found alive, locked fast in her arms, and likely to do well.

Mr. Spry, an auctioneer who had long lived in great respectability at Dock, with his son and god-son, had gone on board to visit a friend, and were all lost.

About half an hour before the frigate blew up, one of her lieutenants, and lieutenant Campbell of the marines, and some of the men got into the boat at the dock-yard stairs, and went off to the ship. Lieutenant Campbell had some business to transact at the Marine barracks in the morning, and continuing there some time, was engaged by the officers to stay to dinner and spend the evening with them. Some persons, however, who had, in the interval, come from the Amphion, informed lieutenant Campbell there were some letters on board for him. As they were some which he was extremely anxious to receive, he left the barracks about half an hour before dinner to fetch them, intending to return immediately;

but while he was on board, the ship blew up. He was a young man universally respected and lamented by the corps, as well as by all who knew him. One of the lieutenants who lost his life was the only support of an aged mother and sister, who, at his death, had neither friend nor relation left to comfort and protect them. The number of people who were afterwards daily seen at Dock, in deep mourning for their lost relatives, was truly melancholy.

Captain Pellow was taken up by the boats and carried to the Commissioner Fanshaw's house, in the dock-yard, very weak with the exertions he had made, and so shocked with the distressing cause of them, that he at first appeared scarcely to know where he was, or to be sensible of his situation. In the course of a day or two, when he was a little recovered, he was removed to the house of a friend, Dr. Hawker of Plymouth.

Sir Richard King had given a public dinner in honor of the coronation. Captain Charles Rowley, of the Unite frigate, calling in the morning, was engaged to stay, and excused himself from dining, as he had previously intended, on board the Amphion.

Captain Darby of the Bellerophon, was also to have dined with captain Pellow, and had come round in his boat from Cawsand Bay; but having to transact some business concerning the ship with Sir Richard King, it detained him half an hour longer at Stone-house than he expected. He had just gone down to the beach, and was stepping into the boat to proceed up to Harmoaze when he heard the fatal explosion. Captain Swaffield was to have sailed the next day, so that the difference of twenty four hours would have saved that much lamented and truly valuable officer. His brother, Mr. J. Swaffield, of the Pay-Office, being asked to the same dinner, had set off with him from Stone-house, but before he had reached the Dock, a person came after him upon business, which obliged him to return, and thus saved him from sharing his brother's untimely fate.

Many conjectures were formed concerning the cause of this catastrophe. Some conceived it to be owing to neglect, as the men were employed in drawing the guns, and contrary to rule, had not extinguished all the fires, though the dinners were over. This, however, the first lieutenant declared to be impossible, as they could not be drawing the guns, the key of the magazine hanging, to his certain knowledge, in his cabin, at the time. Some of the men likewise declared that the guns were drawn in the Sound, before they came to Harmoaze. It was also insinuated, that it was done intentionally, as several of the bodies were afterwards found without clothes, as if they had prepared to jump overboard before the ship could have time to blow up. As no mutiny had ever appeared in the ship, it seems unlikely that such a desperate plot should have been formed, without any one who survived, having the least knowledge of it. It is, besides, a well-known fact, that in almost every case of shipwreck, where there is a chance of plunder, there are wretches so destitute of the common feelings of humanity as to hover round the scene of horror, in hopes, by stripping the bodies of the dead, and seizing whatever they can lay their hands on, to benefit themselves.

It was the fore-magazine which took fire; had it been the after one, much more damage must have ensued. The moment the explosion was heard, Sir Richard arose from dinner, and went in his boat on board the hulk, where the sight he beheld was dreadful; the deck covered with blood, mangled limbs and entrails blackened with gunpowder, the shreds of the Amphion's pendant and rigging hanging about her, and pieces of her shattered timbers strewed all around. Some people at dinner in the Yarmouth, though at a very small distance, declared that the report they heard did not appear to be louder than the firing of a cannon from the Cambridge, which they imagined it to be, and had never risen from dinner, till the confusion upon deck led them to think that some accident had happened.

At low water, the next day, about a foot and a half of one of the masts appeared above water; and for several days, the dock-yard men were employed in collecting the shattered masts and yards, and dragging out what they could procure from the wreck. On the twenty-ninth, part of the fore-chains was hauled, shattered and splintered, also the head and cut-water.

On the 3rd of October, an attempt was made to raise the Amphion, between the two frigates, the Castor and Iphigenia, which were accordingly moored on each side of her; but nothing could be got up, excepting a few pieces of the ship, one or two of her guns, some of the men's chests, chairs, and part of the furniture of the cabin. Some bodies floated out from between decks, and among the rest a midshipman's. These, and all that could be found, were towed round by boats through Stone-house bridge, up to the Royal Hospital stairs, to be interred in the burying-ground. The sight for many weeks was truly dreadful; the change of tide washing out the putrid bodies, which were towed round by the boats when they would scarcely hold together.

Bodies continued to be found so late as the 30th of November, when the Amphion having been dragged round to another part of the dock-yard jetty, to be broken up, the body of a woman was washed out from between decks. A sack was also dragged up, containing gunpowder, covered over at the top with biscuit, and this in some measure confirmed an idea which had before gained ground, that the gunner had been stealing powder to sell, and had concealed what he could get out by degrees, in the above manner; and that, thinking himself safe on a day when every one was entertaining his friends, he had carelessly been among the gunpowder without taking the necessary precautions. As he was said to have been seen at Dock very much in liquor in the morning, it seems probable that this might have been the cause of a calamity as sudden as it was dreadful.

LOSS OF THE HELEN McGREGOR.

The following is a description, by a passenger, of one of the most fatal steam-boat disasters that has ever occurred on the western waters.

"On the morning of the 24th of February, 1830, the Helen M'Gregor stopped at Memphis, on the Mississippi river, to deliver freight, and land a number of passengers, who resided in that section of Tennessee. The time occupied in so doing could not have exceeded three quarters of an hour. When the boat landed, I went ashore to see a gentleman with whom I had some business. I found him on the beach, and after a short conversation, I returned to the boat. I recollect looking at my watch as I passed the gang-way. It was half past eight o'clock. A great number of persons were standing on what is called the boiler-deck, being that part of the upper deck situated immediately over the boilers. It was crowded to excess, and presented one dense mass of human bodies. In a few minutes we sat down to breakfast in the cabin. The table, although extending the whole length of the cabin, was completely filled, there being upwards of sixty cabin passengers, among whom were several ladies and children. The number of passengers on board, deck and cabin united, was between four and five hundred. I had almost finished my breakfast, when the pilot rang his bell for the engineer to put the machinery in motion. The boat having just shoved off, I was in the act of raising my cup to my lips, the tingling of the pilot bell yet on my ear, when I heard an explosion, resembling the discharge of a small piece of artillery—the report was perhaps louder than usual in such cases, for an exclamation was half uttered by me that the gun was well loaded, when the rushing sound of steam, and the rattling of glass in some of the cabin windows, checked my speech and told too well what had occurred. I almost involuntarily bent my head and body down to the floor—a vague idea seemed to shoot across my mind that more than one boiler might burst, and that by assuming this posture, the destroying matter would pass over without touching me.

The general cry of "a boiler has burst" resounded from one end of the table to the other; and, as if by a simultaneous movement, all started on their feet. Then commenced a general race to the ladies' cabin, which lay more towards the stern of the boat. All regard to order or deference to sex seemed to be lost in the struggle for which should be first and farthest removed from the dreaded boilers. The danger had already passed away! I remained standing by the chair on which I had been previously sitting. Only one person or two staid in the cabin with me. As yet no more than half a minute had elapsed since the explosion; but, in that brief space how had the scene changed! In that "drop of time" what confusion, distress and dismay! An instant before, and all were in the quiet repose of security—another, and they were overwhelmed with alarm and consternation. It is but justice to say that in this scene of terror, the ladies exhibited a degree of firmness worthy of all praise. No screaming, no fainting; their fears, when uttered, were for their husbands and children, not for themselves.

I advanced from my position to one of the cabin-doors, for the purpose of inquiring who were injured, when just as I reached it, a man entered at the opposite one, both his hands covering his face, and exclaiming "Oh God, Oh God! I am lost! I am ruined!" He immediately began to tear off his clothes. When stripped, he presented a most shocking and afflicting spectacle; his face was entirely black—his body without a particle of skin. He had been flayed alive. He gave me his name, and place of abode—then sank in a state of exhaustion and agony on the floor. I assisted in placing him on a mattrass taken from one of the berths, and covered him with blankets. He complained of heat and cold as at once oppressing him. He bore his torments with manly fortitude, yet a convulsive shriek would occasionally burst from him. His wife, his children, were his constant theme; it was hard to die without seeing them—"it was hard to go without bidding them one farewell!" Oil and cotton were applied to his wounds; but he soon became insensible to earthly misery. Before I had done attending to him, the whole floor of the cabin was covered with unfortunate sufferers. Some bore up under the horrors of their situation with a degree of resolution amounting to heroism. Others were wholly overcome by the sense of pain, the suddenness of the disaster, and the near approach of death, which even to them was evident—whose pangs they already felt. Some implored us, as an act of humanity, to complete the work of destruction, and free them from present suffering. One entreated the presence of a clergyman to pray by him, declaring he was not fit to die. I inquired; none could be had. On every side were to be heard groans and mingled exclamations of grief and despair.

To add to the confusion, persons were every moment running about to learn the fate of their friends and relatives, fathers, sons, brothers; for, in this scene of unmixed calamity, it was impossible to say who were saved, or who had perished. The countenances of many were so much disfigured as to be past recognition. My attention, after some time, was particularly drawn towards a poor fellow who lay unnoticed on the floor, without uttering a single word of complaint. He was at a little distance removed from the rest. He was not much scalded, but one of his thighs was broken, and a principal artery had been severed, from which the blood was gushing rapidly. He betrayed no displeasure at the apparent neglect with which he was treated—he was perfectly calm. I spoke to him; he said "he was very weak; but felt himself going—it would soon be over." A gentleman ran for one of the physicians; he came, and declared that if expedition were used, he might be preserved by amputating the limb; but that, to effect this, it would be necessary to remove him from the boat. Unfortunately, the boat was not sufficiently near to run a plank ashore. We were obliged to wait until it could be close-hauled. I stood by him calling for help; we placed him on a mattrass, and bore him to the guards; there we were detained some time, from the cause I have mentioned. Never did any thing appear to me so slow as the movement of those engaged in hauling the boat.

I knew and he knew, that delay was death—that life was fast ebbing. I could not take my gaze from his face, there all was coolness and resignation. No word or gesture indicative of impatience escaped him. He perceived by my loud, and perhaps angry tone of voice, how much I was excited by what I thought the barbarous slowness of those around; he begged me not to take so much trouble; that they were doing their best. At length we got him on shore. It was too late; he was too much exhausted, and died immediately after the amputation.

So soon as I was relieved from attending on those in the cabin, I went to examine that part of the boat where the boiler had burst. It was a complete wreck—a picture of destruction. It bore ample testimony of the tremendous force of that power which the ingenuity of man has brought to his aid. The steam had given every thing a whitish hue—the boilers were displaced—the deck had fallen down—the machinery was broken and disordered. Bricks, dirt, and rubbish, were scattered about. Close by the bowsprit was a large rent through which, I was told, the boiler after exploding, had passed out, carrying one or two men in its mouth. Several dead bodies were lying around; their fate had been an enviable one compared with that of others; they could scarcely have been conscious of a pang ere they had ceased to be. On the starboard wheel-house lay a human body, in which life was not yet extinct, though apparently, there was no sensibility remaining. The body must have been thrown from the boiler deck, a distance of thirty feet. The whole of the forehead had been blown away; the brains were still beating. Tufts of hair, shreds of clothing, and splotches of blood might be seen in every direction. A piece of skin was picked up by a gentleman on board, which appeared to have been peeled off by the force of the steam; it extended from the middle of the arm down to the tips of the fingers, the nails adhering to it. So dreadful had been the force that not a particle of the flesh adhered to it; the most skilful operator could scarcely have effected such a result. Several died from inhaling the steam or gas, whose skin was almost uninjured.

The number of lives lost will, in all probability, never be distinctly known. Many were seen flung into the river, most of whom sank to rise no more. Could the survivors have been kept together until the list of passengers was called, the precise loss would have been ascertained; that, however, though it had been attempted, would, under the circumstances, have been next to impossible.

Judging from the crowd which I saw on the boiler-deck immediately before the explosion, and the statement which I received as to the number of those who succeeded in swimming out, after they were cast into the river, I am inclined to believe that between fifty and sixty must have perished.

The cabin passengers escaped, owing to the peculiar construction of the boat. Just behind the boilers were several large iron posts, supporting, I think, the boiler deck; across each post was a large circular plate of iron of between one and two inches in thickness. One of those posts was placed exactly opposite the head of the boiler which burst, being the second one on the starboard side. Against this plate, the head struck, and penetrated to the depth of an inch, then broke and flew off at an angle, entering a cotton-bale to the depth of a foot. The boiler-head was in point blank range with the breakfast-table in the cabin, and had it not been obstructed by the iron post must have made a clear sweep of those who were seated at the table.

To render any satisfactory account of the cause which produced the explosion, can hardly be expected from one who possesses no scientific or practical knowledge on the subject, and who previously thereto was paying no attention to the management of the boat. The captain appeared to be very active and diligent in attending to his duty. He was on the boiler-deck when the explosion occurred; was materially injured by that event, and must have been ignorant of the mismanagement, if any there was.

From the engineer alone, could the true explanation be afforded; and, if indeed it was really attributable to negligence, it can scarcely be supposed he will lay the blame on himself. If I might venture a suggestion in relation thereto, I would assign the following causes:—That the water in the starboard boilers had become low, in consequence of that side of the boat resting upon the ground during our stay at Memphis; that, though the fires were kept up some time before we shoved off, the head which burst had been cracked for a considerable time; that the boiler was extremely heated, and the water thrown in when the boat was again in motion, was at once converted into steam, and the flues not being sufficiently large to carry it off as quickly as it was generated, nor the boiler-head of a strength capable of resisting its action, the explosion was a natural result."

LOSS OF THE SHIP BEVERLY.

The ship Beverly, captain Moore, bound to Valparaiso, was burnt at sea, on the 13th November, 1826. She was upwards of seven hundred tons burthen, owned by Israel Thorndike, of Boston, and the value of the ship and cargo was estimated at one hundred and eighteen thousand dollars.

On the 13th of November, latitude 6, 26, longitude 27, 2, at half past three, P. M., the ship was discovered to be on fire in the fore peak, and every exertion was made to extinguish it, for three hours, but without success. From the inflammable nature of the cargo, (which consisted of tar, rosin, pitch, turpentine, linseed-oil, spirits and cabinet furniture,) the fire spread with alarming rapidity. They succeeded in getting out the boats, into which the officers and crew were divided, and in a few minutes left her, having previously taken in a quantity of provisions. They lay-by to the windward, until about ten o'clock, when the ship had burnt to the water's edge, and then shaped their course for the coast of Brazil. Finding their progress retarded by waiting for each other, they mutually agreed to separate, on the third day after leaving the ship. There were nine in the pinnace, fifteen in the long-boat, and six in the whale-boat, making a total of thirty persons cast adrift on the open ocean.

On the 3d of December, the pinnace landed at Faraibo, three weeks after abandoning the ship. Captain Moore stated that while he was in the boat, he had fine weather, and with the aid of a sail, averaged over ninety miles a day, using the oars but once during the passage. He computed the distance run by the boat at nearly sixteen hundred miles. The fire originated through the carelessness of the cook, who went below with a lantern, and it is supposed took the candle out. The flames spread so rapidly, that he had his clothes and skin burnt, before he could be extricated, and finally died of his wounds in the boat.

One of the boys, who arrived with captain Moore in the pinnace, after having escaped the perils of "fire and flood," was so unfortunate as to have one of his legs bit off by a shark, while bathing, soon after he landed.

LOSS OF THE FRANCES MARY.

The Frances Mary was a new ship, of about four hundred tons burthen, commanded by captain Kendall, and bound from New Brunswick to Liverpool, laden with timber. We publish the following particulars of this dreadful disaster as related by captain Kendall.

Sailed from St. Johns, N. B., January 18, 1826. February 1, strong gales from the W. N. W.; carried away the main-topmast and mizzen-mast head; hove to, got boat's sails in the main rigging, to keep the ship to the wind. At 11, P. M., shipped a heavy sea, which washed away the caboose, jolly-boat, and disabled five men. February 2d, cleared away the wreck and made sail before the wind; strong breezes. February 5, 11, A. M., strong gales, with a heavy sea; clewed up the sails and hove to, head to the southward; shipped a sea, which carried away the long-boat, companion, tiller, the best bower-chain, unshipped the rudder, and washed a man overboard, who was afterwards saved. At 10. P. M. another heavy sea struck us, which stove in our stern. Cut away our foremast and both bower anchors, to keep the ship to the wind. Employed in getting what provision we could, by knocking out the bow-port; saved fifty pounds of bread and five pounds of cheese, which we stowed in the maintop. Got the master's wife and female passenger up, whilst we were clearing away below, lightening the ship; most of the people slept in the top. At daylight, found Patrick Conney hanging by his legs to the cat-harpins, dead from fatigue; committed his body to the deep.

Feburary 6, at 8, A. M., saw a strange sail standing towards us; made signals of distress,—stranger spoke us, and remained in company twenty-four hours, but gave us no assistance; the American making an excuse that the sea was running too high. Made a tent of spare canvass on the forecastle—put the people on an allowance of a quarter of a biscuit a day. February 8, saw a brig to leeward—strong gales. February 9, 10, A. M., observed the same vessel to windward—made the signal of distress; stranger bore up and showed American colors. February 10, she spoke us, asking how long we had been in that situation, and what we intended to do, if we intended leaving the ship? Answered yes. He then asked if we had any rigging? Answered yes. Night coming on, and blowing hard, saw no more of the stranger. Suffered from hunger and thirst.

On the 11th, saw a large ship to the northward—did not speak her; wore head to the northward. At this time all our provisions were out; suffered much from hunger, having received no nourishment for nine days. February 12, departed this life, James Clark, seaman;—read prayers, and committed his body to the deep. We were at this time on a half gill of water a day, and suffered much from hunger. During the whole period of being on the wreck we were wet from top to toe. February 22, John Wilson, seaman, died at 10, A. M.; preserved the body of the deceased, cut him up in quarters, washed them overboard, and hung them up on pins.

February 23, J. Moore died, and was thrown overboard, having eaten part of him, such as the liver and heart. From this date to Saturday, 5th of March, the following number perished from hunger, viz. Henry Davis, a Welsh boy, Alex. Kelley, seaman, John Jones, apprentice boy, nephew of the owner, James Frier, cook, Daniel Jones, seaman, John Hutchinson, seaman, and John Jones, a boy—threw the last named overboard, his blood being bitter.

James Frier was working his passage home, under a promise of marriage to Ann Saunders, the female passenger who attended on the master's wife, and who, when she heard of Frier's death, shrieked a loud yell, then snatching a cup from Clerk, the mate, cut her late intended husband's throat and drank his blood! insisting that she had the greatest right to it. A scuffle ensued, but the heroine got the better of her adversary, and then allowed him to drink one cup to her two.

February 26, on or about this day an English brig hove in sight; hoisted the ensign downward; stranger hauled his wind towards us, and hauled his foresail up when abreast of us; kept his course about one mile distant—set his foresail, and we soon lost sight of him—fresh breeze with a little rain—the sea quite smooth, but he went off, having shown English colors. Had he at this time taken us off the wreck, much of the subsequent dreadful sufferings would have been spared us.

March 7. His B. M. ship Blonde came in sight, and to our relief, in latitude 44, 43, north, longitude 31, 57, west. Words are quite inadequate to express our feelings, as well as those which Lord Byron and our deliverers most evidently possessed, when they had come to rescue six of their fellow-creatures, two of them females, from a most awful, lingering, but certain death. It came on to blow during the night a fresh gale, which would no doubt have swept us all overboard. Lieutenant Gambier came in the ship's cutter to bring us from the wreck. He observed to us, "You have yet, I perceive, fresh meat." To which we were compelled to reply, 'No, sir, it is part of a man, one of our unfortunate crew,—it was our intention to put ourselves on an allowance even of this food, this evening, had not you come to our relief." The master's wife, who underwent all the most horrid sufferings which the human understanding can imagine, bore them much better than could possibly have been expected. She is now, although much emaciated, a respectable, good-looking woman, about twenty-five years of age, and the mother of a boy seven years old. But what must have been the extremity of want to which she was driven, when she ate the brains of one of the apprentices, saying it was the most delicious thing she ever tasted; and it is still more melancholy to relate, that the person, whose brains she was thus forced by hunger to eat, had been three times wrecked before, but was providentially picked up by a vessel, after being twenty-two days on the wreck, water-logged: but in the present instance, he perished, (having survived similar sufferings for a space of twenty-nine days,) and then became food for his remaining shipmates!

Ann Saunders, the other female, had more strength in her calamity than most of the men. She performed the duty of cutting up and cleaning the dead bodies, keeping two knives for the purpose in her monkey jacket; and when the breath was announced to have flown, she would sharpen her knives, bleed the deceased in the neck, drink his blood, and cut him up as usual. From want of water, those who perished drank their own urine and salt water. They became foolish, and crawled upon their hands round the deck when they could, and died, generally, raving mad!

After floating about the ocean for some months, this ill-fated vessel was fallen in with by an English ship, and carried into Jamaica, where she was refitted, and again sent to sea. The putrid remains of human bodies, which had been the only food of the unfortunate survivors, was found on board the vessel.

LOSS OF THE SHIP ALBION.

THE following account of this melancholy shipwreck was given by Henry Cammyer, first mate of the vessel.

We sailed from New York on the first of April, 1822, in the ship Albion, of four hundred and forty-seven tons, with a crew, including officers, of twenty-five in number, besides twenty-three cabin, and six steearge passengers; making in the whole fifty-four persons, only nine of whom now live to relate the melancholy tale. For the first twenty days, we continued our voyage with moderate and favorable weather; and at about half past one o'clock, in the afternoon of Sunday the 21st, we made the land. The Fastnet rock bore by compass, E. N. E., distant about three leagues. At two, made cape Clear, bearing east and by north, distance about two leagues. Thick and foggy, blowing fresh, and heavy squalls from the southward. Ship heading up E. S. E., carrying all prudent sail, to crowd the ship off the land. The gale increasing, shortened sail occasionally. At four o'clock, then under double reefed topsails, foresail, and mainsail, carried away the foreyard, and split the foretopsail. Got the pieces of the yard down, and prepared to get another yard up. Gale increasing, about half past four, took in the mainsail and mizzen-topsail, and set the main-trysail. Night coming on, cleared the decks for working ship. At half past eight, gale still increasing, with a high sea. Shipped a heavy sea, which threw the ship on her beam-ends, and carried away the mainmast by the deck, the head of the mizzen-mast, and fore-topmast, and swept the decks clear of every thing, including boats, caboose house, bulwarks, and compasses, and stove in all the hatches, state rooms, and bulwarks in the cabin, which was nearly filled with water. At the same moment, six of the crew and one cabin passenger, Mr. A. B. Convers, of Troy, N. Y., were swept overboard.

The ship being unmanageable, and the sea making a complete breach over her, we were obliged to lash ourselves to the pumps, and being in total darkness, without correct compasses, could not tell how the ship's head lay. The axes being swept away, had no means of clearing the wreck. About one o'clock, made the light of the Old Head of Kinsale, but could not ascertain how it bore; and at two, found the ship embayed. The captain, anticipating our melancholy fate, called all the passengers up, who had not before been on deck. Many of them had received considerable injury when the sea first struck her, and were scarcely able to come on deck; others had been incessantly assisting at the pumps; and it is an interesting fact, that Miss Powell, an amiable young lady, who was on board, was desirous to be allowed to take her turn. One gentleman, who had been extremely ill during the passage, Mr. William Everhart, of Chester, Penn., was too feeble to crawl to the deck without assistance, but strange to say, he was the only cabin passenger who was saved.

Our situation at that moment, is indescribable, and I can scarcely dwell upon, much less attempt to detail, its horrors. About three o'clock, the ship struck on a reef, her upper works beat in over the rocks, and in about half an hour after coming in over the first reef, she parted midships, and her quarter-deck drifted in on the top of the inside ledge, immediately under the cliffs. Up to the period of her parting, nearly twenty persons were clinging to the wreck, among whom were two females, Mrs. Pye, and Miss Powell. Captain Williams had, with several others, been swept away soon after she struck; a circumstance which may be attributed to the very extraordinary exertions which he used, to the last moment, for the preservation of the lives of the unfortunate passengers and crew.

A short time before she parted, myself and six of the crew got away from the vessel. After gaining a rock in a very exhausted state, I was washed off, but, by the assistance of Providence, was enabled, before the return of the sea, to regain it; and before I could attempt to climb the cliff, which was nearly perpendicular, I was obliged to lie down, to regain a little strength, after the severe bruises and contusions I had received on the body and feet. One of the passengers, colonel Augustine J. Prevost, reached the rock with me alive, but was, together with one of the stewards, washed off and drowned.

Some of the passengers were suffocated on deck and in the fore rigging, and some must have been destroyed by an anchor which was loose on the forecastle before the ship parted. It is scarcely possible to describe the devastation which followed. The entire cargo, consisting of cotton, rice, turpentine, and beeswax, together with a quantity of silver and gold, to a large amount, was in all directions beaten to pieces by the severity of the sea, without a possibility of saving it.

Very soon after we got upon the cliffs, my poor shipmates and myself found our way to a peasant's cottage. Early in the morning, Mr. James B. Gibbens, of Ballinspittle, came to me from the wreck, where he had been since five o'clock, endeavoring to save some of the lives. He most humanely sent Mr. Everhart, Mr. Raymond, the boy, and myself, to his house, about a mile from the spot, where we experienced the kindest and most hospitable attention. The remaining survivors were taken home by Mr. Purcell, steward of Thomas Rochfort, Esq. of Garretstown, where every attention was paid to them. Coffins were provided by Mr. Purcell, according to the orders of Mr. Rochfort, and the bodies that were found, were interred at Templetrine churchyard, about four miles from Kinsale and one from the fatal spot. The Rev. Mr. Evanson kindly officiated on the occasion. On Tuesday, I went to Kinsale to note a protest, and then first met Mr. Mark, the consul for the United States, who happened to be at Kinsale at that time on other business. He came over and gave directions for clothing the sufferers, who were destitute of every thing.

Unremitting exertions were used daily for the recovery of the goods and specie, but without success, as none of the cargo, and but a small part of the materials of the

26

vessel, were saved, together with property in specie to the amount of about five thousand pounds.

The following is a correct list of the crew and passengers.

Crew. John Williams, captain, drowned; Henry Cammyer, first mate, saved; Edward Smith, second mate, drowned; William Hyate, boatswain, saved; Alexander Adams, carpenter, Harman Nelson, Harman Richardson, Henry Whittrell, William Trisserly, James Wiley, Robert McLellan, and Thomas Goodman, drowned; John Simson, John Richards, Francis Bloom, and Ebenezer Warner, saved; Samuel Wilson and William Snow, boys, drowned; William Dockwood, drowned, body found and interred; Hierom Raymond, saved; Lloyd Potter, Samuel Penny, stewards, and Francis Isaac, boy, blacks, all drowned; Thomas Hill and Adam Johnson, cooks, blacks, both drowned, bodies found and interred.

Cabin Passengers. W. Everhart, Esq., of Chester, Penn., saved; lieutenant-colonel Augustine J. Prevost, major William Gough, of the 68th regiment; Rev. G. R. G. Hill, last from Jamaica; Nelson Ross, of Troy, N. Y.; William H. Dwight, of Boston; Mr. Beynon, of London; professor Fisher, of New-Haven college; Mr. William Proctor, of New York; Mr. and Mrs. Hyde Clark, Mrs. Pye and Miss Powell, of Canada, daughter of Judge Powell, all drowned, found and interred; Mr. A. B. Convers, of Troy, N. Y., and madame Gardiner and son, of Paris, drowned; (madame G.'s body was found and interred;) five French gentlemen, names unknown, (except Mr. Victor Millicent,) drowned, found and interred.

Steerage Passengers. Stephen Chase, of Canada, saved; Mrs. Mary Brereton, and Mary Hunt, drowned, found and interred; Mr. Harrison, carpenter, Mr. Baldwin, cotton spinner, from Yorkshire, England, and Dr. Carver, a veterinary surgeon, drowned.

Four bodies were also found and interred that could not be recognised.

The following account of the wreck of the Albion was

communicated to the editor of the Village Record, of Chester, Pennsylvania, by William Everhart, Esq., after his return to the United States. Mr. Everhart, it will be recollected, was the only cabin passenger who was saved, out of twenty-three persons. As his statement affords some additional particulars of the disaster that may be interesting, we publish it entire.

Mr. Everhart says, that up to the 21st of April, the voyage had been prosperous and pleasant for the season, though he had himself suffered much from sea-sickness, and was almost constantly confined to his room. The storm of the day, it was supposed, was over; they were near to the coast, and all hands flattered themselves that in a short time, they should reach their destined harbor; but, about nine o'clock in the evening, a heavy sea struck the ship, swept several seamen from the deck, carried away her masts, and stove in her hatchways, so that every wave which passed over her, ran into the hold without any thing to stop it,—the railings were carried away, and the wheel which aided them to steer. In short, that fatal wave left the Albion a wreck. She was then about twenty miles from the shore, and captain Williams steadily and coolly gave his orders; he cheered the passengers and crew with the hope that the wind would shift, and before morning blow off shore. The sea was very rough, and the vessel unmanageable; and the passengers were obliged to be tied to the pumps, that they might work them. All who could do no good on deck, retired below, but the water was knee deep in the cabin, and the furniture floating about, rendered the situation dangerous and dreadful.

All night long, the wind blew a gale, directly on shore, towards which the Albion was drifting, at the rate of about three miles an hour. The complete hopelessness of their situation was known to few except captain Williams. The coast was familiar to him; and he must have seen in despair and horror, throughout the night, the certainty of their fate. At length, the ocean, dashing and roaring upon the precipice of rocks, told them that their hour was come. Captain Williams summoned all on deck, and briefly told them that the ship must soon strike; it was impossible to preserve her. Mr. Everhart says, that he was the last that left the cabin. Professor Fisher was behind, but he is confident that he never came on deck, but perished below. Some, particularly the females, expressed their terror in wild shrieks. Major Gough, of the British army, remarked, that "death, come as he would, was an unwelcome messenger, but that they must meet him like men." Very little was said by the others; the men waited the expected shock in silence. General Lefevre Desnouetts, during the voyage, had evidently wished to remain without particular observation; and to prevent his being known, besides taking passage under a feigned name, had suffered his beard to grow during the whole voyage. He had the misfortune, before the ship struck, to be much bruised, and one of his arms was broken, which disabled him from exertion if it could have been availing. It is not possible to conceive the horrors of their situation.

The deadly and relentless blast impelling them to destruction; the ship a wreck; the raging of the billows against the precipice, on which they were driving, sending back from the caverns and the rocks, the hoarse and melancholy warnings of death, dark, cold, and wet! In such a situation the stoutest heart must have quaked in utter despair. When there is a ray of hope, there may be a corresponding buoyance of spirit. When there is any thing to be done, the active man may drown the sense of danger while actively exerting himself; but here there was nothing to do but to die! Just at the gray of dawn the Albion struck.

The perpendicular precipice of rocks is nearly two hundred feet in height; the sea beating for ages against it has worn large caverns in its base, into which the waves rushed violently, sending back a deep and hollow sound, then, running out in various directions, formed whirlpools of great violence. For a perch or two from the precipice, rocks rise out of the water, broad at bottom and sharp at top; on one of these, the Albion first struck, the next wave threw her further on the rock, the third further still, until, nearly balanced, she swung round, and her stern was driven against another, near in shore. In this situation, every wave making a complete breach over her, many were drowned on deck. A woman, Mr. Everhart could not distinguish who, fell near him and cried for help. He left his hold and raised her up,—another wave came, but she was too far exhausted to sustain herself, and sank on the deck. Fifteen or sixteen corpses, at one time, Mr. Everhart thought, lay near the bows of the ship.

Perceiving now that the stern was higher out of water, and the sea had less power in its sweep over it, Mr. Everhart went aft. He now perceived that the bottom had been broken out of the ship. The heavy articles must have sunk, and the cotton and lighter articles were floating around, dashed by every wave against the rocks. Presently the ship broke in two, and all those who remained near the bow were lost. Several from the stern of the ship had got on the side of the precipice, and were hanging by the crags as well as they could. Although weakened by previous sickness and present suffering, Mr. Everhart made an effort and got upon the rock and stood upon one foot, the only hold that he could obtain. He saw several around him, and among the rest, colonel Prevost, who observed, on seeing him take his station, "here is another poor fellow." But the waves, rolling heavily against them, and often dashing the spray fifty feet above their heads, gradually swept those who had taken refuge one by one away; and one poor fellow losing his hold, grasped the leg of Mr. Everhart, and nearly pulled him from his place. Weak and sick as he was, Mr. Everhart stood several hours on one foot on a little crag, the billows dashing over him, and he benumbed with cold.

As soon as it was light, and the tide ebbed so as to render it possible, the people descended the rocks as far as they could, and dropped him a rope, which he fastened around his body, and was drawn out to a place of safety. Of twenty-three cabin passengers, he alone escaped! Mr. Everhart mentions numerous instances of the kindness shewn by the people to the survivors. A sailor was drawn ashore naked, and one of the peasants, although a cold rain was falling, took the shirt from his own back, and put it on that of the sufferer. Mr. Everhart himself was taken to the hospitable mansion of Mr. James B. Gibbens, where he lay for several weeks exceedingly ill, receiving the kindest attention. "They could not have treated me more tenderly," said Mr. Everhart, "if I had been a brother."

The attentions paid the survivors, were in the style of true Irish hospitality. Such disinterested kindness exalts the human character, and is calculated to have not a limited effect, but will prove of national advantage.

This terrible wreck and loss of lives, and on the part of Mr. Everhart, such a miraculous preservation, excited the public sensibility throughout Europe and America. When he landed at Liverpool, it was difficult for him to get along the streets, the people crowded around in such numbers to see the only passenger saved from the wreck of the Albion.

LOSS OF THE SHIP LOGAN BY FIRE.

The ship Logan, captain Bunker, was struck by lightning and consumed, on her passage from Savannah to Liverpool, on the 19th December, 1832. The following account of this dreadful accident was furnished by the captain.

The Logan left Tybee on the 16th December, with a fair wind from south, which continued blowing a heavy gale from westward until the 19th, on which day, at forty-five minutes past one o'clock, P. M., she was struck by lightning, which descended the starboard pump; from thence it passed up the after-hatchway and went off. It was immediately observed that the ship was on fire, and the crew commenced breaking out cotton from the main hatchway, for the purpose of extinguishing it. In the course of half an hour, got into the lower hold, and on

The Logan, struck by lightning. Page 307.

the starboard side of the pump-well, found the cotton on fire. They commenced throwing on water and heaving the cotton overboard, first cutting the bales in pieces. After working in this way for some time, and heaving overboard eight or ten bales, it was found that the fire was raging between decks on the larboard side; they then left the lower hold, and commenced breaking out between decks, and in a short time broke out twenty or thirty bales; but the smoke became so suffocating as to oblige the hands to leave the hold and close the hatches.

It was now night, and the ship was under close reefed topsails; after all the hatches were closed up, the upper decks began to grow hot: with the determination, therefore, to save the ship and cargo if possible, holes were cut around the pumps and capstan, and water poured down, which was continued all night. At daylight, found that all the upper deck, from the mainmast to the after-hatch, was on fire, and in some places the deck had burnt through. The main hatches were taken off, and about one hour was spent in heaving down water, when the smoke became so dense that the men could stand it no longer. The hatches were then closed for the last time, and they continued throwing water through the holes that were cut, the fire still gaining so fast that no hope was left of saving the ship.

The long-boat was now ordered out, and 60 gallons of water and what provision could be obtained, put on board, when the officers and crew, 16 in number, embarked in her, (being in lat. 33 N. long. 66 W.) having saved nothing but a chronometer and quadrant, and what clothes they stood in. The nearest land was the island of Bermuda, which bore about S. E., 100 miles distant, which they endeavored to reach, but the wind blowing heavy from W. S. W., could not fetch it, but drifted to the eastward of it, when they fortunately fell in with the Grand Turk, and were rescued from a watery grave, after having been in the boat five days, most of which time it was blowing a gale. Captain Madigan kindly took them on board, and treated them with every attention which their distressed situation required.

LOSS OF THE SHIP MARGARET,

Of Salem, wrecked at sea on the 21st of May, 1810. The following account was published by captain Fairfield, after his arrival at Marblehead.

We sailed from Naples, homeward bound, on the 10th of April, with a crew, including officers, of fifteen in number, together with thirty-one passengers, making forty-six in all, men and boys. We passed through the Gut of Gibraltar the 22d of April; nothing of moment occurred until Sunday, 20th May, when in latitude 40, north, longitude 39, 30, west, having strong breezes of wind at S. E. and E. S. E. and rainy weather; at 10 A. M. took in royals, top-gallant studding-sails, fore and mizzen top-gallant-sails, jibs, stay-sails, and main-sail; at meridian, wind and weather continued as before-mentioned; at one P. M., on the 21st, the foretopmast studding sail halyards parted; the studding-sail fell overboard, filled with water, and carried away the studding-sail boom; we took in lower studding-sail spanker, and mizzen top-sail, by which time it became squally, and we immediately clewed down fore and main top-sail, and let fly the sheets—the wind shifted in an instant from E. S. E. to S. W., and although the helm was hard to weather, we could not get the ship before the wind, but was instantly hove on her beam ends. Every person on board the ship being at this time on deck, reached either the bottom or side of the ship, and held on. We secured an axe, and immediately cut away the weather lanyard of the shrouds, masts, and long-boat, which being done the ship righted, being full of water, her hatches off, chests, water-casks, &c., drifting amongst the wreck; the guns, anchors, caboose, and every article on deck, we hove overboard to lighten the ship, and endeavored to clear the wreck of spars, rigging, &c., which lay beating against her to windward; but our efforts were in vain, the starboard lanyards of the shrouds being deep under water, and fast to the ship, and the sea making a continual breach over her: during this time the long-boat lay beating among the wreck of spars, &c., bottom up, the pinnace being wrecked entirely to pieces except her keel, and about three streaks of the boards of her bottom lay in the same situation as the long-boat, and the stern boat lying at a small distance from the ship, full of water, with her gunwales torn off, butts started and stern about half stove in. It was with the utmost difficulty that we bailed her out, and kept her so far free as to enable us to get a rope fast to the long-boat, by which we hauled her alongside the ship, turned her over and found her to be badly stove, her gunwales and stem broken entirely off, her wood-ends and garboard streak open, and large holes in her bottom, so that we found it impossible to bail her out, and we were under the necessity of upsetting her again in the sea, with the hope of being able to stop a part of the holes in her bottom, which we in part effected by driving the butts together and by putting canvass, &c., into the largest holes in her bottom; after which we turned her over again, and by continual bailing with every bucket, &c., which we could procure, we were enabled to keep her from sinking, still keeping under the lee of the ship. By this time it was about 7 P. M.; when the boat being hauled near to the ship for the purpose of getting canvass and oakum to stop the leak, as many men as could reach the long-boat jumped into her, and finding the boat would be again sunk if we remained so near the ship, we were obliged to veer the boat to leeward of the ship at the distance of fifteen or twenty fathoms, being twelve in number in the boat. We had not been in this situation but a short time, before one man jumped from the ship into the sea and made for the boat; we took him in, but finding that all on board were determined to pursue the same plan, we were obliged to veer the boat further off. We stated to those on board the ship our situation, which was also evident to them, as it required all our exertions to keep the boat from sinking. During the night, we lay with a rope fast from the ship to the boat, and under her lee, when the people on board the ship being exceedingly anxious to get into the boat, (which had they effected we should all have been inevitably lost,) kept hauling the boat towards them; we then bent on another rope, and veered out as they hauled; but finding they were determined to sink the boat by getting into her, we were obliged (after stating repeatedly to them our situation) to tell them, that provided they persisted in getting into the boat, we should be obliged, though very reluctantly, to cut the rope and leave them; after which they desisted from hauling the boat towards the ship. At this time, we were thirteen in number in the long-boat, and two men in the stern-boat lying under the lee of the ship, continually bailing to keep her from sinking, which augmented our number to more than could with any degree of safety attempt to leave the ship, in the long-boat, in the shattered condition she was then in.

Monday morning,—moderate breezes and sea tolerably smooth; at which time the people on the wreck were about half of them on the taffrel rail, and the remainder on the bowsprit and windlass, every other part of her being under water continually. They kept entreating us to take them into the boat; we then told them our determination was to continue by the ship while she kept together, and that the boat was not in a situation to leave them, unless they attempted to come into her; but if any of them once made the attempt, we should be under that necessity, notwithstanding our wretched situation, having no compass, quadrant, or any instrument whatever by which we could direct our course, nor a single drop of fresh water in the boat, and two men continually bailing; all of which circumstances were known to them.

About this time, casks of brandy and sundry other articles of the cargo were drifting from the wreck; amongst which we picked up the mizzen top-gallant sail, two spars, five oars, one cask of oil, one drowned pig, and one goat, one bag of bread, and they hove us a gallon keg of brandy from the ship; we then fixed a sail for the boat from the mizzen top-gallant sail. It being now about 11, A. M. the people on the wreck were again determined to get into the boat, and began by jumping into the sea. Seeing their intention, we veered the boat further from the ship and they again returned to her, after which we repeated to them our determination to continue by them so long as the ship held together, but if any other person attempted to come into the boat, we should that instant leave them, notwithstanding our desperate situation. At this time they had secured on the wreck, two quadrants, two compasses, one hogshead of water, bread, flour, and a plenty of provisions, as they frequently informed us; but they would not spare us any of these articles unless we consented to come alongside the ship with the boat, which had we done, we should have been sunk in an instant, as they were prepared to jump, having oars, chests, &c., ready for the purpose on the taffrel rail. Notwithstanding they knew our determination and the impossibility of our taking them into the boat, they still persisted in trying to get into her, and one of them jumped into the sea and made for the small boat, which lay veered to the leeward of the ship, which he reached; but finding we would not take him into the long-boat, he returned to the ship with the small boat. As they were now all determined to pursue the same plan, we were under the painful necessity of cutting the rope by which we were fast to the ship, and row and sail from them for the preservation of our lives, in the hope of falling in with some vessel to relieve us, which was almost the only hope we had left, being about four hundred miles distant from the nearest land, and in the desperate situation before stated. At this time, it was about meridian, with moderate wind from the southward and westward; we made our course as nearly east as possible, for the island of Corvo or Flores, and the last we saw of the ship she was lying in the same situation as when we parted from her. We continued our course to the eastward, having the winds variable from S. S. E. to N. W., and two men constantly bailing; steering in the night by the stars, when to be seen, and in dark cloudy weather by the heaving of the sea, and in the daytime, by judging from the bearing of the sun, when to be seen, and when not, by the best of our judgment. For four days we continued in this situation without seeing any vessel; but on Saturday, 26th of May, at one P. M., to our great joy we espied a sail, which proved to be the brig Poacher, of Boston, captain James Dunn, from Alicant, who took us on board and treated us with every attention and civility.

As nothing was afterwards heard of the vessel, all that remained on the wreck, (thirty-one in number,) undoubtedly perished.

BURNING OF THE KENT.

The Kent, captain Henry Cobb, a fine new ship of one thousand three hundred and fifty tons, bound to Bengal and China, left the Downs on the 19th of February, with twenty officers, three hundred and forty-four soldiers, forty-three women, and sixty-six children, belonging to the thirty-first regiment; with twenty private passengers, and a crew (including officers) of one hundred and forty-eight men, on board.

On the night of Monday, the 28th of February, 1827, when the Kent was in latitude 47 degrees 30 minutes, longitude 10 degrees, a violent gale blew from the west, and gradually increased during the following morning. The rolling of the vessel became tremendous about midnight, so that the best fastened articles of furniture in the principal cabins were dashed about with violence, and the main-chains were thrown at every lurch under water.

It was a little before this period, that one of the officers of the ship, with the well-meant intention of ascertaining that all was fast below, descended with two of the sailors into the hold, where they carried with them, for safety, a light in the patent lantern; and seeing that the lamp burned dimly, the officer took the precaution to hand it up the orlop-deck to be trimmed. Having afterwards discovered one of the spirit casks to be adrift, he sent the sailors for some billets of wood to secure it; but the ship in their absence having made a heavy lurch, the officer unfortunately dropped the light; and letting go his hold of the cask in his eagerness to recover the lantern, it suddenly stove, and the spirits communicating with the lamp, the whole place was instantly in a blaze.

It so happened that the author went into the cuddy to observe the state of the barometer, when he received from captain Spence, the captain of the day, the alarming information that the ship was on fire in the after hold.

As long as the devouring element appeared to be confined to the spot where the fire originated, and which we were assured was surrounded on all sides by water casks, we ventured to cherish hopes that it might be subdued; but, no sooner was the light blue vapor that at first arose succeeded by volumes of thick dingy smoke, which speedily ascended through all the four hatchways, rolling over every part of the ship, than all farther concealment became impossible, and almost all hope of preserving the vessel was abandoned. "The flames have reached the cable tier," was exclaimed by some individuals, and the strong pitchy smell that pervaded the deck confirmed the truth of the exclamation.

In these awful circumstances, captain Cobb, with an ability and decision of character that seemed to increase with the imminence of the danger, resorted to the only alternative now left him, of ordering the lower deck to be scuttled, the combing of the hatches to be cut, and the lower ports to be opened, for the free admission of the waves.

These instructions were speedily executed by the united efforts of the troops and seamen: but not before some of the sick soldiers, one woman, and several children, unable to gain the upper deck, had perished. On descending to the gun-deck with colonel Fearon, captain Bray, and one or two other officers of the 31st regiment, to assist in opening the ports, I met, staggering towards the hatchway, in an exhausted and nearly senseless state, one of the mates, who informed us that he had just stumbled over the dead bodies of some individuals who must have died from suffocation, to which it was evident that he himself had almost fallen a victim. So dense and oppressive was the smoke, that it was with the utmost difficulty we could remain long enough below to fulfil captain Cobb's wishes; which were no sooner accomplished than the sea rushed in with extraordinary force, carrying away in its resistless progress to the hold, the largest chests, bulk-heads, &c.

On the one hand stood death by fire, on the other, death by water: the dilemma was dreadful. Preferring always the more remote alternative, the unfortunate crew were at one moment attempting to check the fire by means of water; and when the water became the most threatening enemy, their efforts were turned to the exclusion of the waves, and the fire was permitted to rage with all its fury.

The scene of horror that now presented itself, baffles all description. The upper deck was covered with between six and seven hundred human beings, many of whom, from previous sea-sickness, were forced on the first alarm to flee from below in a state of absolute nakedness, and were now running about in quest of husbands, children or parents.

While some were standing in silent resignation, or in stupid insensibility to their impending fate, others were yielding themselves up to the most frantic despair. Some on their knees were earnestly imploring, with significant gesticulations and in noisy supplications, the mercy of Him, whose arm, they exclaimed, was at length outstretched to smite them; others were to be seen hastily crossing themselves, and performing the various external acts required by their peculiar persuasion, while a number of the older and more stout-hearted sailors suddenly took their seats directly over the magazine, hoping, as they stated, that by means of the explosion, which they every instant expected, a speedier termination might thereby be put to their sufferings.

Captain Cobb, with great forethought, ordered the

Burning of the Kent, East-Indiaman. *Page* 315.

deck to be scuttled forward, with a view to draw the fire in that direction, knowing that between it and the magazine were several tiers of water casks; while he hoped that the wet sails, &c., thrown into the after-hold, would prevent it from communicating with the spirit-room abaft.

Several of the soldiers' wives and children, who had fled for temporary shelter into the after-cabins on the upper deck, were engaged in praying and in reading the scriptures with the ladies, some of whom were enabled, with wonderful self-possession, to offer to others those spiritual consolations, which a firm and intelligent trust in the Redeemer of the world appeared at this awful hour to impart to their own breasts.

All hope had departed! the employment of the different individuals indicated utter despair of rescue—one was removing a lock of hair from his writing desk to his bosom—others were awaiting their fate in stupor—some with manly fortitude—others bewailing it with loud and bitter lamentation—and part were occupied in prayer and mutual encouragement.

It was at this appalling instant, when "all hope that we should be saved was taken away," that it occurred to Mr. Thompson, the fourth mate, to send a man to the foretop, rather with the ardent wish than the expectation, that some friendly sail might be discovered on the face of the waters. The sailor, on mounting, threw his eyes round the horizon for a moment—a moment of unutterable suspense—and waving his hat, exclaimed, "A sail on the lee-bow!" The joyful announcement was received with deep-felt thanksgiving, and with three cheers upon deck. Our flags of distress were instantly hoisted, and our minute guns fired: and we endeavored to bear down under our three topsails and foresail upon the stranger, which afterwards proved to be the Cambria, a small brig of two hundred tons burden, captain Cook, bound to Vera Cruz, having on board twenty or thirty Cornish miners, and other agents of the Anglo-Mexican company.

While captain Cobb, colonel Fearon, and major Macgregor of the 31st regiment, were consulting together, as the brig was approaching us, on the necessary preparations for getting out the boats, &c., one of the officers asked major Macgregor in what order it was intended the officers should move off? to which the other replied, "Of course, the funeral order;" which injunction was instantly confirmed by colonel Fearon, who said, "Most undoubtedly the juniors first—but see that any man is cut down who presumes to enter the boats before the means of escape are presented to the women and children."

Arrangements having been considerately made by captain Cobb for placing in the first boat, previous to letting it down, all the ladies, and as many of the soldiers' wives as it could safely contain, they hurriedly wrapt themselves up in whatever article of clothing could be most conveniently found; and I think about two, or half past two o'clock, a most mournful procession advanced from the after cabins to the starboard cuddy-port, outside of which the cutter was suspended. Scarcely a word was heard—not a scream was uttered—even the infants ceased to cry, as if conscious of the unspoken and unspeakable anguish that was at this instant rending the hearts of the parting parents—nor was the silence of voices in any way broken, except in one or two cases, when the ladies plaintively entreated to be left behind with their husbands. But on being assured that every moment's delay might occasion the sacrifice of human life, they successively suffered themselves to be torn from the tender embrace, and with a fortitude which never fails to characterize and adorn their sex on occasions of overwhelming trial, were placed, without a murmur, in the boat, which was immediately lowered into a sea so tempestuous, as to leave us only "to hope against hope" that it should live in it for a single moment. Twice the cry was heard from those on the chains that the boat was swamping. But He who enabled the apostle Peter to walk on the face of the deep, and was graciously attending to the silent but earnest aspirations of those on board, had decreed its safety.

After one or two unsuccessful attempts to place the little frail bark fairly upon the surface of the water, the command was at length given to unhook; the tackle at the stern was in consequence immediately cleared; but the ropes at the bow having got foul, the sailor there found it impossible to obey the order. In vain was the axe applied to the entangled tackle. The moment was inconceivably critical; as the boat, which necessarily followed the motion of the ship, was gradually rising out of the water, and must, in another instant, have been hanging perpendicularly by the bow, and its helpless passengers launched into the deep, had not a most providential wave suddenly struck and lifted up the stern, so as to enable the seaman to disengage the tackle; and the boat being dexterously cleared from the ship, was seen after a little while battling with the billows; now raised, in its progress to the brig, like a speck on their summit, and then disappearing for several seconds, as if engulphed "in the horrid vale" between them.

Two or three soldiers, to relieve their wives of a part of their families, sprang into the water with their children, and perished in their endeavors to save them. One young lady, who had resolutely refused to quit her father, whose sense of duty kept him at his post, was near falling a sacrifice to her filial devotion, not having been picked up by those in the boats, until she had sunk five or six times. Another individual, who was reduced to the frightful alternative of losing his wife, or his children, hastily decided in favor of his duty to the former. His wife was accordingly saved, but his four children, alas! were left to perish. A fine fellow, a soldier, who had neither wife nor child of his own, but who evinced the greatest solicitude for the safety of those of others, insisted on having three children lashed to him, with whom he plunged into the water; not being able to reach the boat, he was drawn again into the ship with his charge, but not before two of the children had expired. One man fell down the hatchway into the flames, and another had his back so completely broken as to have been observed quite doubled falling overboard.

The numerous spectacles of individual loss and suffering were not confined to the entrance upon the perilous voyage between the two ships. One man, who fell between the boat and brig, had his head literally crushed fine—and some others were lost in their attempts to ascend the sides of the Cambria.

When the greater part of the men had been disposed of, the gradual removal of the officers commenced, and was marked by a discipline the most rigid, and an intrepidity the most exemplary: none appearing to be influenced by a vain and ostentatious bravery, which in cases of extreme peril, affords rather a presumptive proof of secret timidity than of fortitude; nor any betraying unmanly or unsoldier-like impatience to quit the ship; but with the becoming deportment of men neither paralyzed by, nor profanely insensible to, the accumulating dangers that encompassed them, they progressively departed in the different boats with their soldiers;—they who happened to proceed first, leaving behind them an example of coolness that could not be unprofitable to those who followed.

Every individual was desired to tie a rope round his waist. While the people were busily occupied in adopting this recommendation, I was surprised, I had almost said amused, by the singular delicacy of one of the Irish recruits, who in searching for a rope in one of the cabins, called out to me that he could find none except the cordage belonging to an officer's cot, and wished to know whether there would be any harm in his appropriating it to his own use.

Again: As an agreeable proof too, of the subordination and good feeling that governed the poor soldiers in the midst of their sufferings, I ought to state that toward the evening, when the melancholy group who were passively seated on the poop, exhausted by previous fatigue, anxiety and fasting, were beginning to experience the pain of intolerable thirst, a box of oranges was accidentally discovered by some of the men, who with a degree of mingled consideration, respect, and affection, that could hardly have been expected at such a moment, refused to partake of the grateful beverage, until they had afforded a share of it to their officers.

The spanker-boom of so large a ship as the Kent, which projects, I should think, sixteen or eighteen feet over the stern, rests on ordinary occasions about nineteen or twenty feet above the water; but in the position in which we were placed, from the great height of the sea, and consequent pitching of the ship, it was frequently lifted to a height of not less than thirty or forty feet from the surface.

To reach the rope, therefore, that hung from its extremity, was an operation that seemed to require the aid of as much dexterity of hand as steadiness of head. For it was not only the nervousness of creeping along the boom itself, or the extreme difficulty of afterwards seizing on and sliding down by the rope, that we had to dread, and that occasioned the loss of some valuable lives, by deterring the men from adopting this mode of escape: but as the boat, which one moment was probably under the boom, might be carried the next, by the force of the waves, fifteen or twenty yards from it, the unhappy individual, whose best calculations were thus defeated, was generally left swinging for some time in mid-air, if he was not repeatedly plunged several feet under water, or dashed with dangerous violence against the sides of the returning boat—or, what not unfrequently happened, was forced to let go his hold of the rope altogether. As there seemed, however, no alternative, I did not hesitate, notwithstanding my comparative inexperience and awkwardness in such a situation, to throw my leg across the perilous stick; and with a heart extremely grateful that such means of deliverance, dangerous as they appeared, were still extended to me; and more grateful still that I had been enabled, in common with others, to discharge my honest duty to my sovereign and to my fellow-soldiers; I proceeded, after confidently committing my spirit, the great object of my solicitude, into the keeping of Him who had formed and redeemed it, to creep slowly forward, feeling at every step the increased difficulty of my situation. On getting nearly to the end of the boom, the young officer whom I followed and myself were met with a squall of wind and rain, so violent as to make us fain to embrace closely the slippery stick, without attempting for some minutes to make any progress, and to excite our apprehension that we must relinquish all hope of reaching the rope. But our fears were disappointed, and after resting for awhile at the boom-end, while my companion was descending to the boat, which he did not find until he had been plunged once or twice over head in the water, I prepared to follow; and instead of lowering myself, as many had imprudently done, at the moment when the boat was inclining towards us—and consequently being unable to descend the whole distance before it again receded—I calculated that while the boat was retiring, I ought to commence my descent, which would probably be completed by the time the returning wave brought it underneath; by which means I was, I believe, almost the only officer or soldier who reached the boat without being either severely bruised or immersed in the water. But my friend colonel Fearon had not been so fortunate; for after swimming for some time, and being repeatedly struck against the side of the boat, and at one time drawn completely under it, he was at last so utterly exhausted, that he must instantly have let go his hold of the rope and perished, had not one in the boat seized him by the hair of the head and dragged him into it, almost senseless and alarmingly bruised.

Captain Cobb, in his immovable resolution to be the last, if possible, to quit his ship, and in his generous anxiety for the preservation of every life entrusted to his charge, refused to seek the boat, until he again endeavored to urge onward the few still around him, who seemed struck dumb and powerless with dismay. But finding all his entreaties fruitless, and hearing the guns, whose tackle was burst asunder by the advancing flames, successively exploding in the hold, into which they had fallen—this gallant officer, after having nobly pursued, for the preservation of others, a course of exertion that has been rarely equalled either in its duration or difficulty, at last felt it right to provide for his own safety, by laying hold on the topping-lift, or rope that connects the driver-boom with the mizzen-top, and thereby getting over the heads of the infatuated men who occupied the boom, unable to go either backward or forward, and ultimately dropping himself into the water.

LOSS OF THE SHIP BOSTON.

An unusual degree of sensation was excited in Boston, on the first of June, by the melancholy tidings of the loss of the packet ship Boston. This strong and elegant ship—one of the finest packets that belonged to this country—was struck by lightning in the Gulf stream, six days out from Charleston, and burnt to the water's edge. We present the details below, as furnished by captain Mackay.

"On Tuesday, the 25th of May, lat. 39, 31, long. 63, 46, commenced with fresh breeze and squally weather—at 2 P. M., heavy rain which continued until about sunset—at 8 P. M., forked lightning in the south-west, and dark and heavy clouds rising from the westward—at 9, the wind hauled to the westward—at 10 P. M., a heavy cloud began to rise in the south-west—at half past 10, sharp lightning, clewed up the topgallant sails, and hauled the mainsail up—at 11, heavy thunder and sharp lightning; the second flash struck the ship, burst the main-royal from the gaskets and burnt it; knocked down the steward and Isaac Hopkins, a sailor, and filled the ship full of electric fluid. We examined the ship immediately, to ascertain if the masts were injured, or the lightning had passed through the deck; but the mast appeared uninjured, a bright complaisance resting on each royal-mast head. We single reefed the main-top sail, and were about to hand the mainsail, when we ascertained that the ship was on fire. We immediately cleared the main and after hatchways, to get at the fire, heaving the cotton overboard and cutting holes in the deck, plying water in every direction—but all in vain; the cotton in the main-hold was on fire, fore and aft, on both sides, burning like tinder. Our only alternative was to clear away the boats and get them out, part of the crew and passengers at work keeping the fire down as much as possible by drawing and heaving water, the scuppers being stopped up; we stove water casks over holes cut in the deck and in the main-hatchway, starting the water, but all to no good purpose, for before we could get the long-boat over the ship's side, the fire had burst through the deck and out the larboard side of the ship. The flames raged with such violence and consumed the vessel so quick, that nothing could be saved from the wreck. We got about forty gallons of water, and provisions sufficient, on a short allowance, to keep the passengers and crew alive for three weeks—almost every thing else was burnt up in the ship, even the money, watches, and clothes—all destroyed. At 3, A. M., the main and mizzen-masts were burnt off below deck, and the masts fell into the water; at half past 3, the passengers and crew were all in the boats; the flames had then reached the forecastle, and the ship was one complete flame of fire, fore and aft. The passengers had exerted themselves to the utmost to assist us. The officers had with unwearied exertion, coolness and persevering activity done all that men could do. The ship's crew worked like horses and behaved like men; but all would not do. About three hours time had changed one of the best ships that ever swam to a complete volcano, and cast twenty-three persons adrift on the open ocean.

"The cabin passengers were admiral Sir Isaac Coffin and servant, Dr. William Boag, and his sister Miss Ansella Boag, Mr. Neil McNeil, and Mr. Samuel S. Osgood. It was then raining, and every person was drenched through with water; in this situation the constitution of Miss Boag, the only lady-passenger, soon gave way. This amiable young lady's firmness of conduct at the first alarm of fire, and during the whole scene, is worthy of the highest praise. To the divine will of her God she submitted without a murmur, and at 11 o'clock on Wednesday, she died in the arms of her brother, in the boat, thanking him in the most affectionate manner for his kindness, giving her blessing to us all. On the following day, she was buried with the church service, our situation not admitting of the corpse being kept longer in the boat. We remained in the boats near the fire of the wreck two days, and at three o'clock P. M. on Thursday, were taken on board the brig Idas, of Liverpool, N. S. from Demarara, bound to Halifax, captain Joseph Barnaby, who with his officers and crew treated us with every kindness and attention. We remained on board the brig two days, when, Sunday morning, May 30th, falling in with the brig Camilla, captain Robert B. Edes, he was good enough to offer us a passage to Boston, and received us on board his vessel."

Admiral Sir Isaac Coffin, after landing from the brig Camilla, authorized his agent to present captain Mackay with a check for five hundred dollars; and subsequently sent him an elegant gold watch, to replace one which he had lost by the destruction of the ship.

LOSS OF THE WHALE SHIP ESSEX.

This vessel sailed from Nantucket on a whaling voyage, commanded by captain Pollard. On the 13th of November, 1820, they were among the whales, and the three boats were lowered down. They succeeded in capturing a young whale, but the mate's boat got stove, and returned to the ship to be repaired. Shortly after, a whale of the largest class, probably the dam of the one they had just taken, struck the ship, knocked part of the false keel off, just abreast of the main channels.

The animal then remained for some time alongside, endeavoring to clasp the ship within her jaws, but could not accomplish it. She then turned, went round the stern, and came up on the other side; and went away ahead about a quarter of a mile. Then suddenly turning, she came at the ship with tremendous velocity, head on. The vessel was going at the rate of five knots, but such was the force with which she struck the ship, which was under the cat-head, that the vessel had sternway, at the rate of three or four knots. The consequence was, that the sea rushed into the cabin windows, every man on deck was knocked down, and, worse than all, the bows were completely stove in. In a few minutes, the vessel filled and went on her beam ends.

At this unhappy juncture, the captain and second mate were both fast to a whale; but on beholding the awful catastrophe that had taken place, immediately cut from the fish and made for the ship. As soon as the captain got on board, he gave orders for cutting away the masts, which was accordingly done, and the vessel righted;—the upper deck was then scuttled, and some water and bread were procured for the two boats, in which they were compelled to remain, as all thoughts of saving the ship were given up. In expectation of falling in with some vessel, they remained by the wreck, making sails, &c., but were finally compelled to abandon it, and stood away to the southward, in hopes of getting the variable winds, and experiencing fine weather; but the wind being constantly from the east and south-east, they made much lee-way and were prevented from keeping to the southward. They continued beating about in this way for thirty days, when they made an island, which they took for Ducie's island, at which place the boats remained one week; but the island affording hardly any nourishment, and in fact, exhibiting nothing but sterility, they resolved on venturing for the coast; leaving behind them three men who preferred remaining there, rather than to venture across the ocean in an open boat.

After a series of disasters, a part of the crew finally reached Valparaiso. Captain Downes, of the U. S. frigate Macedonian, on becoming acquainted with the particulars, resolved to rescue the three unfortunate men. who were left behind on the island. Accordingly he fitted out a schooner, at an expense of a thousand dollars, and sent her in search for them. She was out, however, but one month, and returned dismasted. The ship Surrey, captain Raine, lying at Valparaiso, was on the eve of sailing for New Holland, and as Ducie's island was not far from her track, captain Downes offered her commander three hundred dollars, to call there and take off the men.

On Thursday, the 5th of April, captain Raine, considering himself within a short distance of Ducie's island, which is laid down in Norie's epitome to be in lat. 24 degrees 40 minutes S. and long. 124 deg. 17 minutes W., kept a good look out. About 2, P. M., land was perceived, which turned out to be an island in lat. 24 deg. 26 minutes. As the vessel neared the land, they discharged a gun, and shortly after, the three poor men were seen to issue from the woods. The boats were presently lowered, captain Raine taking one himself. On approaching the shore, it was found not only dangerous, but utterly impracticable to land; of which circumstance they were informed, in weak and tremulous voices, by the almost starved and nearly worn out creatures themselves, who could scarcely, from the miserable plight they were in, articulate a syllable. One poor fellow summoned up courage enough to plunge into the waves, and with great difficulty reached the boat: he said, one of the others only could swim.

After warily backing the boat as near the rocks as possible, amidst a heavy surf, the other two men succeeded in getting on board, much bruised and lacerated by the repeated falls; which object was no sooner effected, when each devoutly expressed his gratitude to that benign Being who had so wonderfully preserved them from sharing in the destruction to which most of their unhappy shipmates had fallen victims. They had been on the island four months, living on wild berries, resembling a cherry, sometimes killing a sea-gull by throwing stones, and no fresh water but when it rained, which was very seldom. On the island they discovered the name of the ship Elisabeth, of London, carved on a tree, and a cave, with eight human skeletons, lying together.

LOSS OF THE ISABELLA, OFF HASTINGS, ENGLAND.

The details below were furnished by one of the passengers, in a letter to a friend, dated

EASTBOURNE, March 15, 1833.

This wreck is still visible; she was a fine ship of 340 tons, and offers an awful evidence of the power of nature over the noblest works of art. My heart still sickens with dismay at the recollection of the dreadful trials I have passed through. I have not before had health and strength enough to give you an outline of the particulars, and, even now, I tremble as they pass in review before me.

All our valuable furniture, plate, books, manuscripts, outfit and necessaries had been put on board the Isabella in the docks, when she dropped down to Gravesend, where I joined her on the evening of Saturday the 16th of February, with my wife and three children, a girl of eighteen months, and two boys of four and six years. We were opposed by contrary winds, and put our pilot on shore on Monday evening. On Tuesday, the wind freshened into a gale; and the dreadful enervating sickness usually attending these scenes, dispossessed my wife and myself of all energy and strength. The wind was now directly against us, and every hour increasing its fearful power; but our captain, full of intrepidity and confidence, determined to proceed, although he left behind a fleet of perhaps an hundred sail. As night closed, the tempest raged yet more fearfully. Our gallant ship was but as a feather on the wave's surface, and all was fearfully dark as any night in the black catalogue of tempests; the wind right ahead; there was equal peril now in advancing or receding; the captain, however, gave his orders with as much precision as if he were exhibiting in a state pageant. The loud voice of the speaking-trumpet was the only sound that could be heard amid the wild roar of contending elements. Between three and four o'clock, our captain entered the cabin: he spoke little. I saw the distressed workings of his mind, and one or two questions constituted all the interruptions I offered. He took brandy and water, threw off his saturated dress, and having sat a little in dry clothes, retired.

From this time, the ship seemed to me to labor and strain more than before, and the hurricane to drive and lay down the ship lower on her side; but as the captain was taking rest, I had fancied more security, and had lain myself on the floor of the cabin in the hope of getting also some repose. I had been lying down I suppose thirty minutes, when I thought I heard or felt the keel of the ship drag. I had been, to this time, sick to death. I was exhausted and listless, almost lifeless, when the dreadful suspicion and announcement of "shore," alarmed me; I was ill no more. I jumped up, and was rushing through the cabin to mention my fears, when the ship beat twice on a rock, and I heard the cry of "The ship has struck!" I called the captain. The dreadful shock and loud cries of alarm, combined to summon all on deck, excepting the ladies and the poor children, who had been roused, at last, by the general crash, and these I would not allow to leave their berths lest they might interrupt the exertions making above. Here, indeed, was redoubled energy. The rudder was unshipped when we first struck, and was abandoned. Now was the loud cry for the speaking-trumpet—now for the axes, which for a time could not be found. I asked if there were no guns to fire signals of distress? No guns. No rockets to let off to acquaint the coast-guard with our condition? No rockets. It was manifest our captain had been, as Napoleon said of Massena, a spoiled child of fortune! Always happy and successful in his adventures, his voyages deservedly fortunate, had superseded all contemplation of disaster. Every effort was now made, by manœuvring the sails, to force the ship once more to sea, and made in vain—we were constrained to wait until daylight enabled us to appreciate our real situation, and procure for us, from the shore, the necessary assistance.

It is difficult to judge of distance on water, but I believe we lay nearly half a mile from the beach. Every succeeding wave raised the ship several feet, and subsiding, we beat with tremendous violence on the rock. An immense quantity of bricks had been shipped in lieu of ballast; between these and the rock, the ship's bottom might represent the metal works between the anvil and the hammer, and strange it would have been had it not severely suffered. Every wave was a fearful mountain, while the hurricane momentarily threatened to shiver us into atoms. Such a storm has not been felt on these shores during the last fifty years. As the ungoverned state of the rudder was now breaking up all within its range, the binnacles were removed below for security, and the rudder lashed to the boom; but the cords were soon rent asunder like threads. After lying in this situation nearly two hours, sometimes fancying we saw boats approaching to our assistance, sometimes that we saw lights as signals, the dawn at length assured us we were descried from the shore, where we saw a general activity corresponding to the peril of our unhappy condition. Not a boat could, however, venture to put out through the frightful surf, and I own I felt little hopes of relief while the elements continued their frightful ravages. The shore was now lined with spectators, but their sympathy could avail us nothing. While this was our condition without, within the ship all was devastation. At each new concussion something was strained and gave way. Bedsteads, lamps, tables and trunks were hurled from side to side with frightful noise, which made the females believe, in spite of our assurances, the ship was breaking up. But now beamed suddenly forth in our extremity, the dawn of our deliverance. We had watched a team laboring along the beach conveying to windward a boat. It was launched, and, in the same moment, manned. It was the God-like life-boat, equipped with the most intrepid crew that ever deserved their country's gratitude. In half an hour of unequalled struggles they were alongside, and boarded us; and now, indeed, I saw countenances where the glad gleam of joy endeavored to penetrate through a mass of suffering and despair; but we had scarcely interchanged congratulations, when I was told the boat had left the ship. I could not believe it. I ran aloft and found it true. I felt I had now a duty to perform to my family, and I asked the captain, if the boat were dismissed, what could be his plan? I represented that as our rudder was useless, he could have no command of the ship if she floated with the coming flood; and if her bottom was pierced, of which there could be no doubt, we must expect that if she dipped into deep water, she would fill and go down, and all would inevitably perish—that it would be impossible, in her present crippled state, to work her into any port, and I submitted, therefore, that our safety should be consulted above all things. Our captain firmly answered, our safety was his principal duty and first care; that I might rely on his word, that he would not hazard our lives; and that if the ship was not in a condition to leave the shore, he would not attempt it. I own I returned to my family with a heavy heart to announce the fearful experiment.

The flood-tide was rolling in, and the trumpet of our vigilant captain was again in full activity. After many mighty workings, an awful blast drove us over the reef, and hurried us to sea. Hope beamed again, but it was found that the ship had made five feet of water in ten minutes. The signal of distress was hoisted, and every possible effort made to put the ship's head to the shore, but without the assistance of her rudder, she was wholly unmanageable, and very soon became water-logged. I now caught the captain's eye; he motioned me, and gave the dreadful intelligence that the ship was sinking, and I must prepare my wife and children for any event! I asked how long it might be before she would go down? He said, "Some time yet." Without making any communication, I conveyed my family on deck, and watched the progress of the ship visibly made in sinking. Efforts were again made to put the ship about, but they were fruitless.

Happily for our safety, the life-boat, better acquainted

with the distressing features of disaster, had kept hovering around. I had grieved at its dismissal, but now suddenly heard it hailing the captain to let go the remaining anchor. After dragging a little, it held on, and threw her stern round; but the ship was water-logged, and made little progress. She was now so low that every wave rolled in one side and discharged itself on the other. We had thrown out a line to the boat, but it had quickly snapped, and we threw others, in the hope of keeping them at a short distance. As it appeared we must in a few seconds go down, I was preparing cords for the safety of my family, when a squall, a hundred times more frightful than any that had yet assailed us, gave hopes, and the crew cried out, "Now—now the masts must go." But still they stood, to our great danger and annoyance. The ship had, however, felt the impulse received from the last blast, and been impelled forward;—and now a shock succeeded which gave the glad, auspicious tidings of shore. The men clasped their hands, and looked towards Heaven with emotions of gratitude. The last nearly overwhelming gale had lifted us forward, and proved our deliverance; and now the exertions of the crew of the boat were increased tenfold, and they were quickly under our stern. Our intrepid captain, lashing himself for security, jumped over the ship's side, and, though overwhelmed by every wave, called aloud for the children first. I had taken them below, lest the fall of the masts should injure them. I flew down, and in an instant my eldest son was in the arms of the captain.—The life-boat was now riding on the brink of the wave, and now was lost in the abyss; but as she was descending my son was caught as the captain loosed his arm, by a dozen eager arms raised for his safety. The second boy met with more facility, and the infant was thrown and caught, when the whole crew, with generous sympathy, cried out, "Now the mother." The mother was soon with her children, and seemed to us protected by these our worldly saviors from destruction. The other females were then handed down, with a youth of fourteen, and I next followed, in agonizing anxiety to share with those I felt dearer to me than life, the yet remaining perils.

Lifted sometimes mountains high, sometimes hidden from all view in the depths into which we descended, we at last reached the shore. The people upon the beach rushed into the surf to receive us, and braved its perils for our security. The boat was soon lighted, and a cart stood ready to convey us to an adjoining house, where dry clothing was soon exchanged for garments long saturated with brine. The captain and crew were left on the wreck with one passenger, and two hours elapsed before the boat could succeed in extricating these from the dangers assailing them. For a considerable period, the sea had been covered with floating packages, carried by the storm and tide many miles along the beach, but at nightfall, began the active work of plunder, and that which had resisted other violence was soon conveyed away from observation.

LOSS OF THE ROTHSAY CASTLE STEAMER.

The Rothsay Castle was a steam-packet which formerly traded on the Clyde. She belonged to the line of steamers which sailed from Liverpool to Beaumaris and Bangor, and was furnished with one engine only. She was commanded by Lieut. Atkinson. At ten o'clock, on the — of August, 1831, the vessel was appointed to sail from the usual place, George's Pierhead, but a casual delay took place in starting, and it was eleven o'clock before she had got every thing in readiness. Whilst taking passengers on board, a carriage arrived at the Pierhead for embarkation. It belonged to M. W. Foster, Esq. of Regent's Park, London, who, with his wife and servant, were conveyed in it to the packet, and took their passage at the same time. They were all subsequently drowned, a little dog which accompanied them being the only survivor of this unfortunate group. When the steamer left the Pierhead, her deck was thronged with passengers. The captain, crew, musicians, &c. amounted to fifteen, in addition to whom, it was supposed by persons who saw the vessel sail, that one hundred and ten or one hundred and twenty souls were on board. The majority of the passengers consisted of holiday and family parties, chiefly from country places; and in one of these companies, who came on a journey of pleasure from Bury, the hand of death committed a merciless devastation. It consisted of twenty-six persons; in the morning, joyous with health and hilarity, they set out upon the waves, and when the shades of that evening approached, every soul but two saw his last of suns go down.

The weather was not particularly boisterous at the time she sailed. A severe storm, however, had raged in the morning, and must have agitated the water on the Banks more than usual. The wind, too, blew strongly from the north-west, and the vessel had to contend with the tide, which began to flow soon after she passed the rock. When the steamer arrived off the floating-light, which is stationed about fifteen miles from Liverpool, the roughness of the sea alarmed many of the passengers. One of the survivors stated, that Mr. Tarry, of Bury, who, with his family, consisting of himself, his wife, their five children and servant, was on board, being, in common with others, greatly alarmed for his own safety and the safety of those dear to him, went down to the cabin, where the captain was at dinner, and requested him to put back. His reply was, "I think there is a great deal of fear on board, and very little danger. If we were to turn back with passengers, it would never do—we should have no profit." To another gentleman who urged him to put back, he is reported to have said very angrily, "I'm not one of those that turn back." He remained in the cabin two whole hours, and peremptorily refused to comply with the repeated requests made to him by the more timid of his passengers, to return to Liverpool; observing that if they knew him, they would not make the request. Before dinner, his behavior had been unexceptionable; but after he had dined, a very striking difference was observed in his conduct. He became violent in his manner, and abusive in his language to the men. When anxiously questioned by the passengers, as to the progress the vessel was making, and the time at which she was likely to reach her destination, he returned trifling, and frequently very contradictory answers. During the early part of the voyage, he had spoken confidently of being able to reach Beaumaris by seven o'clock; but the evening wore away, night came on, and the vessel was still a considerable distance from the termination of her voyage. It was near twelve o'clock, when they arrived at the mouth of the Menai strait, which is about five miles from Beaumaris. The tide, which had been running out of the strait, and which had, consequently, for some time previous retarded the steamer's progress towards her destination, was just on the turn. The vessel, according to the statement of two of the seamen and one of the firemen saved, had got round the buoy on the north end of the Dutchman's bank, and had proceeded up the river as far as the tower on Puffin island; when suddenly the steam got so low that the engine would not keep her on her proper course. When asked why there was not steam on, the fireman said, that a deal of water had been finding its way into the vessel all day, and that sometime before she got into the strait, the bilge-pumps were choked. The water in the hold then overflowed the coals; so that, in renewing the fires, a deal of water went in with the coals, and made it impossible to keep the steam up. It was the duty of the fireman to give notice of this occurrence; but he seems not to have mentioned it to the captain. The vessel, which had evidently come fair into the channel, though there was no light on the coast to guide her, now drifted with the ebb-tide and north-west wind, towards the Dutchman's bank, on the north point of which she struck, her bows sticking fast in the sand. Lieut. Atkinson immediately ordered the man at the helm to put the helm a-starboard. The man refused to do so; but put it to port. The mate perceiving this, ran aft, took the helm from the man, and put it to starboard again. In the meantime, the captain and some of the passengers got the jib up. No doubt he did this intending to wear her round and bring her head to the northward; but, in the opinion of nautical men, it could not make the least difference which way her head was turned, as she was on a lee shore, and there was no steam to work her off. The captain also ordered the passengers first to run aft, in the hope, by removing the pressure from the vessel's stem, to make her float: this failing to produce the desired effect, he then ordered them to run forward. All the exertions of the captain, the crew and passengers united, were unavailing. The ill-fated vessel stuck still faster in the sands, and all gave themselves up for lost. The terror of the passengers became excessive. Several of them urged the captain to hoist lights, and make other signals of distress; but he positively refused to do so, assuring the passengers that there was no danger, and telling them several times, that the packet was afloat and doing well, and on her way; when the passengers knew perfectly well that she was sticking fast in the sand, and her cabins rapidly filling with water. Doubtless the unfortunate man was perfectly aware of the imminence of the danger; but we may charitably suppose that he held such language for the purpose of preventing alarm which might be fatal. The alarm-bell was now rung with so much violence that the clapper broke, and some of the passengers continued to strike it for some time with a stone. The bell was heard, it is said, at Beaumaris, but, as there was no light hoisted on the mast of the steamer, (a fatal neglect!) those who heard the signal were, of course, ignorant whence it proceeded.

The weather, at this awful moment, was boisterous, but perfectly clear. The moon, though slightly overcast, threw considerable light on the surrounding objects. But a strong breeze blew from the north-west, the tide began to set in with great strength, and a heavy sea beat over the bank on which the steam-packet was now firmly and immovably fixed.

We cannot describe the scene which followed. Certain death seemed now to present itself to all on board, and the most affecting scenes were exhibited. The females, in particular, uttered the most piercing shrieks; some locked themselves in each other's arms, while others, losing all self-command, tore off their caps and bonnets, in the wildness of despair. A Liverpool pilot, who happened to be in the packet, now raised his voice and exclaimed, "It is all over—we are all lost!" At these words there was a universal despairing shriek.—The women and children collected in a knot together, and kept embracing each other, keeping up, all the time, the most dismal lamentations. When tired with crying, they lay against each other, with their heads reclined, like inanimate bodies. The steward of the vessel and his wife, who was on board, lashed themselves to the mast, determined to spend their last moments in each other's arms. Several husbands and wives also met their fate locked in each other's arms; whilst parents clung to their beloved children,—several mothers, it is said, having perished with their dear little ones firmly clasped in their arms. A party of the passengers, about fifteen or twenty, lowered the boat and crowded into it. It was impossible for any open boat to live in such a sea, even though not overloaded, and she immediately swamped and went to the bottom, with all who had made this last hopeless effort for self-preservation.

For some time the vessel, though now irrecoverably lost, continued to resist the action of the waves, and the despairing souls on board still struggled with their doom. But hope had forever fled; the packet was beaten and tossed about by the tumultuous waters with a violence which threatened to dash her into fragments at every shock, and the sea now made a continual breach over her. The decks were repeatedly swept by the boiling ocean, and each billow snatched its victims to a watery grave. The unfortunate captain and his mate were among the first that perished. About thirty or forty passengers were standing upon the poop clinging to each other in hopeless agony, and occasionally uttering the most piteous ejaculations. Whilst trembling thus upon the brink of destruction, and expecting every moment to share the fate which had already overtaken so many of their companions in misery, the poop was discovered to give way; another wave rolled on with impetuous fury, and the hinder part of the luckless vessel, with all who sought safety in its frail support, was burst away from its shattered counterpart, and about forty wretched beings hurried through the foaming flood into an eternal world.

'Then rose from sea to sky the wild farewell,
Then shrieked the timid and stood still the brave.'

Those who retained any degree of sensibility endeavored to catch at whatever was floating within their reach, with the vain hope of prolonging their lives, though it was certain that life could only lengthen their sufferings. Many grasped, with frantic despair, at the slightest object they could find, but were either too weak to retain their hold, or were forced to relinquish their grasp by the raging of the surge. The rudder was seized by eight of the sinking creatures at the same time, and some of them were ultimately preserved. The number of those who clung to the portion of the wreck which remained upon the bank, gradually grew thinner and thinner, as they sunk under their fatigues, or were hurled into the deep by the remorseless waves. At length, about an hour and a half from the time when she struck, the remnant of the Rothsay Castle disappeared from the bosom of the ocean, and the remainder of her passengers and crew were precipitated into the foaming abyss.

LOSS OF THE BRIG SALLY.

August 8, 1767, while in latitude 25, having a strong gale of wind, the brig Sally was laid-to under her main-stay-sail till ten o'clock the next morning, when she was hove on her beam-ends, and in less than five minutes turned keel upwards, so that they had only time to cut away the lanyards of her main-mast. There were on board, Anthony Tabry, master; Humphrey Mars, mate; Joseph Sherver, Samuel Bess, John Burna, mariners, who were drowned; six other mariners, viz. Peter Toy, Daniel Cultan, John Davis, Alexander Landerry, Peter Mayes, and William Hammon, having got hold of the top-mast, which floated alongside, tied it to the stern, and supported themselves by it, till about five o'clock in the evening, when the cabin boy swam to the hull and threw them a rope, by which they got on the bottom of the vessel, where they were still in a dismal plight; the first want that invaded them was drink, this drove away all thought of meat. The main-mast, with all the rigging, the lanyards having been cut away, came up alongside, from which they got the wreath, (a square hoop which binds the head of the mast,) with which, and a bolt of a foot long, they went to work on her bottom; in the mean time keeping their mouths moist, as well as they could, by chewing the stuff of her bottom, she not having any barnacles, being lately cleaned, and some lead which was on her bow, and drinking their own water; in four days time Peter Toy died, raving for drink, whose body they threw off the vessel the next day. In this manner did they work for six days, without meat, drink, or sleep, nor daring to lie down for fear of falling off the vessel; the sixth day they got a hole in the brig, where they found a barrel of bottled beer; this they drank very greedily; they soon got another parcel, when one of them put the others on an allowance. The eleventh day of their being on the wreck, they got a barrel of pork, which they were obliged to eat raw. As to sleep, as soon as they got a hole through the vessel's bottom, they pulled out a great number of staves and shingles, and made a platform in the same place, but so small was it, that when they wanted to turn, they were obliged to wait till the sea hoisted the vessel, and when she fell again with the sea, they were almost froze to death. Thus did these poor miserable fellows live for thirteen or fourteen days; after they got the pork, they made a kind of net with a hoop, some shingles, and ropes, which they got from the mast; this they let into the sea, with some pork, and caught a few small fish, which, with two or three mice they caught on board the brig, afforded them several most delicious repasts, raw as they were; this lasted but a few days, as they could not catch any more; when they were obliged to return to their pork, which was become quite putrid by the salt water getting to it. To their great joy, on the 1st of September, in latitude 26, 15, longitude 70, 10, at four o'clock in the afternoon, they could just perceive a vessel to windward of them, which seemed to stand some time for them, but soon put about and stood from them; it was then they despaired, as that morning they had drank the last bottle of their beer, and that one was all they had; for that day they worked hard to get at the casks of water in the hold, but they were so far from them, that they could not have got at them in a long time. About sun half an hour high, the vessel stood for them, and came so near that they perceived a piece of canvass, that they on the wreck supported on a piece of board, bore down for it, and about seven or eight o'clock took them on board; she was the brig Norwich, captain Robert Noyes. Thus were they relieved when death stared them in the face, by a captain who used them very kindly, gave them food and clothes, as their own were rotted off their backs, washed their sores, and gave them plasters, as they were almost raw from head to foot with the heat of the sun and salt water, which, in many places had eaten holes in their flesh.

SUFFERINGS OF EPHRAIM HOW.

On the 25th of August, 1676, Mr. Ephraim How, of New-Haven, in New-England, with his two eldest sons; one Mr. Augur; Caleb Jones, son to Mr. William Jones, one of the magistrates of New-Haven; and a boy; six persons in all, set sail from New-Haven for Boston, in a small ketch, of about seventeen tons.

Having despatched his business there, he sailed for New-Haven on the 10th of September, but was forced back to Boston by contrary winds. Here Mr. How was seized with a violent flux, which continued nearly a month; many being at that time sick, and some dying of the same.

Being in some degree restored to health, he again sailed from Boston, October 10. They went with a fair wind as far as cape Cod; but on a sudden, the weather became very tempestuous, so that they could not pass the cape, but were driven off to sea, where they were in great danger, experiencing terrible storms, with outrageous wind and seas.

His eldest son fell sick and died about the 21st; soon after, his other son was taken ill and died also. This was a bitter cup to the poor father, for these youths were the only assistants in working the vessel. Soon after Caleb Jones died, so that half the company were now no more.

Mr. How continued in a very sickly and weak state, yet was necessitated to stand at the helm twenty-four and thirty-six hours together. During this time, the sea was so boisterous as frequently to break over the vessel, so that if he had not been lashed fast he must have been washed overboard. In this extremity, he was at a loss in his own thoughts, whether he should persist in endeavoring to make for the New-England shore, or bear away for the southern islands. Upon his proposing the question to Mr. Augur, they determined, according to the custom of some in those times, to decide this difficult case by casting lots. They did so, and it fell upon New-England.

Nearly about the 7th of November, they lost their rudder, so that now their only dependence was upon Providence. In this deplorable state they drove up and down for a fortnight longer. During the last six weeks, the poor infirm Mr. How was hardly ever dry, nor had he the benefit of warm food above thrice or thereabouts!

At length, about the 21st of November, early in the morning the vessel was driven on the tailings of a ledge of rocks, where the sea broke violently. Looking out, they saw a dismal, rocky island to the leeward, upon which, if Providence had not by the breakers given them timely warning, they had been dashed to pieces. They immediately let go an anchor, and got out the boat, and the sea became calm. The boat proving leaky, and they being in great terror, they took but little out of the ketch, but got on shore as they could.

Here they could discover neither man nor beast. It was a small, rocky, desolate island, near cape Sable, the southern extremity of Nova Scotia. They now appeared to be in great danger of being starved to death, but the storm returning, beat so violently upon the vessel, as it still lay at anchor, that it was stove to pieces, and several things floated to the shore.

The following articles were all they had towards their future support:—a cask of gunpowder, which received no damage from the water; a barrel of wine; half a barrel of molasses; several useful articles towards building a tent: all the above drifted from the wreck: besides which they had fire-arms and shot; a pot for boiling; and most probably other things not mentioned in the narrative.

Their tent was soon erected, for the cold was now getting severe, but new and great distresses attended them, for though they had arms and ammunition, there were seldom any fowls to be seen, except crows, ravens, and seagulls. These were so few, that they could seldom shoot more than one at a time. Many times half a fowl, with the liquor it was boiled in, served for a meal for all three. Once they lived five days without any sustenance, but did not feel themselves pinched with hunger as at other times; which they esteemed a special favor of Heaven unto them.

When they had lived in this miserable condition twelve weeks, Mr. How's dear friend and companion, Mr. Augur, died, about the middle of February, 1677; so that he had none left to converse with but the lad, who likewise departed on the 2d of April.

Mr. How was now the sole inhabitant of this desolate spot, during April, May, and June, and saw fishing vessels every now and then, sailing by; some of which came even nearer to the island than that which at last took him off. He used all the means in his power to make them acquainted with his distress; but they either did not see him, or were afraid to approach close to the island, lest some of those Indians should be quartered there, who were at that time in hostility against the English, viz., the North-east Indians, who held out after the death of the famous Philip, king of the Wompanoags.

At length a vessel belonging to Salem, in New-England, providentially passed by, and seeing this poor fellow, they sent their boat on shore, and took him away. He had been on the island more than seven months, and above a quarter of a year by himself. On the 18th of July, he arrived at Salem, and at last returned to his family at New-Haven. They for a twelvemonth had supposed him dead; by which it appears he did not get home till the end of August, or perhaps later.

LOSS OF THE TRANSPORT HARPOONER.

The hired transport Harpooner was lost, near Newfoundland, in November, 1818; she had on board three hundred and eighty-five men, women and children, including the ship's company. The passengers consisted of detachments of several regiments, with their families, who were on their way to Quebec. On Saturday evening, November 10th, a few minutes after nine o'clock, the second mate on watch called out, "the ship 's aground;" at which she slightly struck on the outermost rock of St. Shotts, in the island of Newfoundland. She beat over, and proceeding a short distance, she struck again, and filled; encircled among rocks, the wind blowing strong, the night dark, and a very heavy sea rolling, she soon fell over on her larboard beam end; and, to heighten the terror and alarm, a lighted candle communicated fire to some spirits in the master's cabin, which, in the confusion, was with difficulty extinguished.

The ship still driving over the rocks, her masts were cut away, by which some men were carried overboard. The vessel drifted over, near the high rocks, towards the main. In this situation, every one became terrified: the suddenness of the sea rushing in, carried away the berths and stanchions between decks, when men, women and children were drowned, and many were killed by the force with which they were driven against the loose baggage, casks, and staves, which floated below. All that possibly could, got upon deck, but from the crowd and confusion that prevailed, the orders of the officers and masters to the soldiers and seamen were unavailing; death stared every one in the face; the ship striking on the rocks, as though she would instantly upset. The shrieking and pressing of the people to the starboard side was so violent, that several were much hurt. About eleven o'clock, the boats on the deck were washed overboard by a heavy sea: but even from the commencement of the disaster, the hopes of any individual being saved were but very small.

From this time, until four o'clock the next morning, all on the wreck were anxiously praying for the light to break upon them. The boat from the stern was in the meanwhile lowered down, when the first mate and four seamen, at the risk of their lives, pushed off to the shore. They with difficulty effected a landing upon the main land, behind a high rock, nearest to where the stern of the vessel had been driven. The log-line was thrown from the wreck, with a hope that they might lay hold of it; but darkness, and the tremendous surf that beat, rendered it impracticable. During this awful time of suspense, the possibility of sending a line to them by a dog occurred to the master; the animal was brought aft, and thrown into the sea with a line tied round his middle, and with it he swam towards the rock upon which the mate and seamen were standing. It is impossible to describe the sensations which were excited at seeing this faithful dog struggling with the waves; and on reaching the summit of the rock repeatedly dashed back again by the surf into the sea; until at length, by unceasing exertions, he effected a landing. One end of the line being on board, a stronger rope was hauled and fastened to the rock.

At about six o'clock in the morning of the 11th, the first person was landed by this means; and afterwards, by an improvement in rigging the rope, and placing each individual in slings, they were with greater facility extricated from the wreck; but during this passage, it was with the utmost difficulty that the unfortunate sufferers could maintain their hold, as the sea beat over them, and some were dragged to the shore in a state of insensibility. Lieutenant Wilson was lost, being unable to hold on the rope with his hands; he was twice struck by the sea, fell backwards out of the slings, and after swimming for a considerable time amongst the floating wreck, by which he was struck on the head, he perished. Many who threw themselves overboard, trusting for their safety to swimming, were lost; they were dashed to pieces by the surf on the rocks, or by the floating pieces of the wreck.

The rope, at length, by constant working, and by swinging across the sharp rock, was cut in two: and there being no means of replacing it, the spectacle became more than ever terrific; the sea beating over the wreck with great violence, washed numbers overboard; and at last the wreck, breaking up at the stern from midships and forecastle, precipitated all that remained into one common destruction.

The parting of the ship was noticed by those on shore

and signified with the most dreadful cry of "Go forward!" It is difficult to paint the horror of the scene; children clinging to their parents for help; parents themselves struggling with death, and stretching out their feeble arms to save their children, dying within their grasp.

The total number of persons lost was two hundred and eight, and one hundred and seventy-seven were saved.

Lieutenant Mylrea, of the 4th Veteran Battalion, one of the oldest subalterns in the service, and then upwards of seventy years of age, was the last person who quitted the wreck; when he had seen every other person either safe, or beyond the power of assistance, he threw himself on to a rock, from which he was afterwards rescued.

Among the severest sufferers, was the daughter of surgeon Armstrong, who lost on this fatal night her father, mother, brother, and two sisters.

The rock which the survivors were landed upon, was about one hundred feet above the water, surrounded at the flowing of the tide. On the top of this rock they were obliged to remain during the whole of the night, without shelter, food, or nourishment, exposed to wind and rain, and many without shoes. The only comfort that presented itself was a fire, which was made from pieces of the wreck that had been washed ashore.

At daylight on the morning of the 12th, at low water, their removal to the opposite land was effected, some being let down by a rope, others slipping down a ladder to the bottom. After they crossed over, they directed their course to a house or fisherman's shed, distant a mile and a half from the wreck, where they remained until the next day; the proprietor of this miserable shed not having the means of supplying relief to so considerable a number as took refuge, a party went over land to Trepassy, about fourteen miles distant, through a marshy country, not inhabited by any human creature. This party arrived at Trepassy, and reported the event to Messrs. Jackson, Burke, Sims, and the Rev. Mr. Brown, who immediately took measures for alleviating the distressed, by despatching men with provisions and spirits, and to assist in bringing all those forward to Trepassy who could walk.

On the 13th, in the evening, the major part of the survivors (assisted by the inhabitants, who, during the journey carried the weak and feeble upon their backs) arrived at Trepassy, where they were billeted, by order of the magistrate, proportionably upon each house.

There still remained at St. Shotts, the wife of a sergeant of the Veteran Battalion; with a child, of which she was delivered on the top of the rocks shortly after she was saved. A private, whose leg was broken, and a woman severely bruised by the wreck, were also necessarily left there.

Immediately after the arrival at Trepassy, measures were adopted for the comfort and refreshment of the detachments, and boats were provided for their removal to St. John's, where they ultimately arrived in safety.

LOSS OF THE BRIG POLLY.

The Brig Polly, of one hundred and thirty tons burthen, sailed from Boston, with a cargo of lumber and provisions, on a voyage to Santa Croix, on the 12th of December, 1811, under the command of Capt. W. L. Cazneau—with a mate, four seamen and a cook; Mr. I. S. Hunt, and a negro girl of nine years of age, passengers. Nothing material happened until the 15th, when they had cleared cape Cod, the shoal of Georges, and nearly, as they supposed, crossed the gulf stream, when there came on a violent gale from the south-east, in which the brig labored very hard, which produced a leak that so gained on the pumps as to sound nearly six feet, —when about midnight she was upset, and Mr. Hunt washed overboard! Not having any reason to hope for her righting, by much exertion the weather-lanyards were cut away, the deck load having been before thrown over, and the lashings all gone; in about half an hour the mainmast went by the board, and soon after, the foremast, when she righted, though full of water, a dreadful sea making a fair breach over her from stem to stern.—In this situation the night wore away, and daylight found all alive except the passengers, and upon close search, the little girl was found clinging to the skylight, and so saved from drowning in the cabin. The glass and grating of the skylight having gone away, while on her beam ends, the little girl was drawn through the openings, but so much chilled that she survived but a few hours. In this situation they remained, without fire, as near as the captain can recollect, twelve days, when the cook, an Indian from Canton, near Boston, suggested the operation of rubbing two sticks together, which succeeded. Very fortunately, the caboose did not go overboard with the deck load: this was got to windward, a fire kindled, and some provisions cooked, which was the first they had tasted, except raw pork, for the whole time. They now got up a barrel of pork, part of a barrel of beef, and one half barrel of beef. A small pig had been saved alive, which they now dressed, not having any thing to feed it with. But at this time no apprehension was entertained of suffering for meat, there being several barrels stowed in the run, and upwards of one hundred under deck. With this impression, the people used the provisions very imprudently, till they discovered that the stern-post was gone, and the gale continuing for a long time, the barrels had stove, and their contents were all lost forever.

There happened to be a cask of water lashed on the quarter-deck, which was saved, containing about thirty gallons; all the rest was lost. This lasted about eighteen days, when the crew were reduced to the necessity of catching what rain they could, and having no more. At the end of forty days, the meat was all gone, and absolute famine stared them in the face. The first victim to this destroyer was Mr. Paddock, the mate, whose exquisite distress seemed to redouble the sufferings of his companions. He was a man of a robust constitution, who had spent his life in the Bank fishing, had suffered many hardships and appeared the most capable of standing the shocks of misfortune of any of the crew. In the meridian of life, being about thirty-five years old, it was reasonable to suppose that, instead of the first, he would have been the last to have fallen a sacrifice to cold and hunger: but Heaven ordered it otherwise—he became delirious, and death relieved him from his sufferings the fiftieth day of his shipwreck. During all this time, the storms continued, and would often overwhelm them so as to keep them always drenched with sea-water, having nothing to screen them, except a temporary kind of cabin which they built up of boards between the windlass and nighthead on the larboard side of the forecastle. The next who sunk under this horrid press of disasters was Howes, a young man of about thirty, who likewise was a fisherman by profession, and tall, spare, and as smart and active a seaman as any aboard. He likewise died delirious and in dreadful distress, six days after Paddock, being the fifty-sixth day of the wreck. It was soon perceived that this must evidently be the fate of all the survivors in a short time, if something was not done to procure water. About this time, good luck, or more probably, kind Providence, enabled them to fish up the tea-kettle, and one of the captain's pistols; and necessity, the mother of invention, suggested the plan of distillation. Accordingly, a piece of board was very nicely fitted to the mouth of the boiler, a small hole made in it, and the tea-kettle, bottom-upwards, fixed to the upper side of the board, the pistol-barrel was fixed to the nose of the kettle and kept cool by the constant application of cold water. This completely succeeded, and the survivors, without a doubt, owe their preservation to this simple experiment. But all that could be obtained by this very imperfect distillation, was a scanty allowance of water for five men; yet it would sustain life and that was all. The impression that there was meat enough under the deck, induced them to use every exertion to obtain it; but by getting up pieces of bone, entirely bare of meat and in a putrid state, they found that nothing was left for them but to rely on Heaven for food, and be contented with whatever came to hand, till relief should come. Their only sustenance now, was barnacles gathered from the sides of the vessel which were eaten raw that the distilling might not be interrupted, which would give them no more than four wine glasses of water each per day. The next food which they obtained was a large shark caught by means of a running bow-line. This was a very great relief and lasted some time. Two advantages arose from this signal interposition of kind Providence; for while they lived upon their shark, the barnacles were growing larger and more nutritive. They likewise found many small crabs among the sea-weed which often floated around the wreck, which were very pleasant food. But from the necessity of chewing them raw and sucking out the nourishment, they brought on an obstinate costiveness, which became extremely painful and probably much exasperated by the want of water.

On the 15th of March, according to their computation, poor Moho, the cook, expired, evidently from want of water, though with much less distress than the others and in the full exercise of his reason: he very devoutly prayed and appeared perfectly resigned to the will of the God who afflicted him. Their constant study was directed to the improvement of their still, which was made much better by the addition of the other pistol barrel, which was found by fishing with the grain they made by fixing nails into a piece of a stave. With this barrel they so far perfected the still as to obtain eight junk bot-bottles full of water in twenty-four hours. But from the death of Moho to the death of Johnson, which happened about the middle of April, they seemed to be denied every kind of food. The barnacles were all gone, and no friendly gale wafted to their side the sea-weed from which they could obtain crabs or insects. It seemed as if all hope was gone forever, and they had nothing before them but death, or the horrid alternative of eating the flesh of their dead companion. One expedient was left, that was to try to decoy a shark, if happily there might be one about the wreck, by part of the corpse of their shipmate! This succeeded, and they caught a large shark, and from that time had many fish till their happy deliverance. Very fortunately, a cask of nails which was on deck, lodged in the lea-scuppers while on their beam ends: with these they were enabled to fasten the shingles on their cabin, which by constant improvement, had become much more commodious, and when reduced to two only, they had a better supply of water.

They had now drifted above two thousand miles, and were in latitude 28 North, and longitude 13 West, when to their unspeakable joy they saw three ships bearing down upon them. The ships came as near as was convenient, and then hailed, which captain Cazneau answered with all the force of his lungs. The ship which hailed, proved to be the Fame, of Hull, captain Featherstone, bound from Rio Janeiro home. It so happened that the three captains had dined together that day and were all on board the Fame. Humanity immediately sent a boat, which put an end to the dreadful thraldom of captain Cazneau and Samuel Badger, the only surviving persons who were received by these humane Englishmen with exalted sensibility. Thus was ended the most shocking catastrophe which our naval history has recorded for many years, after a series of distresses from December 15th to the 20th of June, a period of one hundred and ninety-one days! Every attention was paid to the sufferers that generosity warmed with pity and fellow-feeling could dictate, on board the Fame. They were cherished, comforted, fed, clothed and nursed until the 9th of July, when they fell in with captain Perkins, of the brig Dromo, in the chops of the channel of England, who generously took them on board and carefully perfected the work of goodness begun by the generous Englishmen, and safely landed them in Kennebunk.

It is natural to inquire how they could float such a vast distance upon the most frequented part of the Atlantic and not be discovered all this time? They were passed by more than a dozen sail, one of which came so nigh them that they could distinctly see the people on deck and on the rigging looking at them: but to the inexpressible disappointment of the starving and freezing men, they stifled the dictates of compassion, hoisted sail, and cruelly abandoned them to their fate.

THE LOSS OF HIS MAJESTY'S SHIP, QUEEN CHARLOTTE.

The queen Charlotte was, perhaps, one of the finest ships in the British navy. She was launched in 1790, and her first cruise was with the fleet fitted out against Spain, in consequence of the dispute respecting Nootka sound. Lord Howe, who was the commander and chief of the fleet, was then on board of her; and she also bore his lordships flag on the first of June. After which she was sent to the Mediterranean, and was the flag-ship of the commander-in-chief on that station. In March, 1800, she was despatched by that nobleman to reconnoitre the island of Cabrera, about thirty leagues from Leghorn, then in the possession of the French, and which it was his lordship's intention to attack. On the morning of the 17th, the ship was discovered to be on fire, at the distance of three or four leagues from Leghorn. Every assistance was promptly forwarded from the shore, but a number of boats, it appears, were deterred from approaching the wreck, in consequence of the guns, which were shotted, and which, when heated by the fire, discharged their contents in every direction.

The only consolation that presents itself under the pressure of so calamitous a disaster is, that it was not the effect either of treachery or wilful neglect, as will appear by the following official statement of the carpenter:—

"Mr. John Braid, carpenter of the queen Charlotte, reports, that twenty minutes after 6 o'clock in the morning, as he was dressing himself he heard throughout the ship a general cry of "fire." On which he immediately ran up the after-ladder to get upon deck, and found the whole half-deck, the front bulk-head of the admiral's cabin, the main-mast's coat, and boat's covering on the booms, all in flames; which, from every report and probability, he apprehends was occasioned by some hay, which was lying under the half-deck, having been set on fire by a match in a tub, which was usually kept there for signal guns.—The main-sail at this time was set, and almost entirely caught fire; the people not being able to come to the clue garnets on account of the flames.

"He immediately went to the forecastle, and found lieutenant Dundas and the boatswain encouraging the people to get water to extinguish the fire. He applied to Mr. Dundas, seeing no other officer in the forepart of the ship (and being unable to see any on the quarter-deck, from the flames and smoke between them) to give him assistance to drown the lower-decks, and secure the hatches, to prevent the fire falling down. Lieutenant Dundas accordingly went down himself, with as many people as he could prevail upon to follow him: and the lower-deck ports were opened, the scuppers plugged, the main and fore-hatches secured, the cocks turned, and water drawn in at the ports, and the pumps kept going by the people who came down, as long as they could stand at them.

"He thinks that by these exertions the lower-deck was kept free from fire, and the magazines preserved for a long time from danger; nor did lieutenant Dundas, or he, quit this station, but remained there with all the people who could be prevailed upon to stay, till several of the middle-deck guns came through that deck.

"About nine o'clock, lieutenant Dundas and he, finding it impossible to remain any longer below, went out at the fore-most lower deck port, and got upon the forecastle; on which he apprehends there were then about one hundred and fifty of the people drawing water, and throwing it as far aft as possible upon the fire.

"He continued about an hour on the fore-castle; and finding all efforts to extinguish the flames unavailing, he jumped from the jib-boom, and swam to an American boat approaching the ship, by which he was picked up and put into a Tartan, then in the charge of lieutenant Stewart, who had come off to the assistance of the ship.

(Signed) "JOHN BRAID."

Leghorn, March 18, 1800.

Captain Todd remained upon deck, with his first lieutenant, to the last moment, giving orders for saving the crew, without thinking of his own safety. Before he fell a sacrifice to the flames, he had time and courage to write down the particulars of this melancholy event, for the information of lord Keith, of which he gave copies to different sailors, entreating them, that whoever should escape might deliver it to the admiral.

Thus fell victims to perhaps a too severe duty, the captain and his first lieutenant, at a time when they still had it in their power to save themselves; but self-preservation is never a matter of consideration in the exalted mind of a British naval officer, when the safety of his crew is at stake.

Lord Keith and some of the officers were providentially on shore at Leghorn, when the dreadful accident occurred. Twenty commissioned and warrant officers, two servants and one hundred and forty-two seamen, are the whole of the crew that escaped desruction out of nearly nine hundred souls on board, that for nearly four hours exerted every nerve to avoid that dreadful termination which too surely awaited them.

LOSS OF THE AMPHITRITE CONVICT SHIP.

The following particulars of the loss of this vessel are copied from a letter dated Boulogne-sur-mer, September 1, 1833.

The shocking event which is announced by the title to this letter, has, I assure you, filled the town with dismay, and must lead to a most narrow and rigid investigation. I cannot attempt to describe the afflictions not only of the English, but the French, at this most distressing event, and I only express the general opinion when I say that the British public demands that an inquiry be instituted into the conduct of all parties concerned in this deplorable affair.

The Amphitrite convict ship sailed for New South Wales from Woolwich on the 25th of August. Captain Hunter was the commander; Mr. Forrester the surgeon; and there were one hundred and eight female convicts, twelve children, and a crew of sixteen persons. The captain was part owner of the vessel. When the ship arrived off Dungeness, the gale of the 29th began. On Friday morning the captain hove the ship to, the gale being too heavy to sail. The vessel was about three miles to the east from Boulogne harbor on Saturday at noon, when they made land. The captain set the topsail and main-foresail in hopes of keeping her off shore.

From three o'clock she was in sight of Boulogne, and certainly the sea was most heavy and the wind extremely strong; but no pilot boat went out to her, and no life-boats or other assistance were dispatched. I observed her from three o'clock till about half past four in the afternoon, when she came round into Boulogne harbor and struck on the sands. By four o'clock it was known that it was a British ship, but some said it was a brig; others said it was a merchant vessel, though all said it was English.

It appears from the statement of three men who have been saved out of the crew—all the rest having perished—that the captain ordered the anchor to be let go, in hopes of swinging round with the tide.

In a few minutes after the vessel had gone aground, multitudes rushed to the beach, and a brave French sailor, named Pierre Henin, who has already received the thanks of the Humane society, of London, addressed himself to the captain of the port, and said that he was resolved to go alone, and to reach the vessel, in order to tell the captain that he had not a moment to lose, but must, as it was low water, send all his crew and passengers on shore.

You will recollect that up to the time of her running aground no measure was adopted, and the captain was not warned from shore of her danger.

As soon as she had struck, however, a pilot-boat, commanded by Francois Heuret, who has on many occasions shown much courage and talent, was dispatched, and by a little after five came under her bows. The captain of the vessel refused to avail himself of the assistance of Heuret and his brave companions, and when a portion of the crew proposed going on shore the captain prevented them. Two of the men saved, state that they knew the boat was under the bows, but that the rest were below making up their bundles. The crew could then have got on shore and all the unfortunate women and children.

When the French boat had gone, the surgeon sent for Owen, one of the crew, and ordered him to get out the long-boat. This was about half past five. The surgeon discussed the matter with his wife and with the captain. They were afraid of allowing the prisoners to go on shore. The wife of the surgeon is said to have proposed to leave the convicts there, and to go on shore without them.

In consequence of the discussion, no long-boat was sent out. Three of the convict women told Owen, that they heard the surgeon persuaded the captain not to accept the assistance of the French boat, on account of the prisoners who were on board.

Let us now return to Pierre Henin. The French pilot-boat had been refused by the surgeon and captain —the long-boat had been put out, through a discussion as to saving the convicts—and it was now nearly six o'clock. At that time Henin went to the beach, stripped himself, took a line, swam naked for about three quarters of an hour or an hour, and arrived at the vessel at a little after seven. On reaching the right side of the vessel, he hailed the crew, and said, "Give me a line to conduct you on land, or you are lost, as the sea is coming in." He spoke English plain enough to be heard. He touched the vessel and told them to speak to the captain. They threw (that is, some of the crew, but not the surgeon or captain) two lines, one from the stern and one from the bow. The one from the stern he could not seize—the one from the bow he did. He then went towards the shore, but the rope was stopped. This was, it is believed, the act of the surgeon and captain. He (Henin) then swam back, and told them to give him more rope to get on shore. The captain and surgeon would not. They then tried to haul him in, but his strength failed and he got on shore.

You perceive, then, that up to this moment also the same obstacle existed in the minds of the captain and surgeon. They did not dare, without authority, to land the convicts, and rather than leave them on board, or land them without such authority, they perished with them.

The female convicts, who were battened down under the hatches, on the vessel's running aground, broke away the half deck hatch, and frantic, rushed on deck. Of course they entreated the captain and surgeon to let them go on shore in the long-boat, but they were not listened to, as the captain and surgeon did not feel authorized to liberate prisoners committed to their care.

At seven o'clock the flood tide began. The crew seeing that there were no hopes, clung to the rigging. The poor one hundred and eight women and twelve children remainedon deck, uttering the most piteous cries. The vessel was about three quarters of a mile English from the shore, and no more. Owen, one of the three men saved, thinks that the women remained on deck in this state about an hour and a half. Owen and four others were on the spars, and thinks they remained there three quarters of an hour, but, seeing no hope of being saved, he took to swimming, and was brought in a state of insensibility to the hotel. Towsey, another of the men saved, was on a plank with the captain. Towsey asked who he was? He said "I am the captain," but the next moment he was gone. Rice, the third man, floated ashore on a ladder. He was in the aft when the other men took to the raft. When the French pilot-boat rowed away, after being rejected by the captain, he (Rice) saw a man waving his hat on the beach, and remarked to the captain that a gentleman was waving to them to come on shore. The captain turned away and made no answer. At that moment the women all disappeared, the ship broke in two.

These are the facts of this awful case. The French Marine Humane society immediately placed hundreds of men on the beach; and the office, or lodging, being close to the shore, as soon as the corpses were picked up they were brought to the rooms, where I assisted many of my countrymen in endeavoring to restore them to life. Our efforts were fruitless, except in the cases of the three men, Owen, Rice, and Towsey. I never saw so many fine and beautiful bodies in my life. Some of the women were the most perfectly made; and French and English wept together at such a horrible loss of life in sight of—ay, and even close to, the port and town. Body after body has been brought in. More than sixty have been found; they will be buried to-morrow. But alas! after all our efforts, only three lives have been saved out of one hundred and thirty-six.

LOSS OF THE LADY OF THE LAKE.

The ship Lady of the Lake, sailed from Belfast, on the 8th of April 1833, bound to Quebec, with two hundred and thirty passengers. The following particulars were furnished by captain Grant.

On the 11th May, in latitude 46. 50, north, and longitude 47. 10, west, at five A. M., steering per compass W. S. W. with a strong wind at N. N. E. we fell in with several pieces of ice; at eight, A. M. the ice getting closer, I judged it prudent to haul the ship out to the eastward under easy sail to avoid it; while endeavoring to pass between two large pieces, a tongue under water in the lee ice struck our starboard bow and stove it entirely in. We immediately wore the ship round, expecting to get the leak out of the water, but did not succeed; the ship now filling fast, the mate, with seven or eight of the crew, got into the stern-boat—after getting bread, beef, compass, &c. &c. we pulled away to the north-west—the scene that then took place is beyond description; after getting the long-boat out, the passengers crowded into her with such mad desperation, that she was twice upset alongside, drowning about eighty of them. I now attempted to save my own life and succeeded in getting the boat clear of the ship half full of water, with thirty-three souls in her, without oars, sails, or a mouthful of provisions. The last time I saw the brig, (the ice coming between her and us) she was sunk up to the tops, and about thirty of the passengers in the main-top-mast rigging. We then tried to pull after the other boat, with the bottom boards and thufts, but got beset with the ice. We now expected a worse fate than those who were in the vessel, viz. to perish with cold and hunger. The next morning the wind changed to the westward and we got clear of most of the ice. We then pulled to the eastward, in the faint hope of some vessel picking us up, and at noon saw a brig lying-to under her two top-sails—at four got on board of her, and found the crew just leaving her, the brig in the same state as our own, sinking. We, however, got some provisions out of her, and there being a boat lying on her decks, I got part of the passengers out of our own boat into it. In the course of the night it came on to blow from the south-west and the other boat foundered. All that now remained alive, to the best of my belief or knowledge, out of a crew and passengers of two hundred and eighty, is myself, one seamen, two boys, nine male passengers and two female, fifteen in all. At noon on the 14th, we fell in with the master and mate of the brig Harvest Home, of Newcastle, the vessel we had previously been on board of; and on the evening of the same day both got on board of a loaded brig bound to St. Johns, Newfoundland, after we had been seventy-five hours in an open boat, half-dressed, wet, and frost bitten; next morning, I, with the remainder of the crew and passengers, left the brig and was kindly received on board the ship Amazon, of Hull, bound to Quebec, where we arrived in safety.

LOSS OF THE BRITISH BRIG JESSE.

The following are the particulars respecting the wreck of the British ship or brig Jesse, captain Gilmour, under very distressing circumstances:—

The Jesse, timber laden, left St. John's, Newfoundland, on the 14th of May, 1835, for Belfast, and on the 17th, encountered a heavy gale, which strained the vessel, and occasioned her to make a great deal of water. No danger was apprehended till the 25th of May, when a tremendous gale sprang up from the North and East, and the ship was hove to under close reefed maintopsail and storm trysail—all hands pumping, but the water still gained on her and she shipped some heavy seas.

On Sunday, 24th of May, although all hands were at the pumps, the leaks still increased; at half past eleven, A. M., had reached the cabin floor. A few buckets of bread were got out of the cabin, also a barrel of bread and a cask of water, all of which were hoisted into the maintop. The captain ordered the long-boat to be cleared. On Monday, the vessel began to break up rapidly, and the cargo to float out; about nine, P. M., the foremast fell through the bottom, until brought up by the lower yard resting on the rail. About half an hour afterwards, the mainmast got out of the step, and shortly after, was carried away a few feet above the deck; by this accident, the provisions secured in the foretop were lost.

The captain and crew, fifteen in number, with six steerage passengers, then embarked in the long-boat, with about five gallons of water, a few pieces of salt beef, and a little bread so saturated with salt water, that it was of the consistency of pap; a dog was also taken into the boat, which. in the sequel, they killed, and the flesh devoured, after drinking his blood, which afforded them great relief.

The compass was unfortunately broken in putting it into the boat, so that they had nothing to steer by, but the stars and the sun. This occurred in lat. 41 30 N. long. 25 20 W.—cape Rae being about four hundred and fifty miles distant. From the time of leaving the ship, until the Saturday following, May 30, the boat was kept before the wind, a heavy sea running all the time, which threatened to swamp the long-boat.

On this day, James Savage, seaman, became insane and jumped overboard, all efforts to save him were unavailing. Shortly after, James Robinson, seaman, expired, and on the next day, William Robinson, the cook, also died. On Monday, Mrs. McCartney, passenger, and her two infant children, expired, exhausted with their sufferings; on Tuesday, Samuel Nugent, a passenger, James Scott, apprentice, and William Savage, apprentice, died.

On Wednesday, at three, P. M., saw a sail to the E. N. E. which proved the Ythan, of New-Castle, captain W. Davidson, who received the survivors, twelve in number, on board. Hugh Macanelly, seaman, died shortly after, and on Thursday, 4th of June, John Mullin, seaman. On the Wednesday following, 10th of June, Charles Stevens, Robert Jones, J. McKnabb, were put on board the Wansbeck, captain Young. The remainder have since arrived; two have been sent to the hospital, and the others are still in a weak state, from their sufferings. The whole of those who died, drank salt water to excess, and became insane before death ensued.

The following is a list of the survivors:—Capt. Gilmour, W. Kelley, first mate, Hugh Smith, second do., John McKnabb, carpenter, Charles Stevens, R. Jones, Alexander Stuart, seaman, and Andrew Close, apprentice; Samuel McCartney, husband and father of the female and children who died in the boat, and Margaret Crouch passengers. McCartney has since been taken to the marine hospital, in a very exhausted state, as have two of the crew.

INDEX.